India on the Growth Turnpike

Dr. Vijay L. Kelkar

# India on the Growth Turnpike

*Essays in Honour of Vijay L. Kelkar*

*Editor*

SAMEER KOCHHAR

ACADEMIC FOUNDATION
NEW DELHI

First published in 2010
by

**ACADEMIC FOUNDATION**
4772-73 / 23 Bharat Ram Road, (23 Ansari Road),
Darya Ganj, New Delhi - 110 002 (India).
Phones : 23245001 / 02 / 03 / 04.
Fax : +91-11-23245005.
E-mail : books@academicfoundation.com
www. academicfoundation.com

*in association with*

SKOCH

Skoch Consultancy Services
www.skoch.in

SKOCH
DEVELOPMENT FOUNDATION

Skoch Development Foundation
www.skoch.org



Cataloging in Publication Data--DK
Courtesy: D.K. Agencies (P) Ltd. <docinfo@dkagencies.com>

**India on the growth turnpike** : essays in honour of Dr. Vijay Kelkar / edited by Sameer Kochar.
p. cm.

**ISBN 13: 9788171888306**
**ISBN 10: 8171888305**

1. Economic development--India. 2. India--Economic policy--1991- I. Kelkar, Vijay L. II. Kochar, Sameer.

DDC 338.954 22

Typeset and cover design: Italics India, New Delhi.
Printed and bound in India.

# Contents

# List of Tables, Figures and Appendices

## Tables

## Figures

**Appendices**

# About the Editor/ Contributors

*Editor:*

**Sameer Kochhar** is President of Skoch Development Foundation which is the leading think tank on digital, social and financial inclusion issues in India. He has been passionately working towards promoting participatory democracy, empowerment, and bringing improvements in delivery systems. He is CEO, Skoch Consultancy Services, and is an industry veteran with a multifaceted career spanning over two and a half decades. He is India strategy and management consultant to several Fortune 500 as well as large Indian companies for over a decade. He is also Chief Editor of *Inclusion*—a quarterly publication focused on development economics issues. He is considered to be one of the most respected independent voices on inclusive development and citizenship issues in India. He is a member of several expert groups and committees and his research opinion and writings have shaped many a public policy dialogue. He is also a Member of the Expert Group constituted by the Ministry of Panchayati Raj, Government of India advocating a case for strengthening of Panchayati Raj Institutions (village councils) through use of technology. He has written extensively on areas of emerging management practices, infrastructure, governance, technology, finance, economics, e-Governance, *Panchayati Raj* and ICT for development. He has recently published four widely acclaimed books titled *Infrastructure and Governance* (2008); *Financial Inclusion* (2009); *Urban Renewal: Policy and Response* (2009) and, *Speeding Financial Inclusion* (2009).

*Contributors:*

**Surjit S. Bhalla** obtained his Ph.D in Economics from Princeton University. He has worked as a research economist at Rand Corporation, Brookings Institution, the World Bank and The Policy Group; as a proprietary trader/strategist/portfolio manager at the World Bank, Goldman Sachs, Deutsche Bank and Oxus Investments. Presently, he is Chairman of Oxus Investments, a New Delhi based "hedge fund" and emerging markets advisory firm. Dr. Bhalla has served on several committees of the Government of India. He is author of several academic articles as well as three books on globalisation and its effects on the world economy: *Imagine There's No Country: Poverty, Inequality, and Growth in the Era of Globalization* (2002); *Devaluing Your Way to Prosperity: Misaligned Currencies and Their Growth Consequences* (forthcoming, 2010) and *Second Among Equals: The Middle Class Kingdoms of China and India* (2007, also forthcoming, 2010).

**Laveesh Bhandari** is Founder Director of Indicus Analytics Pvt. Ltd. He has led policy-oriented studies for nationally and internationally reputed organisations such as the Finance Commission, World Bank, UNICEF, ADB, FAO, etc. He has published extensively and many newspapers and newsmagazines carry his columns regularly. His work on inequality, education and regional growth is frequently referred to in the policy debate in India. He has received a number of awards: EXIM Bank Award for his work on international joint ventures and the Hite Fellowship for his work on international finance. He has also served as visiting faculty at the Indian Institute of Technology, Delhi and as Managing Editor, *Journal of Emerging Market Finance*.

**K.C. Chakrabarty,** a seasoned banker with an accomplished banking career spanning over three decades donned the role of a Central Banker on June 15, 2009 after he assumed charge of the office of Deputy Governor in Reserve Bank of India (RBI). His current assignments at RBI include guiding and overseeing the areas pertaining to rural and urban cooperative banks, information technology, payment and settlement systems, customer services, human resource and personnel management. Before taking over as the Deputy Governor, Dr. Chakrabarty graced the seat of Chairman & Managing Director (CMD),

Punjab National Bank for over two years and before that, the CMD, Indian Bank for two years. He was also the Chairman of the Indian Banks' Association (IBA) for a brief period. He has recently published a widely acclaimed book with Sameer Kochhar, R. Chandrashekar and Deepak B. Phatak entitled *Financial Inclusion*.

**Bibek Debroy** is Distinguished Fellow, Skoch Development Foundation, an economist and currently Research Professor, Centre for Policy Research, and Contributing Editor, *Indian Express* group. He has worked in teaching and research institutes, for the government, and an industry chamber. He is the author of several popular articles, papers and books. His interests include law reform and indology.

**Nitin Desai,** a graduate of LSE, taught economics at two UK universities, worked briefly in the private sector, had a long stint as a government official in India and then joined the UN in 1990. In India, he joined the Planning Commission in 1973, and worked there till 1988. Later he joined the Ministry of Finance as the Chief Economic Advisor (1988-1990). In the UN, which he joined in 1990, he was Under-Secretary-General for Economic and Social Affairs. After his retirement, he has been involved in a variety of public policy activities nationally and internationally. He is a member of the National Security Advisory Board and the Prime Minister's Council on Climate Change. He is a Distinguished Fellow of TERI and an Honorary Fellow of the LSE. He writes a monthly column in the *Business Standard*.

**Shubhashis Gangopadhyay** is Managing Trustee and Research Director of India Development Foundation. In 2008, he was Advisor to the Finance Minister, Government of India, and was the youngest ever Secretary in the Government. He got his Ph.D in Economics from Cornell University, USA, in 1983 and his Bachelor's degree from Presidency College, Kolkata in 1978. He joined the Indian Statistical Institute as a lecturer in 1983 and was promoted to fulltime professor in 1991. He took over as founder-director of IDF, an independent research organisation, in 2002. He was awarded an honorary doctorate by the University of Gothenburg, Sweden, in October 2006 where he is currently a Visiting Professor. He is the Chief Editor of the *Journal of Emerging Market Finance* (Sage Publications), and an Associate Editor of the *Journal of Financial Stability* (Elsevier). He is a member of the South Asia Chief Economist's Advisory Council of the World Bank. He is also the Founder-President of the Society for the Promotion of Game Theory and its Applications. He has published widely in international journals and has a number of books, in economics and finance.

**Sumita Kale** is Chief Economist with Indicus Analytics. She has been visiting faculty at the Department of Economics, University of Pune, and at the National Insurance Academy, Pune. She obtained her Ph.D from the University of Pune and M.Phil. in Economics of Developing Countries, from the University of Cambridge, UK. Dr. Kale has a number of publications to her credit including chapters in edited volumes, papers in journals and regular articles published in *Mint*, *Business Standard*, *Financial Express*, *The Indian Express* and *Outlook Money*.

**Arvind Panagariya** is the Jagdish Bhagwati Professor of Indian Political Economy & Professor of Economics at Columbia University. In the past, he has been the Chief Economist of the Asian Development Bank and Professor of Economics and Co-director, Center for International Economics, University of Maryland at College Park. He has also worked with the World Bank, IMF, WTO and UNCTAD in various capacities. He holds a Ph.D degree in Economics from Princeton University. Dr. Panagariya has written or edited a dozen books. He is an editor of the *India Policy Forum*, a journal co-founded by the Brookings Institution, Washington DC and the National Council on Applied Economic Research, New Delhi. He is also the founding editor of the *Journal of Policy Reform*, which he edited with Dani Rodrik during 1996-2001. He is currently an Associate Editor of *Economics and Politics* and the *Journal of International Trade and Economic Development*. Panagariya writes a monthly column in *The Economic Times*.

**Ila Patnaik** works in the field of international macroeconomics and international finance in India and in some other emerging markets. On one hand, her research is about issues of business cycle stabilisation and the exchange rate regime in terms of macroeconomics. This has involved work on measurement of the exchange rate regime, and on the macroeconomic consequences of the exchange rate inflexibility which many developing countries have favoured. On the other, her research is about the international finance issues associated with the internationalisation of corporations in emerging markets. This leads into the use of microeconomic data for addressing macroeconomic issues such as exchange rate exposure and crisis propagation. In all these areas, she has worked on a combination of doing original research and writing academic papers, of getting involved in policy formulation in India, and in advocating sound policies in the Indian policy discourse.

**Indira Rajaraman** is presently Honorary Visiting Professor at the Indian Statistical Institute, Delhi and was a Member of the Thirteenth Finance Commission over its two-year term starting December 2007. She was awarded her Ph.D in Economics from Cornell University in January 1974. She taught for 18 years at the Indian Institute of Management in Bangalore. From 1994 until her retirement in 2007, she held the Reserve Bank of India Chair at the National Institute of Public Finance and Policy, Delhi, and the NABARD Chair for a year on deputation at the Institute of Economic Growth, Delhi. She has been a Visiting Scholar at Harvard and Stanford Universities on sabbatical, and has taught at the University of Illinois at Urbana-Champaign. Dr. Rajaraman's research papers have been published in journals and books published by Elsevier, Springer Verlag, John Wiley, the Brookings Institution and Oxford University Press on a wide range of issues covering trade policy, rural labour markets, formal and informal financial institutions, and fiscal policy. She has disseminated her research by delivering talks at a number of institutions. Most recently, she was invited to speak at a conference on "Transparency in Financial Institutions" at Columbia University in April 2009 and at the annual conference of the European Union Development Network at Paris, on "Fragmentation in a Globalised World", in December 2009. She has been active in policy formulation in India at national and state levels. She writes on policy issues in the financial press.

**Hari Sankaran** is the Managing Director & CEO of Infrastructure Leasing & Financial Services Limited (IL&FS). After completing his Masters in Economics from the London School of Economics, Sankaran developed a career in the areas of project finance, infrastructure development and management, regulation and public policy. His primary interest has been to understand the relationship between communities, infrastructure development and economic growth.

**Ajay Shah** works on fiscal, financial and monetary institutions with a focus on the new policy aspects associated with India's rapid evolution into a high growth market economy, which is increasingly integrated into the world economy. His academic research has emphasised bringing analytical ideas and datasets about financial markets and firms to obtain fresh insights into questions of macroeconomic policy. In finance, he has worked on a domestic financial reform in the areas of banking, securities markets, derivatives and pension reform. In public finance, he has worked on a roadmap to fiscal consolidation in recent years, on the goods and services tax, and the establishment of the debt management office. He has begun work on Indian taxation of capital income and financial transactions in the context of cross-border finance. In all these areas, he has written policy papers, served as member of many of the critical expert commissions appointed by the Indian government in the last 15 years, and has been actively involved in translating ideas into action in the Indian policy landscape.

**Arvind Subramanian** is Senior Fellow jointly at the Peterson Institute for International Economics and the Center for Global Development, and Senior Research Professor at the Johns Hopkins University. He was Assistant Director in the Research Department of the International Monetary Fund. During his career at the Fund, he worked on trade, development, Africa, India and the Middle East. He served at the GATT (1988-1992) during the Uruguay Round of Trade Negotiations and taught at Harvard University's Kennedy School of Government (1999-2000). He has written on growth, trade, development, institutions, aid, oil, India, Africa, the WTO, and intellectual property. He has published widely in academic and other journals. He has also published or been cited in leading magazines and newspapers. He has been interviewed on PBS's *Charlie Rose Show* and is a columnist for India's leading financial daily, *Business Standard*. His book, *India's Turn: Understanding the Economic Transformation*, was published in 2008 (OUP). He is co-editor of *Efficiency, Equity, and Legitimacy: The Multilateral Trading System at the Millennium* (Brookings/Harvard University Press, 2002). He obtained his undergraduate degree from St. Stephens College, Delhi;

his MBA from the Indian Institute of Management at Ahmedabad, India; and his M.Phil and D.Phil from the University of Oxford, UK.

**S.S.Tarapore,** Distinguished Fellow, Skoch Development Foundation, has a B.A. (Economics) from Sheffield University (1958) and M.Sc. (Economics) from London University (1960). He was awarded the degree of Doctor of Laws *honoris causa* from Sheffield University (1996). He joined the Reserve Bank of India in 1961 as Research Officer and retired in 1996 as Deputy Governor. He was on deputation from 1971-1979, first in the IMF Research Department and subsequently under the IMF Central Banking Service with the Bank of Mauritius as Advisor to the Governor. He has chaired a number of official committees including the Committee on Capital Account Convertibility (1997), the Unit Trust of India Inquiry (2001), the Committee on Procedures and Performance Audit of Public Services (2004-05) and the Committee on Fuller Capital Account Convertibility (2006). He was a member of the Committee on Banking Sector Reforms (1998) and the Advisory Group on Transparency of Monetary Policy (2000).

# Introduction

Sameer Kochhar

## I

My first association with Dr. Vijay Laxman Kelkar came about when I critiqued some of his recommendations on indirect taxes in 2002. It led me to explore my natural curiosity about the person behind the well-known name and triggered a discovery process that has lasted a lifetime, leaving me rich in knowledge and honoured in friendship of this remarkable human. The high point of this journey is this festschrift that has been put together to commemorate his being conferred the Skoch Challenger Lifetime Achievement Award 2010.

In a remarkable, 33 year-long career in public policy, Dr. Kelkar has been one of the key players in the vanguard of India's economic reforms, making lasting contributions in shaping the development of the economy to this day. His uniqueness lies in the fact that even after his retirement, both the public and private sectors continue to compete for his talent.

Among his early contributions was India's trade policy, as member secretary of the committee that drew up the roadmap for reform of the policy. From that time to his current responsibility of chairing the 13$^{th}$ Finance Commission, causes espoused by Dr. Kelkar exhibit his deep understanding of and dedication to the forces of growth and development. His core competence, however, remains prices and fiscal reform, where he has made waves through petroleum price reform, tax committee recommendations, the Fiscal Reform and Budget Management Act, and now the far-reaching 13$^{th}$ Finance Commission report.

In the words of Dr. Kelkar himself, "I am really grateful to this country for giving me an opportunity to work on some of very important economic policy issues and contribute towards alleviating some of the constraints so that our economy can grow at a double digit growth rate or be an India on the growth turnpike."

A Ph.D in development economics from the University of California at Berkeley, Dr. Kelkar began his career as a senior faculty member at the Administrative Staff College of India, Hyderabad. His long tryst with the government started in 1973, when he was persuaded by no less than D.P. Dhar to join the Planning Commission as a consultant. In 1977, Dr. Kelkar became Economic Advisor, Ministry of Commerce, at the very young age of 35 and rose steadily to occupy some of the highest posts in the government, including Secretary to the Economic Advisory Council to the Prime Minister during 1985-1988, Chair of the Bureau of Industrial Cost and Prices (BICP), Secretary to the Ministry of Petroleum and Natural Gas, Tariff Commission Chairman, Finance Secretary, Executive Director to the IMF, Advisor to finance minister Yashwant Sinha and so on. He has chaired many key reform bodies including the Task Force for Implementation of the Fiscal Responsibility and Budget Management Act as well as the Task Forces on Direct and Indirect Taxes.

Ila Patnaik says, "Dr. Kelkar is a visionary and one of the best economic thinkers in India." His vision remains as valuable today as when he began in the government. Writing in the EPW in 1977, Dr. Kelkar said, "The initial conditions for the sixth five year plan are substantially different compared to the earlier experience and consequently, the possibilities of growth are much wider. Among other changes most notable are: i) the nature, structure and levels of private remittance that are being recorded in the Indian economy, ii) large utilised capacity in the capital goods sector, iii) the ability of the Indian economy to increase exports due to its diversified base, iv) the existence of a large stock of technical manpower, and v) the existence of buffer stocks of critical commodities, e.g. cereals and foreign exchange."[1]

At the BICP (1987-1991), he laid the foundation for changes in the drug policy. Several excellent sector studies were done under his stewardship, with him pushing for knowledge-based industrial policies to take advantage of the enormous base of human capital. He advocated that

1. "Growth Possibilities in the Indian Economy", *Economic and Political Weekly*, December 1977.

20 per cent deduction in import duty would lead to a substantial acceleration in economic activity. At the Tariff Commission, he worked in association with the NCAER to outline tariff barriers and develop a model for future action in this area.

Bibek Debroy talks about the immense influence of Dr. Kelkar's writings, even when he was a newbie in the government. "I remember one of his papers published in the EPW when he was chairman of the BICP. It was a pretty influential paper by him, pointing out the abuse that had resulted from the discretionary system, especially the misallocation of resources."

From 1994-1997, he served as secretary to the Ministry of Petroleum and Natural Gas, which was a bit unusual because, like the current Planning Commission deputy chairman Montek Singh Ahluwalia who was finance secretary, he too did not belong to the IAS. There, he became the chief architect of the move away from the APM (Administered Price Mechanism) regime in petroleum pricing. He also introduced the New Exploration Licensing Policy (NELP), which took away the monopoly of the ONGC and other state-owned companies, bringing in much-needed competition in the sector. Among all the oil sector reforms, this has been the most significant in terms of economic impact. India has added more reserves in the last 10 years after launching NELP than it had in the previous 40.

Although he has moved on from the Ministry of Petroleum and Natural Gas, he continues to be abreast of all the new developments and initiatives in the sector. In his speech at PETROTECH 2009 on 12 January, he says, "...my successors have taken the oil industry to newer heights. Our oil industry has scored spectacular successes... Our oil industry now is working at the cutting edge of new technologies such as gas hydrates, GTL technology, use of productivity enhancing catalysts and many others. Perhaps there is one area where our industry has not done enough and that is the area of knowledge creation and innovation... Surely, this is not a very happy state of affairs. Hence, this is the next frontier for our industry to conquer."

His ability to arrive at a smooth consensus worked very well in the government system. This was especially seen in the hydrocarbon sector where he took it upon himself to convince the oil PSUs that a move towards privatisation was not only in the larger interest of the nation but also in their own enlightened self-interest. He made them realise that the Indian hydrocarbon sector was large enough for all and had massive growth potential to accommodate the private sector without hurting the public sector. In retrospect, privatisation and liberalisation came as a godsend to the PSUs in the hydrocarbon sector. The vibrancy in these organisations today only serves to vindicate Dr. Kelkar's vision.

His leadership qualities are evident from the fact that in spite of being an outsider to the Civil Service, he was able to quietly but thoroughly transform India's hydrocarbon sector. His colleagues in the PSUs that reported to him and bureaucrats in related ministries regularly consulted him before making any decisions.

From petroleum, Dr. Kelkar arrived at the North Block in 1998 to take the place of Montek Singh Ahluwalia. The shift surprised many, and the going thereafter could not have been easy for him, an outsider among the career bureaucrats. From there, he was nominated to the board of the IMF; as an executive director, he oversaw the Fund's South Asia operations during 1999-2002, after which he returned to the finance ministry as advisor to the Finance Minister in the rank of a Minister of State till September 2004.

In his farewell speech[2] at the IMF in 2002, Dr. Kelkar was remarkably prescient when he said that, "the first half of the 21st century is set to see further expansion in global capital flows and in economic growth rate which means even further rise in the economic potential of developing countries. Other important implications of these forces are more volatility, increased vulnerabilities and consequent heightened downside risks due to what Professor Calvo calls 'globalisation hazard'. Volatility and vulnerabilities come from external shocks such as sharp movements in exchange rates, sudden reversals in capital flows, synchronised downturns and asset price bubbles. In this age of mobile capital, the incidence of economic costs of these shocks will be much less equitable."

2. Farewell speech by Dr. Vijay Kelkar, Executive Director for India, Sri Lanka, Bangladesh and Bhutan, International Monetary Fund, 31 July 2002.

But he proved to be more on the ball on the fiscal constraints to India's growth potential. He outlined them in his celebrated K.R. Narayanan Oration at the Australian National University, Canberra in 2004, called "India: On the Growth Turnpike". "The essence of this problem," he said, "has been stagnation in the tax-GDP ratio. From 1990-1991 to 2003-04, we did obtain progress on direct taxes, which went up from 1.9 per cent of GDP to 3.5 per cent. The phasing out of customs duties has inevitably given poor growth in indirect taxes, which went from 7.9 per cent of GDP to 5.7 per cent. The fiscal difficulties at the states have given a fresh impetus to state-level tax efforts, which have yielded some progress, with growth from 5.3 per cent of GDP to 6.3 per cent of GDP. However, the overall picture has been unchanged, with the tax/GDP ratio being stable at 15.5 per cent of GDP in 2003-04 and in 1990-91. The combination of large fiscal deficits with a stagnant tax/GDP ratio has given sharp growth in the debt/GDP ratio. Since 1998, the debt/GDP ratio...has resumed an extremely rapid climb to the present level of 80 per cent of GDP. This has fuelled concerns about the possibility of India facing the problem of debt trap as interest payments have steadily become a bigger fraction of tax revenues."

Ajay Shah says Dr. Kelkar's major achievement lies in his work on fiscal reforms. Three extremely important reports in this area were done under his stewardship, Reports of the Task Forces on Direct Taxes and Indirect Taxes as well as on the implementation of the FRBM Act, 2003. By streamlining and simplifying the indirect tax structure by cutting through the excise maze, and by focusing on expanding the equity of the tax system and elimination of incentives and other distortions in the savings system, he proved that, "a modern, transparent and efficient tax system encompassing the best international practices is certainly possible to implement in the short run." Getting FRBM passed by Parliament was a remarkable achievement of India's democracy. Dr. Kelkar's review stressed how it was important to focus on both revenue income and expenditure to monitor fiscal consolidation, which would in the long run expand aggregate demand, encourage private investment and depress interest rates.

As advisor to the then Finance Minister Yashwant Sinha, Dr. Kelkar also pioneered the establishment of tax information network (TIN) and enhanced the role of computer technology by getting the National

Securities Depository Ltd. (NSDL) as the implementing agency, which for the first time stared doing reconciliation of the TDS, says Ajay Shah. Such a network was to enable taxmen to focus on inspection and assessment only. He was confident that the government could outsource NSDL's hardware and software infrastructure, which could be readied within four months. This was one major step towards digital inclusion of the whole tax system. Acknowledging Dr. Kelkar's contribution, C.B. Bhave says, "concept of TIN and ability to see that the project comes to execution was where, I think, he made a huge contribution. That is not just a contribution to the NSDL, it is really a contribution to the country."

The challenge then was to keep the government budget as balanced as possible, keeping the fiscal deficit under a tight leash. Dr. Kelkar travelled across India to different universities, and institutions to discuss how the budget should be.

Most of Dr. Kelkar's work on fiscal consolidation was done after he returned from the IMF. That successive governments, cutting across political affiliations, have handed him key assignments is a measure of the respect that he commands among political formations. His ability to identify bright sparks in the system to get the work done also helped greatly in his continued success as policy maker.

Till the time he took up the chairmanship of the 13$^{th}$ Finance Commission, in the rank of a Union Cabinet Minister, in January 2008, Dr. Kelkar has been active on top of the rung corporate boards and chairing the private equity arm of IDFC, straddling both public and private sectors with equal ease. The recently released Report of the Commission is an evidence of how well he carried out the mandate of the Commission, by: a) laying down a critical roadmap of fiscal consolidation both at the states and the Centre, b) by furthering the cause of devolution both at the state as well as local government level, and c) by also focusing on sustaining the commitment to social expenditures, particularly education and health.

Greater financial inclusion, Dr. Kelkar has always believed, is only possible with fiscal discipline as well as fiscal federalism and decentralisation, a fact that shows up in the Commission report. The clear and significant devolution of revenues to local bodies and the stringency built into the system to ensure state compliance marks a landmark shift in federal relations. For the first time have local governments been guaranteed a share of central revenues.

Beginning this year, Dr. Kelkar is the unanimously elected chair of the Forum of Federations, an international organisation headquartered in Ottawa which seeks to strengthen democratic governance by promoting dialogue on the practices, principles, and possibilities of federalism through partner governments. A strong believer in democracy, Dr. Kelkar discards the view that democracy impedes economic growth and India might eliminate poverty faster were we to sacrifice freedom and democracy. More important, he believes in effective conflict management within our democracy.

Dr. Kelkar modestly calls himself as "a policy economist", with a "comparative advantage" in fiscal reform.[3] Yet, to describe him as one of the best economists, thinkers and policy makers of this country would be merely stating the obvious. Whether articulating a vision for the role of markets and government, or stressing the importance of a sound public sector balance sheet, or arguing for fiscal reform and fiscal federalism, or tirelessly working on and building consensus for policy change, his contributions will continue to impact the Indian economy for years to come. In his convocation address at IGIDR last year he remarked: "that skills, acuity and professional training be available not just in the marketplace of ideas, but also in the toolroom of policy reforms. It is here that you can make a professional difference to the welfare of the citizens of this country, and I can assure you that there is no more rewarding terrain to forge your professional careers."

A lifetime of brilliant service that still endures clearly, there could not have been a better contender this year for the Skoch Challenger Lifetime Achievement Award 2010[4] than Dr. Vijay Laxman Kelkar.

---

3. Convocation address at Indira Gandhi Institute of Development Research, Mumbai, 6 February 2009 *http://fincomindia.nic.in/ShowContentOne.aspx?id=26&Section=1*

4. Skoch Challenger Awards are conferred annually on people, projects and institutions for their extraordinary achievements in contribution to the society. Past recipients include Sam Pitroda, C. Rangarajan, C.B. Bhave, Aruna Roy, R.H. Patil and Deepak B. Phatak.

## II

This section gives a brief introduction to the essays in this book, written to felicitate Dr. Kelkar's remarkable career in public policy planning and implementation.

On 11 May 2000, India's billionth citizen, Aastha was born. In 2001, every second Indian was under the age of 20, making India the next big growth target for business. Some even predicted that India would be among the three biggest economies by 2050. The simple extrapolation being, the largest number of working age people equals highest or close to highest gross domestic output. Ten years on, evidences of the promise are on show. India recorded 9-plus per cent growth for three years in a row and nearly 8 per cent in the past five years. Today, India has a population of 1,162 million, projected to be 1,341 million by 2020. Will India's true potential now be weighed down by the challenges it faces? The economics of need often dominates development debates. One of three Indians today cannot afford two square meals. Many are yet to be enrolled in a school or have dropped out. Poverty remains persistent and acute in large areas, confining India to the category of low-income economy.

Transforming India into a developed nation implies that every citizen of the country lives well above the poverty line, their education and health is of a high standard, national security is assured, and its core competence in certain major areas enable production as well as export of quality goods competitively, bringing prosperity for all.

Many of the contributors to this book have known him longer than I have. They have worked closely with him on various issues and I am indeed grateful that they took the time out to write on topics close to our hearts. Their insights into the process of economic development and reforms only highlight that India is poised for a crucial period in its growth trajectory.

A decade of opening up of the economy has produced new energy and dynamism. The world is waking up to India's crucial role as the largest democracy and as a dynamic economy on the verge of greatness. The new technologies, especially information technology and biotechnology, give new opportunities for economic and social development. India's political system is more than ever in consensus about the basic direction of reforms. The current government enjoys a strong electoral mandate. Clearly, the time is ripe.

India is expected to grow at 9 per cent per annum on an average in the next few years. Accompanying this growth will be an increase in demand for infrastructure services. Economic growth and population growth prospects are expected to place additional pressure on existing infrastructure facilities. Therefore, addressing these challenges will be essential if the infrastructure sector is to continue fostering economic growth rather than remaining a constraint. Failure to respond to this demand will create bottlenecks to growth and hamper poverty alleviation efforts.

As a nation, to quote Nobel Laureate Amartya Sen, we are "argumentative" and this applies with even greater force to Indian economists. Dr. Kelkar is a unique example of an Indian economist who cannot be classified under this category. Despite significant achievements, Dr. Kelkar stands out as an incredibly unassuming and humane person, who consistently refuses to brandish his outstanding achievements. A unique feature of Dr. Kelkar's personality is to listen to what others have to say and only after deep reflection does he air his views. Had more economists in India imbibed Dr. Kelkar's characteristics, the quality of Indian economic thought would have been greatly enriched, remarks S.S. Tarapore.

Having worked closely with Dr. Kelkar, Tarapore in his essay discusses some of the more enduring issues in Indian macroeconomic management and emphasises the need for consistency in fiscal, monetary and external sector policies so as to enable the country to achieve sustained growth.

Arvind Panagariya admits that while he likes to claim the credit for being the first to predict India's shift to 5 to 7 per cent growth path in a paper "India: A New Tiger on the Block?" in view of the fragility of reform process at that time, Dr. Kelkar was perhaps the first to predict the shift to the current near-double-digit growth path in his 2004 K.R. Narayanan Oration. He was clearly among the first to appreciate the breadth and depth of the reforms put in place cumulatively by former prime ministers Rajiv

Gandhi, Narasimha Rao and Atal Bihari Vajpayee. It might be worthwhile to recall the concluding paragraph of Kelkar's oration:

> Thanks to painstaking policy reforms initiated over the last two decades by successive Governments, I believe that India is at the threshold of 'a golden age of growth', with India's democratic framework being a key growth fundamental. It seems to me that, over time, India has paid the 'fixed costs' of democracy in terms of the creation of institutional infrastructure, traditions and conventions. Further, India's democratic system has also internalised what Prime Minister Vajpayee calls Coalition Dharma, showing that coalitions can provide stable government and push economic reforms. This means that in the future, the economy can reap the dividends from the resultant systemic stability. Thus, India—riding the wave of growth fundamentals such as demographic transition, human capital accumulation, improved incentive structures, diffusion of new technologies such as IT, total factor productivity accelerators through 'network industries', and an improved security environment—will be growing at growth rates which can be above 10 per cent per annum i.e. double-digit growth rates. There is an ineffable sense of joy for me personally, and professionally, to see India embark on this growth odyssey, a journey that I call 'India: On the growth turnpike'.[5]

Panagariya goes on to say that while the shift to double-digit or even higher growth has so far not happened, something very close to it has indeed taken place. India clocked a steady annual average growth of 8.5 per cent for six years beginning in 2003-04 and ending in 2008-09. Even during the crisis year of 2008-09, the country pulled off an impressive 6.7 per cent growth and recovered in the second quarter of 2009-10—the latest quarter for which we have the data—to 7.9 per cent. The country is almost certain to perform even better in the remaining two quarters of the financial year 2009-10.

An important aspect of this impressive growth story is the phenomenal growth that some of the poorest states have experienced in recent years, argues Panagariya. Three of the bottom six states among the larger states have grown 8 per cent or more annually during 2003-04 to 2008-09. Rajasthan and Orissa have grown 9.4 per cent each and Bihar 8.4

5. "India: On the Growth Turnpike", K.R. Narayanan Oration, Australian National University, Canberra, April 27, 2004.

per cent. Likewise, all three of the newest states, which were carved out of three of the poorest four larger states have grown at rates exceeding 9 per cent. "In concluding this extraordinary story, I can justifiably join Vijay Kelkar in expressing 'personal and professional joy' in seeing India not only push ahead full-speed on the growth turnpike but also carry all its parts—big and small and rich and poor—with it," says Panagariya.

Ajay Shah and Ila Patnaik, in their essay, "Stabilising the Indian Business Cycle", note that the framework of fiscal and monetary policy in India was established before the business cycle fluctuations of a market economy came about. In the new setting, it is important to carefully design the legal and institutional frameworks for fiscal and monetary policy so as to reduce the extent of business cycle fluctuations.

They argue that accelerating broad-based economic reforms is an important tool for stabilisation. In a downturn, it can induce greater optimism about India, and yield increased private corporate investment. The magnitudes involved here are larger than those which can be mustered through monetary or fiscal policy.

Shah and Patnaik also emphasise that, "the focus on financial inclusion has traditionally been motivated by the agenda of poverty reduction. However, financial inclusion, and the full integration between the formal financial system and the world of informal finance, should legitimately be a part of the policy agenda for building an effective monetary policy transmission. Recent innovations in financial engineering connected with informal finance, such as linking up micro finance institutions to the wholesale bond market through securitisation, would help improve integration between formal finance and informal finance, and thus help further this agenda of creating a meaningful monetary policy transmission."

Surjit S. Bhalla minces no words when he writes, "As India embarks on implementing some radical changes in direct and indirect taxes, it owes an enormous debt of gratitude to Kelkar's thinking and research for the better part of the last decade." The major reforms in the next few years will be with regard to public finance, where Dr. Kelkar has had a deep involvement. Once the proposed new direct and indirect tax codes (goods and services tax or GST) become policy, the economy will move to a more efficient growth path. Bhalla's essay examines the economics and the likely impact of the proposed new direct tax code. The results suggest that not only will tax collections be revenue neutral in the face of a large tax cut, they will be revenue enhancing.

Indira Rajaraman focuses on the issue of transparency, redefined after the global economic and financial crisis of 2008. Fiscal transparency undoubtedly finds very wide support in general. More and better information about public expenditure and revenue intent is sought by both market-friendly reformers and supporters of the role of the state. The case for fiscal transparency is atheoretic. It is not shaped by theory, nor constrained by issues other than the need to protect the identity of individual taxpayers and perhaps national security considerations.

Monetary policy, on the other hand, relies on the control of levers affecting private market players. The issue of what should be revealed therefore becomes amenable to theorising on the reactions of market players to information. Present-day prescriptions for monetary policy transparency are based on stylised models. She argues that the standards beamed at developing countries, for what constitutes transparent functioning and accountability in the conduct of monetary and regulatory policy, carry some components that are diagnostically flawed and unsuited to the economic structures and political economy pressures found in these countries.

Nitin Desai examines how growth can and may be sustained. The optimism about growth prospects rests to a large degree on the acceleration in growth seen since 1980 and even more so since 2003-04. He reviews the growth record of the Indian economy since 1950, the reasons that underlie the acceleration and the prospects at present. The case for more rapid growth also rests to some extent on a comparison with other developing countries, particularly with some fast growing economies in Asia. Looking at some international comparisons, Desai seeks to draw some lessons from this review of the past and tries to highlight some of the key conditions for sustaining high growth over long periods. The real question is whether we have a political system that is capable of leading and directing us in that direction. The paper ends with a discussion of what India would be like if we were to succeed.

According to Hari Sankaran, the case for using PPP as a delivery mechanism in infrastructure is well-supported by both domestic and international experience. For India, the next phase of infrastructure development will require a more holistic, integrated and strategic approach to PPP. With its legislative and policy framework largely in place, the focus now needs to shift to enabling genuine partnerships that build institutional capacity across sectors. The response of the private sector to projects offered till date would certainly appear to suggest their willingness to support such a drive.

"As an intellectual-practitioner, he remains unsurpassed," writes Arvind Subramanian. Terming Dr. Kelkar as a visionary, Subramanian's essay discusses what he would have made of the recent global financial crisis. It goes on to say how policy makers should be rattled enough by the crisis to attempt to draw lessons, albeit provisional or interim, from it and in thinking about preventing and responding to the next crisis—the crisis of 2018.

As the world economy slowly takes to the upswing, we must be ahead of the curve in terms of growth and value creation so that we are able to supplement the domestic growth momentum with the global push when it comes, says Subramanian. High economic growth is a prerequisite to achieve inclusive growth.

Inclusive growth as a strategy of economic development received attention owing to a rising concern that the benefits of economic growth have not been equitably shared. The onus of making financial inclusion happen is on policy makers and that finacial inclusion is a quasi-public good as Dr. Kelkar remarked in his N.P. Sen Memorial Lecture (January 2008):

> Increasingly, in developing countries, access to finance is positioned as a public good, which is as important and basic as access to safe water or primary education. The pertinent question to ask here is whether 'Financial Inclusion' can be construed a public good? A good is considered a 'public good' if it meets the conditions of non-rivalness in consumption and non-excludability. The degree of 'publicness' in 'financial inclusion' maybe different from the stand point of a typical

> public good like say 'defense', but there is little doubt that financial inclusion meets the above two criteria to a large measure and to that extent is a 'quasi public good'.[6]

There are a number of positive externalities of financial inclusion. One of the important effect is that one is able to reap the advantages of network externality of financial inclusion as the value of the entire national financial system increases. Yet another reason why financial inclusion is a quasi-public good is that the consequent fuller participation by all in the financial system makes monetary policy more effective and thus, enhances the prospects of non-inflationary growth.

K.C. Chakrabarty writes that inclusive growth is essential for creating an equitable society. Well-designed and effectively implemented poverty alleviation programmes not only supplement the poverty-reducing effects of growth but could also promote pro-poor growth. There is a need to design financial instruments that would help people to reduce their risk and vulnerability whether it is for smoothening incomes or ensuring higher education for family members or reducing exposure to health shocks. With the arrival of modern banking technology and the realisation that the poor are bankable with good business prospects, financial inclusion initiatives will strengthen financial deepening further and provide resources to the banks to expand credit delivery.

Laveesh Bhandari and Sumita Kale take the argument further to discuss "Financial Inclusion via Universal Access to Electronic Payments". They argue that universal access to electronic transactions is critical for ensuring financial inclusion. In several steps taken recently, the RBI has created a highly progressive regulatory regime that would enable both innovation and entry of new providers of financial and e-transaction services. Moreover, the ideal mode or 'pipe' through which such services can be provided—the mobile phone—is already widely accessible for the underprivileged.

However, constraints in the mobile value-added services (VAS) sector are preventing further movement in this space. An enabling environment requires the mobile service providers (MSPs) to be receptive to entry of non-

6. "Financial Inclusion for 'Inclusive' Growth", N.P. Sen Memorial Lecture, Administrative Staff College of India, Hyderabad, January 13, 2008.

MSP entities, competition and transparency, without which regulatory action in this sector will become essential to ensure greater financial inclusion. Just as the RBI has created an enabling environment in the financial regulation space, the TRAI and/or the cellular phone industry needs to create an enabling environment in the electronic communication space. Only after this is achieved, the authors argue, we can expect further cost-efficient innovations in the microcredit space that will ensure financial services for all. "We really do not know which kind of services and which type of models will be able to profitably meet the micro-credit requirements of the masses. But by loosening competitive forces at all points in the chain, we would have created a highly enabling environment for innovations to occur," remark Bhandari and Kale.

Shubhashis Gangopadhyay deliberates on "Developing the Market for Land". Land, he says, is becoming the most important factor in India's struggle to achieve a set of development goals: increased urbanisation, improved infrastructure, establishment of new industrial and commercial facilities, and the setting up of Special Economic Zones (SEZs). Focusing on government acquisition of privately owned land, he uses Singur as a case study to raise some issues that are important to resolve before land transactions can become more meaningfully smooth in a development context.

There seems to be no area of reform and development that Dr. Kelkar has not deliberated on, or worked on. Bibek Debroy in his paper on elementary education, argues that education itself is a continuum and cuts across the categories of elementary education, secondary education, vocational education and higher education. He discusses it in the context of India's "demographic dividend", flagged among others by Dr. Kelkar in the 2004 K.R. Narayanan Oration, for instance, where he talked about incremental growth that comes from increased quantity as well as quality of the labour force.

This theme is explored in greater detail in another paper he wrote for the Strategic Studies Institute, where educational reforms are flagged under the head of meso-economic reforms.[7] "In addition to its intrinsic value," he

7. *http://aparc.stanford.edu/publications/south_asia_in_2020_future_strategic_balances_and_alliances/*

writes, "education is also valued for what it can do in terms of human resource capabilities...Compared to 1951, when more than four-fifths of its adults were illiterate, India reached a remarkable level of achievement by 1997, when almost two-thirds of its adult population had attained literacy. Compared to China, however, the gap is huge: with an equally large population and similar size of illiterate population in the 1950s, the PRC has now virtually eliminated illiteracy among its younger population and raised adult literacy to 80 per cent. To reduce such a gap requires an enormous effort with resources on a matching scale. It is estimated that an additional amount equal to 1.9 per cent of GDP would be required annually to provide schooling to those who are not currently in school."

This, in fact, is what he has tried to do through the 13th Finance Commission awards. In an effort to promote greater inclusiveness via education, the ultimate leveller, the Finance Commission has allocated Rs. 24,068 crore for the Sarva Shiksha Abhiyan (SSA). More importantly, unlike the 12th Finance Commission that allocated funds for only eight states, this money has been given for all the states. The funds to be disbursed over the next five years are part of the equalisation grant to states, which will be equivalent of 15 per cent of the assessed requirement. This is mainly intended at taking care of the recurring expenditure in terms of salary, training and similar other heads under SSA. This generosity has been complemented by a strict dictum: states have been told not to use these funds as current expenditure and that they need to grow their own SSA spending by at least 8 per cent.

Clearly, education has come up as the sector that could make or break India. India's expected demographic dividend could rapidly turn into a demographic nightmare unless the country promptly addresses the many structural and systemic problems in its education and training system. And few would disagree that in order to continually clock a 9 per cent growth rate, India must dramatically improve both the quantity and quality of its skilled workforce. Strategies exist to exploit the demographic window of opportunity that India has today. But they need to be adopted and implemented. By 2025, India's window of opportunity will close and a reversal might begin. Rising life expectancy and declining fertility will cause an almost three-fold increase in the proportion of elderly by 2050. In a

# 1 India on the Growth Turnpike

## *No State Left Behind*

Arvind Panagariya*

Vijay Kelkar is that rare policy economist who can see economic policy reforms necessary to promote growth and poverty alleviation before anyone else, effectively communicate the rationale behind them to policy makers and wider public and sometimes even successfully implement them himself. In a paper published in 1999 (Kelkar, 1999), Vijay spelt out the entire gamut of reforms necessary to place the economy on a higher-growth path. While the then National Democratic Alliance (NDA) government implemented many of these reforms, many others remain on the current agenda of most reform-minded economists.[1]

In this remarkably succinct four-page article, published in the *Economic and Political Weekly*, Vijay even called for "innovative measures for creating a social safety net, such as the employment guarantee schemes

* Work on this paper has been supported by Columbia University's Program on Indian Economic Policies, funded by a generous grant from the John Templeton Foundation. The opinions expressed in the paper are those of the author and do not necessarily reflect the views of the John Templeton Foundation. Grateful thanks are due to R.C. Mody for pointing out an important error in an earlier draft of the paper.

1. In the paper, Kelkar (1999) emphasised the need for the "parliament to adopt the Fiscal Responsibility Act," "simultaneous action both at the center and the states to increase user charges particularly of electricity, water, transport, etc," "privatisation of non-strategic public sector enterprises including banking sector," promotion of "transparency and good governance," "an independent monetary authority by giving greater independence to the Reserve Bank of India," "strengthening of independent regulatory agencies such as SEBI, TRAI, CERC, etc., and treating their independence at par with that of the judiciary," "reduction of both short-term and long-term real interest rates," "competition in product markets and the services sector by allowing free entry and freer international trade," "flexibility in labor markets, reform of "laws of bankruptcy and corporate control" and "financial markets," "innovative measures for creating a social safety net, such as the employment guarantee schemes of Maharashtra," replacing product based subsidies including food subsidies by "food stamps and education vouchers for meeting the needs of the socially disadvantaged and weaker sections of society" ("government can be a financier but need not be a producer of such services") and taking the reforms "to the level of the states".

of Maharashtra" that the United Progressive Alliance (UPA) went on to introduce years later under the title of the "National Rural Employment Guarantee Scheme". In the paper, Vijay also pointed out that India needed to replace product based subsidies including those on food by "food stamps and education vouchers" that find overwhelming support among economists today but unfortunately, meet resistance from politicians who instinctively go for more opaque instruments.

Kelkar (1999) also understood and emphasised before most others the connection between reforms and the demographic pattern in the Indian context. But rather than mindlessly claim the inevitability of accelerated growth just because India now had a younger labour force that was getting younger by the day, as many commentators erroneously do, he powerfully cited this phenomenon as the reason for the urgency of reforms. Putting his background in physics to good use, he argued (Kelkar, 1999: 2329):

> The reason for emphasising urgency [of reforms] is the unique state of our demographic transition. In the next couple of decades India will have the once-in-a-lifetime chance of having a population structure where the share of the working population will be the largest. After these decades, the process of aging will catch up and the vigor of the working population will decline. When a satellite is put into orbit, it requires high velocity to ensure exit from the earth's gravitational force, similarly, if our economy is to exit from the gravitational pull of poverty, it requires an exit velocity of double-digit growth rate over the next two decades.

Vijay also has an uncanny ability to predict big economic changes before other analysts, even when the latter are armed with large-scale forecasting models. While I like to claim the credit for being the first to predict India's shift to 5 to 7 per cent growth path in a paper (Panagariya, 1994) cautiously titled "India: A New Tiger on the Block?" in view of the fragility of reform process at the time, Vijay was perhaps the first to predict the shift to the current near-double-digit growth path in his K.R. Narayanan Oration (Kelkar, 2004) boldly titled "India: On the Growth Turnpike". He was clearly among the first to appreciate the breadth and depth of the reforms Prime Ministers Rajiv Gandhi, Narasimha Rao and Atal Bihari Vajpayee had by then cumulatively put in place. To underline the point, it is worthwhile to recall the concluding paragraph of his oration in its entirety:

> Now, I would like to sum up. Thanks to painstaking policy reforms initiated over the last two decades by successive Governments, I believe that India is at the threshold of 'a golden age of growth', with India's democratic framework being a key growth fundamental. It seems to me that, over time, India has paid the 'fixed costs' of democracy in terms of the creation of institutional infrastructure, traditions and conventions. Further, India's democratic system has also internalised what Prime Minister Vajpayee calls *Coalition Dharma*, showing that coalitions can provide stable government and push economic reforms. This means that in the future, the economy can reap the dividends from the resultant systemic stability. Thus, India—riding the wave of growth fundamentals such as demographic transition, human capital accumulation, improved incentive structures, diffusion of new technologies such as IT, total factor productivity accelerators through 'network industries', and an improved security environment—will be growing at growth rates which can be above 10 per cent per annum i.e. double digit growth rates. There is an ineffable sense of joy for me personally, and professionally, to see India embark on this growth odyssey, a journey that I call 'India: On the growth turnpike'.

The shift to double-digit or even higher growth Vijay had predicted has so far not come true but something very close to it has happened. India clocked the steady annual average growth of 8.5 per cent for six years beginning in 2003-04 and ending in 2008-09. Even during the crisis year of 2008-09, the country pulled off an impressive 6.7 per cent growth and recovered in the second quarter of 2009-10—the latest quarter for which we have the data—to 7.9 per cent. The country is almost certain to perform even better in the forthcoming years.

Against the backdrop of these developments, I recently asked Vijay whether in his view India could transition to growth rates of 10 per cent or higher, even recognising the reluctance of the UPA to carry forward the reform agenda. His answer was an emphatic yes. The reason, according to him, is the momentum and energy he has witnessed in almost every one of India's states that he visited as the Chairman, Thirteenth Finance Commission as a mandatory part of the Commission's consultation process.

This then is the long-winded background to the present paper. The paper honours Vijay by undertaking a detailed investigation of growth in various states of India in recent years to throw light on his hypothesis of

India's impending transition to double-digit growth. My conclusion, in a nutshell, is that data support Vijay's observation during his state visits in one important respect: growth momentum has reached almost all states in India. Since 2003-04, the year in which the national shift to 8 to 9 per cent took place, virtually every state has grown faster than in any of the previous periods for which data are available. Nearly all of them have also crossed the 6 per cent threshold of growth. If we combine this shift with the hypothesis Jagdish Bhagwati and I offered in our *Wall Street Journal* article (Bhagwati and Panagariya, 2004) that increased prospects of change turn the electorate more demanding and therefore create a more favourable environment for growth-enhancing reforms, especially at the level of the state, a sound basis for Vijay's optimism is established.

The remainder of the paper is divided into four sections. In the first section, I identify large and small states and union territories and examine the growth experience in 18 larger states representing 93 per cent of India's population. I show that every single one of these states has seen its growth accelerate during 2003-04 to 2008-09 relative to all prior periods no matter how we define these periods. In the second section, I consider the impact on poverty in these same states. I show that between 1993-94 and 2004-05, which can be largely identified as the post-reform period, poverty fell in every one of these states. In the third, I repeat this analysis for the smaller states and UTs accounting for the remaining 7 per cent of the country's population. The smaller states include the three newest states carved out of Madhya Pradesh, Bihar and Uttar Pradesh in November 2000, six tiny states created out of Assam beginning with Nagaland in 1963, Sikkim and Goa. I demonstrate that the same broad pattern found in the larger states applies to smaller states. With rare exceptions, growth has significantly accelerated in all smaller states and UTs during 2003-2009 and poverty has declined uniformly between 1993-94 and 2004-05. Indeed, data exhibit such an impressive decline in poverty in the six states carved out of Assam that I feel forced to speculate whether this may not have resulted from sampling and non-sampling errors. In the final section, I conclude the paper.

## Growth: No State Left Behind

Any state level analysis must begin with the qualification that the quality of the data for states is not as good as that for the country as a whole.[2] The Central Statistical Organisation (CSO), which compiles the data, specifically warns at the bottom of each table that the data are not strictly comparable across states and union territories (UTs) due to differences in "methodology of compilation". There are also bound to be differences in the underlying prices at which output is valued in different states. Additionally, we encounter difficulties in comparison over time since the CSO provides data for different periods using different base years. Nevertheless, these data being the only ones available and surely of much better quality than those available for most developing countries, there is ample justification for inferring some broad trends from them.

I begin with a broad perspective on the Indian states and UTs from the economic standpoint. Table 1.1 reports the net state domestic product (NSDP) in all 28 states (except Nagaland) and four UTs (Andaman & Nicobar Islands, Chandigarh, Delhi and Puducherry) in the descending order in the year 2006-07.[3] While data for many states and UTs are available for years 2007-08 and 2008-09, 2006-07 is the latest year for which they are available for all states except Nagaland and for the four UTs.

The key observation from Table 1.1 is that once we get past Jammu and Kashmir, the remaining states and UTs are tiny from the national perspective. Of the 31 states and UTs listed, the last 10 produced output worth less than 100 billion rupees or $2 billion. Going by the information available for 2005-06, Nagaland also falls below these thresholds. This leaves only 20 states and Delhi with NSDP exceeding 100 billion rupees. Whereas it is important to analyse the smaller entities—8 states and 3 UTs—from the standpoint of welfare of their respective citizens, at least in an accounting sense, economic outcomes in them have very limited consequences for the country as a whole. This conclusion calls for focusing at least the initial analysis on the 20 larger states and Delhi. Out of this

2. Although formally the Central Statistical Organisation (CSO) is the source of the state-level data, the latter are actually compiled by respective states. CSO simply reproduces the data it receives from the states.

3. The remaining UTs—Dadra and Nagar Haveli, Daman and Diu and Lakshadweep—are tiny and not considered in this paper.

**Table 1.1**

*Net State Domestic Product (NSDP) at Factor Cost in 2006-07 at 1999-2000 Prices in Descending Order of Magnitude*

| *State* | *NSDP in 2006-07 (Billion Rupees at 1999-2000 Prices)* | *NSDP in 2006-07 ($Billion)** |
|---|---|---|
| Maharashtra | 3276.0 | 72.3 |
| Uttar Pradesh | 2100.4 | 46.4 |
| West Bengal | 1865.7 | 41.2 |
| Andhra Pradesh | 1854.6 | 41.0 |
| Tamil Nadu | 1853.1 | 40.9 |
| Gujarat | 1499.3 | 33.1 |
| Karnataka | 1300.2 | 28.7 |
| Rajasthan | 1036.2 | 22.9 |
| Kerala | 1004.3 | 22.2 |
| Delhi | 893.1 | 19.7 |
| Haryana | 879.4 | 19.4 |
| Madhya Pradesh | 864.3 | 19.1 |
| Punjab | 810.6 | 17.9 |
| Bihar | 748.3 | 16.5 |
| Orissa | 607.5 | 13.4 |
| Assam | 437.8 | 9.7 |
| Jharkhand | 421.4 | 9.3 |
| Chhattisgarh | 361.8 | 8.0 |
| Uttarakhand | 206.4 | 4.6 |
| Himachal Pradesh | 193.1 | 4.3 |
| Jammu & Kashmir | 185.6 | 4.1 |
| Goa | 85.0 | 1.9 |
| Chandigarh | 79.9 | 1.8 |
| Tripura | 78.9 | 1.7 |
| Meghalaya | 48.0 | 1.1 |
| Puducherry | 41.6 | 0.9 |
| Manipur | 38.7 | 0.9 |
| Arunachal Pradesh | 23.7 | 0.5 |
| Mizoram | 19.7 | 0.4 |
| Andaman & Nicobar Islands | 13.2 | 0.3 |
| Sikkim | 13.0 | 0.3 |
| Total | 22840.5 | 504.4 |

*Note:* *The conversion into US dollars is done at the average financial year exchange rate of rupees 45.2849 per dollar reported in Table 149 in RBI (2009).

*Source:* State related tables in RBI (2009).

smaller group, three states—Chhattisgarh, Jharkhand and Uttarakhand—were created only recently in November 2000. Therefore, our initial focus is on 17 states and Delhi, which together accounted for 93 per cent of the population as per 2001 census. We will return to the small states and UTs and the recently created states later.

Before I turn to the growth experience of the restricted set of states and Delhi, however, it is useful to examine the pattern of per capita NSDP across all 28 states and four UTs. The latest year for which we have NSDP data for all states and UTs is 2006-07. For most but not all states and UTs, it is also available for the following two years. Therefore, in Table 1.2, I report per capita NSDP for years 2005-06, 2006-07 and 2007-08 at 1999-2000 prices for all states and UTs when available. The states and UTs are now ranked from the highest to lowest per capita NSDP in the year 2005-2006. There are occasional shifts in the rankings between two adjacent entities during 2006-07 and 2007-08 but not drastic movements.

Three points regarding per capita NSDP may be gleaned from Table 1.2. First, Chandigarh, Goa and Delhi in that order exhibit per capita income levels that are exceptionally high relative to all other states and UTs. Chandigarh is the capital of both Punjab and Haryana—two of the most prosperous states—and Delhi of India. Goa is the smallest state by area and attracts tourists from around the world. Given these special circumstances of the top three, substantively speaking, Haryana and Maharashtra in that order are the richest states. Even in these cases, the closeness of Haryana to Delhi and the presence of Mumbai in Maharashtra play a crucial role. Second, based on 2005-06 data, strictly speaking, only 43 per cent of the population enjoys income above the countrywide average. Andhra Pradesh is the last state to qualify as having income above India-wide average. If we take a slightly more relaxed attitude, however, and count Sikkim, Uttarakhand and West Bengal as more or less having income equal to the countrywide average, the proportion of population enjoying the national per capita income rises to 51.8 per cent. Finally, Madhya Pradesh, Uttar Pradesh and Bihar, accounting for 30.1 per cent of India's population, remain the three poorest states of India. Per capita incomes in these states at 1999-2000 prices remained below 15,000 rupees in 2007-08. In considering the growth experience below, special attention will have to be

**Table 1.2**

*Per Capita NSDP at Factor Cost in Descending Order of Per Capita NSDP in 2005-06*

| *State/Union Territory* | *Per Capita NSDP (Rupees Per Year at 1999-2000 Prices)* | | | *Share in Population (2001 Census)* |
|---|---|---|---|---|
| | *2005-06* | *2006-07* | *2007-08* | |
| Chandigarh | 66134 | 70361 | 75480 | 0.09 |
| Goa | 52201 | 56021 | 60232 | 0.13 |
| Delhi | 48885 | 54821 | 60189 | 1.35 |
| Puducherry | 36397 | 38488 | 40931 | 0.09 |
| Haryana | 32975 | 37314 | 39796 | 2.06 |
| Maharashtra | 28683 | 30982 | 33302 | 9.42 |
| Andaman & Nicobar Islands | 28637 | 31009 | . | 0.03 |
| Punjab | 28487 | 30041 | 31439 | 2.37 |
| Himachal Pradesh | 27443 | 28639 | 30586 | 0.59 |
| Kerala | 27220 | 30044 | 32961 | 3.1 |
| Tamil Nadu | 25558 | 28320 | 29445 | 6.07 |
| Gujarat | 25487 | 27027 | . | 4.93 |
| Karnataka | 21913 | 22952 | 25226 | 5.14 |
| Tripura | 21524 | 22987 | . | 0.31 |
| Andhra Pradesh | 21334 | 22835 | 25044 | 7.41 |
| Sikkim | 20777 | 22167 | 23761 | 0.05 |
| Uttarakhand | 20355 | 22178 | . | 0.83 |
| West Bengal | 20212 | 21753 | 23229 | 7.79 |
| Mizoram | 18616 | 19220 | 19750 | 0.09 |
| Meghalaya | 18501 | 19292 | 20094 | 0.23 |
| Nagaland | 18318 | . | . | 0.19 |
| Arunachal Pradesh | 18081 | 20087 | 20570 | 0.11 |
| Jammu & Kashmir | 16086 | 16817 | 17590 | 0.99 |
| Rajasthan | 15541 | 16460 | 17334 | 5.49 |
| Chhattisgarh | 14694 | 15660 | 16740 | 2.03 |
| Manipur | 14559 | 15047 | 15270 | 0.21 |
| Assam | 14419 | 15152 | 15857 | 2.59 |
| Orissa | 13957 | 15528 | 16149 | 3.58 |
| Jharkhand | 12950 | 14252 | 15303 | 2.62 |
| Madhya Pradesh | 12567 | 12881 | 13299 | 5.87 |
| Uttar Pradesh | 10758 | 11334 | 11939 | 16.16 |
| Bihar | 6719 | 8167 | 8703 | 8.07 |
| All-India | 20868 | 22580 | 24295 | 100 |

*Source:* Tables related to macro and state-level data in RBI (2009).

paid to these and other states at the low end of per capita income spectrum.

I finally turn to the growth experience of the 17 largest states and Delhi. For expositional convenience, in the rest of the paper, I will refer to Delhi as a state as well. Given that this UT has its own Chief Minister and cabinet to look after most aspects of its local administration, this is not altogether without justification. Table 1.3 reports the average annual growth rates of NSDP for selected periods between 1981-82 and 2008-09 for the 18 states. Based on the sharpness of differences in the national growth rates, I have divided the post-1980 period into two parts in my book *India: The Emerging Giant* (Panagariya, 2008: Chapter 1): 1981-82 to 1987-1988 and 1988-89 and beyond. Given the smaller number of years exhibiting 8 to 9 per cent growth rate at the time I wrote the book, I also

**Table 1.3**

*Annual Average Growth Rates of NSDP at Factor Cost with States Listed in the Descending Order of Per Capita NSDP at Factor Cost in 2005-06*

| *Year* | *1981-1988* | *1988-2003* | *2003-2009* | *1981-1992* | *1992-2003* | *1981-2009* |
|---|---|---|---|---|---|---|
| Delhi | 7.7 | 7.8 | 11.2* | 7.9 | 7.6 | 8.4 |
| Haryana | 4.6 | 6.6 | 10.0 | 5.9 | 6.1 | 6.8 |
| Maharashtra | 4.2 | 6.7 | 8.9* | 6.3 | 5.4 | 6.5 |
| Punjab | 5.5 | 4.2 | 6.1 | 5.3 | 3.8 | 4.9 |
| Himachal Pradesh | 3.3 | 6.5 | 7.5* | 4.6 | 6.6 | 5.9 |
| Kerala | 1.3 | 6.1 | 9.4* | 3.5 | 5.8 | 5.5 |
| Tamil Nadu | 4.8 | 5.5 | 8.6 | 5.4 | 5.1 | 6.0 |
| Gujarat | 2.8 | 7.8 | 10.3# | 7.0 | 5.3 | 6.8 |
| Karnataka | 5.1 | 6.0 | 7.7 | 5.5 | 6.0 | 6.1 |
| Andhra Pradesh | 5.2 | 6.2 | 8.6* | 5.7 | 6.0 | 6.4 |
| West Bengal | 4.2 | 5.9 | 6.9* | 4.4 | 6.5 | 5.7 |
| Jammu & Kashmir | 0.9 | 4.7 | 5.7* | 2.9 | 4.3 | 3.9 |
| Rajasthan | 4.1 | 6.7 | 9.4 | 7.6 | 3.8 | 6.6 |
| Assam | 4.1 | 3.0 | 5.5 | 3.9 | 2.6 | 3.8 |
| Orissa | 2.7 | 3.9 | 9.4 | 3.4 | 3.7 | 4.8 |
| Madhya Pradesh | 3.6 | 4.3 | 6.0* | 4.1 | 4.1 | 4.5 |
| Uttar Pradesh | 4.1 | 3.7 | 6.1 | 4.3 | 3.2 | 4.3 |
| Bihar | 4.3 | 4.2 | 8.4 | 3.3 | 5.4 | 5.1 |

*Note:* *This growth rate is based on the average of growth rates from 2003-04 to 2007-08 since the NSDP for this state for 2008-09 is still not reported.

# This growth rate is based on the average of growth rates from 2003-04 to 2006-07 since the NSDP for this state for 2007-08 and 2008-09 are still not reported.

*Source:* Author's calculations using state-level data in RBI (2009).

hypothesised the emergence of a second break in the growth rate in the year 2003-04. This hypothesis is now a reality requiring a division of post-1980 period into 1981-82 to 1987-88, 1988-89 to 2002-03 and 2003-04 to 2008-09.[4] Accordingly, in the first three columns with numbers in Table 1.3, I report the average annual growth rates during these periods labeled 1981-1988, 1988-2003 and 2003-2009, respectively. For those who like to think of 1991-92, the year in which systematic reforms at the national level began, as defining the dividing line, I also report the average growth rates for periods 1981-82 to 1991-92 and 1992-93 to 2002-03 in the last two columns of Table 1.3, respectively. The states are listed in the declining order of per capita NSDP in the year 2005-06.

Several points emerge from the growth rates in Table 1.3. First and most strikingly, for every single state in the table, growth rate during 2003-2009 exceeded that in every preceding period, however defined. Growth momentum has now penetrated all large states, which together account for 93 per cent of the total population as per 2001 census. Second and related, with the exception of Jammu and Kashmir and Assam, both of which have been subject to insurgencies, every single large state and Delhi have grown 6 per cent or faster during the last six financial years. Even Jammu and Kashmir and Assam are not far behind, respectively growing 5.7 and 5.5 per cent annually during this period. In comparison, only one state (Delhi) during 1981-1988 and nine states during 1988-2003 grew at rates of 6 per cent or higher. Third, some of the poorest states have shown some of the highest growth rates during 2003-2009. Rajasthan, Orissa and Bihar, all of them among bottom six states (respectively ranking 13$^{th}$, 15$^{th}$ and 18$^{th}$), grew at annual rates of 9.4, 9.4 and 8.4 per cent, respectively. Growth rates in Orissa and Rajasthan exceed those in all states except Delhi, Gujarat and Haryana. Finally, the bottom six states, which account for 41.8 per cent of the population as per 2001 census, have together grown at the

4. The CSO does not provide a single series of the NSDP at the state level. Instead, the NSDP data for 1980-81 to 1993-94 are provided at 1980-81 prices, those for 1993-94 to 1999-2000 at 1993-94 prices and those for 1999-2000 to 2008-09 at 1999-2000 prices. I use these data to first compute the annual growth rate for each year and then, treating the resulting growth rates as a single series, compute the average annual growth rates shown in Table 1.3.

5. Because the NSDP for Madhya Pradesh for 2008-09 is not available, the underlying six-state growth rate for this last year is computed on the basis of the remaining five states only.

annual average rate of 7.1 per cent during 2003-2009.[5] This rate is in contrast to 3.8 per cent during 1981-1988 and 4.0 per cent during 1988-2003. A major breakthrough for the bottom two-fifths of India seems clearly to be in the making.

As a footnote, I may state that in my book, published two years ago, I had already noted the signs of a turnaround in the bottom six states in Table 1.3. The evidence emerging in the recent years more firmly establishes that trend. In a key paragraph in the book (Panagariya, 2008: 164), I had stated,

> According to Table 8.2, among the six bottom states, only Assam saw a clear decline in its growth rate in Phase IV [1988-2004] over Phase III [1981-88]. Among the remaining five, Rajasthan, Madhya Pradesh and Orissa saw a clear and significant rise in the growth rates of per-capita net domestic product in Phase IV. Bihar saw a sharp decline from 2.1 per cent during Phase III to –0.3 per cent during 1988-94 but recovered to 2.8 per cent during the longer phase of 1994-04. Uttar Pradesh had the opposite fate: its growth rate rose from 1.7 per cent in Phase III to 2.2 per cent during 1988-94 but fell to 1.2 per cent during 1994-04.

## Poverty: Progress Everywhere

Development economists have seen growth not as an objective in itself but as an instrument of poverty alleviation. It is therefore important to ask if rising incomes have been translating into reduced poverty. Here it is important to remind at the outset that while rapid growth is likely to speed up poverty alleviation, even slow growth is expected to eventually eradicate poverty. While low per capita incomes in the states such as Bihar, Uttar Pradesh and Madhya Pradesh are likely to be associated with higher poverty levels, rising income levels even in these states are likely to be associated with reduced poverty.

Table 1.4 reports the proportion of the population below the official poverty line in the 18 largest states in 1983, 1993-94 and 2004-05. Two clear observations follow from the data. First, poverty declined or remained unchanged in every single state shown in Table 1.4 in the post-reform decade of 1993-94 to 2004-05. Growth during this period has been inclusive across the board. Poverty also declined in most states between 1983 and 1993-94 but there are four exceptions: Haryana, Himachal Pradesh, Jammu and Kashmir and Assam. The rise in Assam and Jammu and Kashmir was 1 percentage point or less but larger in Haryana and Himachal Pradesh. If we consider the entire period from 1983 to 2004-05, poverty declined in every single state.

The second observation flowing from Table 1.4 is that while one can hardly expect the ranking according to poverty rates to match that according to per capita income, there is broad correspondence between the two. High per capita income states, listed in the upper half of Table 1.4, exhibit lower poverty levels on the average than lower per capita income states, listed in the lower half of the table. Madhya Pradesh, Uttar Pradesh and Bihar are the bottom three states by per capita income and they have the highest poverty ratios. Delhi, Haryana, Punjab, Himachal Pradesh and Kerala are among the states with highest per capita incomes and lowest poverty ratios. Maharashtra, Tamil Nadu and Karnataka are the three exceptions that show high poverty ratios despite their relatively high per capita incomes. Precise reasons why this is the case requires closer investigation.

**Table 1.4**

*Poverty Ratios with States Listed in the Descending Order of Per Capita NSDP in 2005-06*

| *States/UT* | *1983* | *1993-94* | *2004-05* |
|---|---|---|---|
| Delhi | 26.2 | 14.7 | 14.7 |
| Haryana | 21.4 | 25.1 | 14 |
| Maharashtra | 43.4 | 36.9 | 30.7 |
| Punjab | 16.2 | 11.8 | 8.4 |
| Himachal Pradesh | 16.4 | 28.4 | 10 |
| Kerala | 40.4 | 25.4 | 15 |
| Tamil Nadu | 51.7 | 35.0 | 22.5 |
| Gujarat | 32.8 | 24.2 | 16.8 |
| Karnataka | 38.2 | 33.2 | 25 |
| Andhra Pradesh | 28.9 | 22.2 | 15.8 |
| West Bengal | 54.9 | 35.7 | 24.7 |
| Jammu & Kashmir | 24.2 | 25.2 | 5.4 |
| Rajasthan | 34.5 | 27.4 | 22.1 |
| Assam | 40.5 | 40.9 | 19.7 |
| Orissa | 65.3 | 48.6 | 46.4 |
| Madhya Pradesh | 49.8 | 42.5 | 38.3 |
| Uttar Pradesh | 47.1 | 40.9 | 32.8 |
| Bihar | 62.2 | 55.0 | 41.4 |
| All-India | 44.5 | 36.0 | 27.5 |

*Source:* Adapted from Table 18 posted on the Planning Commission website accessed on January 10, 2010.

Before I conclude the discussion, it is useful to check the relationship of per capita incomes to another possible, even if, crude indicator of poverty: the number of telephones per hundred individuals or teledensity. Even if the absolute level of this indicator does not reflect poverty since it has been almost surely rising much faster than poverty is declining over time, it may still give us some idea of relative magnitudes of poverty across states. It may be hypothesised that most people want to own a telephone but are unable to do so unless they reach a minimum level of income. If this hypothesis is correct, in a phase when the cost of owning a telephone is rapidly declining, teledensity will achieve higher levels in states with lower poverty ratios than those with higher poverty ratios.

Table 1.5 reports teledensity for the 18 largest states with the states continuing to be listed in the declining order of per capita NSDP in 2005-2006. The pattern turns out to be remarkably consistent with the above hypothesis. In broad terms, states in the upper half of the table show higher teledensity than those in the lower half. Setting aside the anomalous case of Assam, which is richer than Orissa, Madhya Pradesh and Uttar Pradesh but has a slightly lower teledensity than them, the bottom four states by per capita income also exhibit the lowest teledensity and highest poverty ratios.

## Smaller and Newer States and Union Territories

Let me now briefly turn to the remaining 14 smaller and newer states and union territories that I have excluded from the discussion up to this point. At 7 per cent, these states and UTs represent only a tiny proportion of Indian population. Nevertheless, given the large absolute size of the country, their inhabitants currently number approximately 80 million. Of the 14 entities to be discussed in this section, 11 enjoy statehood and 3 are union territories. The states in this group were conferred statehood at different times, the earliest one being Nagaland in 1963 and the latest ones Chhattisgarh, Jharkhand and Uttarakhand in 2000. The three union territories are Andaman and Nicobar Islands, Chandigarh and Puducherry. I first consider the three largest states among the group of 11 to be covered in this section: Jharkhand, Chhattisgarh and Uttarakhand. These are also the newest states.

**Table 1.5**

*Teledensity [Number of Phones Per 100 People] as of March 31, 2009 with States Listed in Descending Order of Per Capita NSDP in 2005-06*

| *State* | *Telephones per 100 Individuals* |
|---|---|
| Delhi | 140.18 |
| Haryana | 43.67 |
| Maharashtra | 50.95 |
| Punjab | 58.25 |
| Himachal Pradesh | 55.80 |
| Kerala | 58.48 |
| Tamil Nadu | 59.92 |
| Gujarat | 45.16 |
| Karnataka | 45.21 |
| Andhra Pradesh | 39.59 |
| West Bengal | 33.60 |
| J&K | 32.76 |
| Rajasthan | 37.15 |
| Assam | 20.65 |
| Orissa | 23.30 |
| Madhya Pradesh | 23.79 |
| Uttar Pradesh | 24.28 |
| Bihar | 17.78 |
| National Average | 36.98 |

*Source:* Telecom Regulatory Authority of India (2009).

## Three Newest States

Jharkhand, Chhattisgarh and Uttarakhand were created out of Bihar, Madhya Pradesh and Uttar Pradesh, respectively, in November 2000. As per 2001 census, the three states together accounted for 5.48 per cent of the country's population. This means the remaining states and UTs account for just 1.5 per cent of the country's population.

One way to judge the performance of these new states is to compare them to respective mother states. This is partially done in Table 1.6, which provides per capita incomes of the new states, their respective mother states and how the former stack up relative to the latter in years 1999-2000 and 2005-06 to 2008-09.[6] Uttarakhand began at a per capita income level

6. Even though the states were actually created in November 2000, the Central Statistical Organisation is able to compute and report the data for them beginning in 1993-94 presumably because it has data at the level of the districts.

1.4 times that of Uttar Pradesh in 1999-2000. By 2006-07, the latest year for which the necessary information is available, it had raced off to per capita income twice that of its mother state. Chhattisgarh began at per capita income nine-tenths that of Madhya Pradesh but steadily bridged the gap and achieved an impressive 30 per cent lead over the latter by 2007-08. Finally, Jharkhand began at per capita income twice that of Bihar and has lost ground relative to it since its creation. It rebounded in 2008-09 in relative terms but not enough to recover its original 1999-2000 lead. Based on press accounts, it is almost certain that during the years under consideration, Uttarakhand and Chhattisgarh were led by administrations superior to the respective mother states while in the case of Jharkhand, the opposite was true.

**Table 1.6**

*Three Newest States: Real and Relative Per Capita NSDP*

| *State/Union Territory* | *Per Capita NSDP (Rupees Per Year)* | | | | | |
|---|---|---|---|---|---|---|
| | *1999-2000* | *2005-06* | *2006-07* | *2007-08* | *2008-09* | *Share in Population (2001 Census)* |
| Uttarakhand (2000) | 13516 | 20355 | 22178 | N.A. | N.A. | 0.83 |
| Chhattisgarh (2000) | 11629 | 14694 | 15660 | 16740 | 17684 | 2.03 |
| Jharkhand (2000) | 13260 | 12950 | 14252 | 15303 | 16294 | 2.62 |
| Uttar Pradesh | 9749 | 10758 | 11334 | 11939 | 12481 | 16.16 |
| Madhya Pradesh | 12384 | 12567 | 12881 | 13299 | N.A. | 5.87 |
| Bihar | 5786 | 6719 | 8167 | 8703 | 9586 | 8.07 |
| Uttarakhand/ Uttar Pradesh | 1.4 | 1.9 | 2.0 | N.A. | N.A. | N.A. |
| Chhattisgarh/ Madhya Pradesh | 0.9 | 1.2 | 1.2 | 1.3 | N.A. | N.A. |
| Jharkhand/Bihar | 2.0 | 1.6 | 1.6 | 1.8 | 1.7 | N.A. |

*Note:* N.A. stands for "not available".

*Source:* RBI (2009) and the author's calculations.

Next compare the relative growth rates of NSDP and poverty ratios for the three newest states and their respective mother states shown in Table 1.7. Three observations follow from this table. First, the three newest states have fully shared in the rapid growth during 2003-2009, each of them growing faster than 9 per cent per year. These rates exceed the growth rates in the prior period by wide margins. Second, all three states have grown faster than their respective mother states during 2003-2009. Finally, the poverty ratio in each of the three newest states remains extraordinarily high. In two cases (Uttarakhand and Chhattisgarh), the poverty ratio is higher than the corresponding mother state. But since we do not have the poverty data in a prior period, we cannot judge the performance of the newest states relative to the mother states in poverty alleviation. It is possible that they were born with larger poverty ratios.

**Table 1.7**

*Three Newest States: Growth and Poverty*

| *State* | *Growth Rate of NSDP* | | *Poverty Ratio* |
|---|---|---|---|
| | *1994-2003* | *2003-2009* | *2004-05* |
| Uttarakhand | 4.8 | 9.4* | 39.6 |
| Chhattisgarh | 2.0 | 9.1 | 40.9 |
| Jharkhand | 3.7 | 9.3 | 40.3 |
| Uttar Pradesh | 3.3 | 6.1 | 32.8 |
| Madhya Pradesh | 3.4 | 6.0^ | 38.3 |
| Bihar | 5.7 | 8.4 | 41.4 |

*Note:* *Based on data until 2006-07 only.
^Based on data until 2007-08 only.

*Source:* Growth rates are calculated by the author using NSDP figures in the tables in RBI (2009) and poverty figures are from the Planning Commission website.

## Smaller Northeastern States, Sikkim, Goa and UTs

I finally turn to the remaining eight states and three UTs accounting for 1.53 per cent of the country's population as per the 2001 census. Of the former, six—Arunachal Pradesh, Manipur, Meghalaya, Mizoram, Nagaland and Tripura—have been carved out of Assam at various times beginning with Nagaland in 1963 and account for 1.14 per cent of India's population. Goa was turned from a UT to state in 1987 and Sikkim was turned from an autonomous region within the Indian Union to a state in 1975. As already noted, the three smaller UTs are: Chandigarh, Andaman and Nicobar Islands and Puducherry.

Table 1.8 reports per capita incomes of the eight states and three UTs in three recent years. I first list the six states carved out of Assam followed by Sikkim and Goa and then the three UTs in alphabetical order. In each case, the name of the state is followed by the year in which it was created

The differences between Goa and the three UTs on the one hand and the remaining states on the other are stark. The former group enjoys per capita incomes well above the national average while the latter systematically falls below it. Indeed, Chandigarh and Goa in that order have the highest per capita NSDP in the country (followed by Delhi). It is quite clear that a long history of insurgencies and conflicts in various tribal regions of Assam have led to a division of the original state into ever-smaller states without delivering significant income gains.

**Table 1.8**

*Per Capita NSDP at 1999-2000 Prices in Smaller States and UTs*

| State*/Union Territory | Per Capita NSDP (Rupees Per Year) | | | | | Share in Population (2001 Census) |
|---|---|---|---|---|---|---|
| | 1999-2000 | 2005-06 | 2006-07 | 2007-08 | 2008-09 | |
| Arunachal Pradesh (1987) | 13990 | 18081 | 20087 | 20570 | | 0.11 |
| Manipur (1972) | 11549 | 14559 | 15047 | 15270 | | 0.21 |
| Meghalaya (1972) | 14355 | 18501 | 19292 | 20094 | | 0.23 |
| Mizoram (1986) | 16443 | 18616 | 19220 | 19750 | 20483 | 0.09 |
| Nagaland (1963) | 13819 | 18318 | — | — | | 0.19 |
| Tripura (1972) | 14119 | 21524 | 22987 | — | | 0.31 |
| Sikkim (1975) | 14890 | 20777 | 22167 | 23761 | | 0.05 |
| Goa (1987) | 42296 | 52201 | 56021 | 60232 | | 0.13 |
| Andaman & Nicobar Islands | 24005 | 28637 | 31009 | — | | 0.03 |
| Chandigarh | 44502 | 66134 | 70361 | 75480 | | 0.09 |
| Puducherry | 30865 | 36397 | 38488 | 40931 | | 0.09 |
| All-India | 15881 | 20868 | 22580 | 24295 | 25494 | 100 |

*Note:* *Year next to a state's name indicates the time of conferral of statehood.

*Source:* RBI (2009).

In Table 1.9, I report the growth rates as well as poverty ratios for the eight smallest states and three UTs. The pattern we have observed for larger states continues to reproduce itself here as well. With rare exceptions, growth rates during 2003-2008 are significantly higher than in the prior period. The only anomalous case is that of Puducherry, which experienced a large 11.9 per cent decline in its NSDP in 2004-05 leading to an overall low growth of 3.1 per cent during 2003-2008. Poverty rates spring something of a surprise. In all six states carved out of Assam and

**Table 1.9**

*Smaller States and UTs: Growth and Poverty*

| State*/UT | Annual Growth in NSDP | | Poverty Ratio | | |
|---|---|---|---|---|---|
| | 1994-2003 | 2003-2008 | 1983 | 1993-94 | 2004-05 |
| Arunachal Pradesh (1987) | 3.9 | 6.9 | 40.9 | 39.4 | 17.6 |
| Manipur (1972) | 3.7 | 6.5 | 37.0 | 33.8 | 17.3 |
| Meghalaya (1972) | 6.7 | 6.1 | 38.8 | 37.9 | 18.5 |
| Mizoram (1986) | 6.6 | 4.0 | 36.0 | 25.7 | 12.6 |
| Nagaland (1963) | 7.3 | 7.5^ | 39.3 | 37.9 | 19.0 |
| Tripura (1972) | 8.2 | 8.0^ | 40.0 | 39.0 | 18.9 |
| Sikkim (1975) | 6.3 | 8.3 | 39.7 | 41.4 | 20.1 |
| Goa (1987) | 6.7 | 10.2 | 18.9 | 14.9 | 13.8 |
| Andaman & Nicobar Islands | 4.1 | 8.8^ | 52.1 | 34.5 | 22.6 |
| Chandigarh | 10.0 | 11.5 | 23.8 | 11.4 | 7.1 |
| Puducherry | 13.5 | 3.1 | 50.1 | 37.4 | 22.4 |

*Note:* *Year next to a state's name indicates the time of conferral of statehood.
^Excludes year 2007-08.

*Source:* Per capita incomes and population from tables in the RBI Handbook, 2009. The year of statehood is from official websites of various states.

Sikkim, poverty rates have been cut in half or less between 1993-94 and 2004-05. Whether this change is real or the outcome of some statistical quirk needs to be investigated.

## Conclusions

Perhaps the single most important and robust conclusion to come out of the detailed exercise undertaken in this paper is that as India has moved on to the growth turnpike, accelerated growth has reached every single state. On the poverty front, all states have seen the rate of poverty decline between 1993-94 and 2004-05 largely representing the post-reform period. Of course, poverty rates from 2004-05 do not reflect the full effect of the accelerated growth since this phenomenon had just set in prior to the 2004-05 survey.

An important aspect of this impressive growth story is the phenomenal growth some of the poorest states have experienced in recent years. Three of the bottom six states among the larger states have grown 8 per cent or more annually during 2003-04 to 2008-09. Rajasthan and Orissa have grown 9.4 per cent each and Bihar 8.4 per cent. Likewise, all three of the newest states, which were carved out of three of the poorest four larger states have grown at rates exceeding 9 per cent. In concluding this extraordinary story, I can justifiably join Vijay Kelkar in expressing "personal and professional joy" in seeing India not only push ahead full-speed on the growth turnpike but also carry all its parts—big and small and rich and poor—with it.

## References

Bhagwati, Jagdish and Arvind Panagariya (2004). "Great expectations", *Wall Street Journal*, May 24.

Kelkar, Vijay (1999). "India's emerging economic challenges", *Economic and Political Weekly* 34(33): 2326-29, August 14-20.

———. (2004). "India: On the growth turnpike", *Narayanan Oration*, Australian National University, April.

Panagariya, Arvind (1994). "India: A new tiger on the block?", *Journal of International Affairs* 48(1): 193-221, Summer.

———. (2008). *India: The Emerging Giant*. New York: Oxford University Press.

Reserve Bank of India (RBI). (2009). *Handbook of Statistics on Indian Economy*. Available at *http://www.rbi.org.in/home.aspx*

Telecom Regulatory Authority of India (TRAI) (2009). *The Indian Telecom Services Performance Indicators April-June 2009*. New Delhi, India, October 1.

# 2 Sustaining High Growth

Nitin Desai

I have had the good fortune to have had Dr. Vijay Kelkar as a friend and collaborator for some 35 years now. In many ways, our ideas about priorities for India's development have evolved in remarkably similar ways. Dr. Kelkar has also had the opportunity to bring some of these ideas closer to fruition in the positions he has held in the past decade and a half. His work as Special Advisor to the Finance Minister who put together the framework for fiscal stability and tax reform and more recently, as Chairman of the 13th Finance Commission will be long remembered.

There are many things about India today which are different from the India that we knew when we were young and at the wheel. One big difference is in the growth prospects of the Indian economy. Today's controversies about whether 7 or 9 per cent is a more realistic estimate of the trend growth rate seem quite extraordinary to those of us who struggled to promote policies that would move the trend growth rate up from 4 per cent to 5-6 per cent or so. Dr. Kelkar was an early believer in the change in the growth prospects for the Indian economy. In his K.R. Narayanan lecture in 2004 (Kelkar, 2006), Dr. Vijay Kelkar saw a 10 per cent growth rate coming from a larger, better educated workforce, higher savings and investment because of the fall in the dependency ratio and fiscal consolidation, productivity gains, greater international interest in India and improved infrastructure. Hence, this contribution to the essays in his honour is focused on the sustainability of the high growth path that the Indian economy is now traversing. The focus is largely on the macroeconomics of growth.

The optimism about growth prospects rests to a large degree on the acceleration in growth seen since 1980 and even more so since 2003-04. Hence, the first part of the paper reviews the growth record of the Indian economy since 1950, the reasons that underlie the acceleration and the prospects at present. The case for more rapid growth also rests to some extent on a comparision with other developing countries, particularly with some fast growing economies in Asia. Hence, the second part deals with some international comparisons. The third part draws some lessons from this review of the past and tries to highlight some of the key conditions for sustaining high growth over long periods. The paper ends with a discussion in the last part of what India would be like if we were to succeed.

## The Growth Record

The record of GDP growth in the post-Independence era has been the subject of a vigorous academic debate.[1] The starting point for the debate is usually an assessment of when a structural break occurred in the growth path of the economy. The first and most obvious point to make is that the most important structural break took place with Independence (Hatekar and Dongre, 2005; Nayyar, 2006). Estimates of pre-Independence growth (available only for undivided India) vary a little and range between 0.8 per cent and 1.0 per cent (Sivasubramaniam, 2000; Maddison, 2003). As against this, the growth rate since Independence has averaged 4.7 per cent in the 55 years since 1950-51.[2]

The structural break that came with Independence is not just a statistical descriptor of the data. It reflects a thorough change in the degree of political autonomy, a radically transformed environment for business enterprises and a profound change in the goals of policy.[3] That break is now history and the real issue is whether there is a structural change in the growth path since then.

The record of growth since 1950-51 seems to show a structural break around 1980-81 according to most analysts who have looked at this.[4] The

1. The literature is too vast to cite. However, see Acharya *et al.* (2006), Nayyar (2006) and Virmani and Mittal (2006) and the references cited therein.
2. The years between Independence and the start of planning are a sort of grey area that rarely figures in these calculations. However, for the record the average growth rate of GDP in the three years from 1948 to 1950 was 1.3 per cent according to Maddison (2003).
3. This point is made forcefully in Nayyar (2006).
4. See Virmani (2004), Rodrik and Subramaniam (2004) among others.

growth statistics do not show a further structural break after 1991-92 with the massive dose of delicensing and trade liberalisation that came with the new economic policy. But, with the recent spurt in growth to 8 per cent plus there are some who argue that a structural break has occurred sometime between 2003-04 and 2006-07.[5]

Though there is general agreement that there was a break in the growth path around 1980-81, there is no real agreement on the narrative that could explain this break.[6] Since the primary purpose of these narratives is to attack or defend particular policy stances, analysts have looked for an explanation in policy changes. More particularly, the point at issue is the extent to which growth acceleration from 1980-81 onwards can be attributed to industrial delicensing and trade liberalisation.

A periodisation based on a statistical analysis of break points is helpful. However, in order to learn lessons from performance it is useful to try a different type of periodisation based on when the policy regime changed substantially.[7] Looked at this way the Indian growth experience can be broken up into the periods indicated in Table 2.1.

**Table 2.1**

*Periodisation of Indian Growth Experience*

| *Period* | *Characterisation* | *GDP Growth (Annual Average)* | *GFCF Percentage (Annual Average)* | *ICOR (Column 4 Divided by Column 3)* |
|---|---|---|---|---|
| *(1)* | *(2)* | *(3)* | *(4)* | *(5)* |
| 1951-52 to 1964-65 | The foundational years | 4.1 | 11.6 | 2.8 |
| 1965-66 to 1969-70 | The crisis years | 3.0 | 14.2 | 4.7 |
| 1970-71 to 1979-80 | The turbulent years | 2.9 | 15.7 | 5.4 |
| 1980-81 to 1990-91 | The transitional years | 5.6 | 20.4 | 3.6 |
| 1991-92 to 2002-03 | The reform years | 5.5 | 22.9 | 4.1 |
| 2003-04 to 2007-08 | The high growth years | 8.8 | 30.2 | 3.4 |

*Note:* Based on data from Tables 1.4 and 1.6 of the *Economic Survey 2008-09*, Ministry of Finance.

5. This has been asserted by Surjit Bhalla (2007).
6. Rodrik and Subramanian (2004) evaluates a variety of explanations for the 1980s' growth acceleration.
7. A similar periodisation can be found in Virmani and Mittal (2006).

The first three plan periods up to the drought and war crisis of 1965-1966 were the foundational years in which the institutional infrastructure and the policy regimes for development were put in place. These were the years when the government launched community development and rural credit cooperatives, industrial and import licensing and industrial development banks, IITs and many research establishments, and many other institutional and policy initiatives.

An import substituting heavy industry-oriented strategy was put in place with the Second Plan and large investments were made in public sector projects for steel and machine building, major power and river valley developments and the transport infrastructure. The public sector grew with fresh investment rather than nationalisation. The private sector had ample room to grow and the government was proactive providing technical advice and political support. The growth performance of the economy in this first phase is good in comparision with India's pre-Independence record.

The twin droughts of 1965 and 1966 were a major shock for which the economy was ill-prepared. Food aid prevented large-scale distress but the ambitious development strategy of the foundational years was more or less abandoned. The focus was on agricultural development with substantial results in the form of the green revolution. There was also some liberalisation of licensing for agriculture-related industries. But the overhang of the earlier strategy led to a continued investment in heavy industries, now including fertilisers. This was also the period which saw the real beginnings of the subsidy burden with the growth of the food and fertiliser subsidies.

In terms of policy regimes, 1970-71 is an important break point. By 1970-71, the green revolution had stabilised and India was past the worst when it came to food security. The Congress split was over and Mrs. Gandhi was firmly in the saddle, *garibi hatao* had become the slogan of the day, poverty eradication rather than growth became the dominating consideration in public policy and a public sector-oriented strategy was in place. The MRTP Act was tightened, state trading was actively promoted and for a brief period, the food grain trade was nationalised. The banking system, which was nationalised in 1969, was put under direct bureaucratic control and directed credit with differential interest rates was instituted.

The upheavals of the oil crisis of 1973-74 and the emergency intervened in mid-decade followed by the Janata Party government, which, though more business-friendly, continued to pursue an anti-poverty strategy in the guise of employment orientation. These were the years of turbulence when the state was in charge but the governments in charge of the state were buffeted by political currents that made it difficult for them to steer the economy with any sense of long-term purpose.

These middle years between 1965-66 and 1979-80 were the ones when Indian development performance was at its worst. This can be seen in the low growth rates despite relatively high levels of investment. The public investment programme was poorly managed with delays and cost overruns, inefficiencies imposed by multiple lines of tied credits being used for a single plant and input bottlenecks which could not be relieved through trade because of foreign exchange shortages.[8]

The return of the Congress Party to power in 1980 marks a shift in policy relative to the earlier years. Though the rhetoric of *garibi hatao* continued, there were some changes in policy in Mrs. Indira Gandhi's second administration that signaled a changed attitude to the private sector.[9] A series of high-level committees under leading figures like L.K. Jha, Vadilal Dagli, Abid Hussain and M. Narasimham laid out an agenda for a more pro-private sector and pro-market policy. But the changes made in the eighties are nowhere near as deep and far-reaching as the bonfire of controls in 1991.

Many of the more important substantive changes came later in mid-decade in Mr. Rajiv Gandhi's administration and Mr. V.P. Singh's budgets. The tax reductions that started with the 1985-86 budget conveyed a positive signal to capital markets and may even have led to improved collections as the tax-GDP ratio rose. But public expenditure rose even more rapidly and the combined deficit of the Central and state

8. Virmani and Mittal (2006) describes these as the years of "legislative-bureacratic socialism". I have chosen to break the period into two to distinguish the years when the focus was largely on getting out of the food crisis and the seventies which, at least in the first half was characterised by a commitment to a hard socialist doctrine. The mood in Delhi started changing after the oil crisis when the take-over of food grain trade was reversed and some hesitant moves towards liberalisation taken.

9. Rodrik and Subramanian (2004) attribute the improvement in growth performance largely to this attitudinal change.

governments rose from 7.5 per cent in 1980-81 to 9.9 per cent in 1986-87 and fell only slightly to 9.4 per cent by 1990-91.

There was a distinct improvement in growth performance beginning in 1980-81. This improvement cannot really be attributed to liberalisation as such, since there was very little of it any how though the big tax reform of the 1985 may have made a difference. The main reason for the change was the improved performance in the public sector and the entrepreneurial drive of a new breed of entrepreneurs who had come up in the seventies when the "big houses" were held in check by MRTP controls. Public investment rose as a proportion of GDP at market prices from 8.4 per cent in 1980-81 to 9.3 per cent by 1990-91. Power availability improved as an average of 4000 MW of power capacity was added per year in the eighties, which is as much in absolute terms and much more in percentage terms as was added per year in the nineties.

Despite a good growth performance why did the Indian economy hit a crisis in 1991? Basically India had not built up a viable relationship with the international economy. Industry remained highly protected and was not subject to competitive pressures though some licensing and MRTP constraints were eased after 1985. Exports had not taken off despite a substantial devaluation of the rupee in the latter half of the decade. Perhaps the large increases in oil production from Bombay High had reduced the sense of urgency. The more immediate reasons for the foreign exchange crisis of 1990-91 were the increase in free foreign exchange needed to replace rupee trade imports lost with the collapse of the Soviet Union, the oil price hike and the inability to go to the IMF before the crisis because of the political upheavals following the break between Rajiv Gandhi and V.P. Singh.

The big change in the policy regime comes after the deep foreign exchange crisis of 1991 when the newly elected Congress government, with Dr. Manmohan Singh as Finance Minister reversed four decades of state control on the private sector and high levels of protection with massive changes in the license-permit system and sharp reductions in tariff rates. Along with this, there was a major change in the policy on foreign investment. The policy regime in India now looked more like the regimes in the export-oriented economies of East and South-East Asia. In the financial sector, SEBI was established and the NSE started leading to a sharp shift away from a bureaucratically directed capital market.[10]

Yet the growth performance in the years after liberalisation does not look much better than the performance in the eighties until recently. There was a boom immediately after liberalisation and a marked slowdown after 1995-96. In part this was due to the boom and bust in the stock market and in part to the weather-related slowdown in the agricultural economy.

The narrative presented above is broadly consistent with most analysis of sources of growth in a growth accounting framework. The source of growth in the eighties and nineties was a substantial improvement in capital productivity, measured crudely by the ICORs reported earlier and more systematically in calculations of total factor productivity[11] reported in Table 2.2.

**Table 2.2**

*Total Factor Productivity Growth*

*(Per cent per annum)*

| | *1950s* | *1960s* | *1970s* | *1980s* | *1990s* |
|---|---|---|---|---|---|
| **Growth (% p.a.)** | | | | | |
| Net domestic product | 3.9 | 4.0 | 2.8 | 5.9 | 5.8 |
| Total factor productivity (1) | 1.4 | 1.3 | -0.1 | 3.0 | 2.3 |
| Total factor productivity (2) | 1.7 | 0.8 | 0.7 | 2.2 | 2.6 |
| **Contribution to Growth (%)** | | | | | |
| Total factor productivity (1) | 70 | 76 | -33 | 84 | 66 |
| Capital per worker | 7 | 42 | 221 | 15 | 32 |
| Rainfall deviation from mean | 23 | -18 | -88 | 1 | 2 |

*Note:* (1) TFP (1) is from an unfiltered time series of estimates and TFP (2) filters out temporary factors like variations in capacity utilisation.

(2) The rainfall deviation factor in the last row arises from the use of a rainfall dummy in the estimates equations linking per capita NDP growth to per capita growth in capital per worker.

*Source:* Virmani (2004b: Table A1).

10. For a more complete listing of policy changes in this period, see Acharya *et al.* (2006: Box 3.1) and Virmani and Mittal (2006).

11. Total factor productivity calculations are generally based on an underlying production function with unit elasticity of substitution between capital and labour and fixed shares of the two factors in value added. Both assumptions are questionable. Hence, estimates of TFP presented should be treated as illustrative rather than precise.

The prospects for growth look much better in the past few years. The break in 2003-04 is not so much a change in the policy regime as a marked shift in performance. The most striking break from the past is the phenomenal growth in corporate savings from around 4 per cent of GDP at the end of the nineties to 8.8 per cent of GDP in 2007-08. This fuelled a big increase in private sector investment from around 16.5 per cent of GDP at the end of the nineties to 25.7 per cent of GDP by 2007-08. Since then the global crisis has intervened and the growth rates of GDP in 2008-09 fell to 6.7 per cent with some signs of recovery as the advance estimates for 2009-10 indicate a GDP growth rate of 7.2 per cent.

The moot question is whether and how soon the economy can get back to the 9 per cent growth path projected in the 11th Plan. Actual performance of some macro variables is presented in Table 2.3.

**Table 2.3**

*Macroeconomic Performance during 11th Plan*

*(All figures are averages for the Plan period)*

| | *Plan Target* | *2007-08* | *2008-09 Quick Est.* | *2009-10 Advance Est.* |
|---|---|---|---|---|
| 1. GDP growth | 9.0 | 9.2 | 6.7 | 7.2 |
| 2. Investment rate (GDCF as % of GDPmp) | 36.7 | 37.6 | 35.6 | 34.5 |
| Public | 8.0 | 7.9 | 8.5 | NA |
| Private | 28.7 | 28.6 | 26.2 | NA |
| 3. Fixed investment rate (GFCF as % of GDPmp) | - | 33.0 | 33.0 | 32.3 |
| Public | | 8.1 | 8.6 | NA |
| Private | | 24.9 | 24.4 | NA |
| 4. Savings rate (GDS as % of GDPmp) | 34.8 | 36.4 | 32.5 | NA |
| Households | 23.0 | 22.6 | 22.6 | NA |
| Corporate | 7.3 | 8.7 | 8.4 | NA |
| Public | 4.5 | 5.1 | 1.4 | NA |
| 5. Exports as % of GDPmp | 22.5 | 13.5 | 13.8 | NA |
| 6. Imports as % of GDPmp | 38.5 | 20.5 | 23.4 | NA |

*Source:* Data from Press Notes on Quick Estimates 2008-09 (dated 29 January 2010) and Advance Estimates 2009-10 (dated 8 February 2010).

These figures suggest that the sharp increase in investment that underlies the high growth of the four years after 2003-04 has been maintained and fixed investment in particular seems to be on track. The fixed investment rate would suggest that with an ICOR of around 4, a growth rate of 8 per cent is readily achievable. But for 9 per cent growth the investment rate may have to be a little higher than what the Plan projects, particularly if the substantial investment needs for infrastructure are taken into account. Two areas of macro policy may require a special effort: getting government savings back on track and ensuring that capital inflows contribute to real investment growth.

The projections of government savings and the revenue deficit in the 11$^{th}$ Plan involve a major shift. But they are implied by the goals set under the Fiscal Responsibility and Budget Management (FRBM) Act. The key lies in the management of the combined revenue deficit of the Centre and the state deficits which rose to a peak of nearly 7 per cent of GDP in 2001-02, has fallen steadily since then and is projected to fall to 0.48 per cent of GDP in the Budget Estimates for 2008-09 for the Centre and the states. But the actual outcome may well be different, given the amounts pushed out as a stimulus for flagging growth and the slowdown in revenue growth.

As for capital inflows, the absolute amount of inward flow implied by the projection amounts to about $30 billion a year. This looked plausible given the rate at which foreign portfolio and direct investment were flowing when the Plan was formulated, with the actual flow in 2005-06 being around $20 billion. The real challenge is to ensure that these flows are revived, that they focus much more on direct rather than portfolio investment and that they do not end up in even more reserve accumulation. If they do, the Plan investment rate may not be realised, the exchange rate will tend to appreciate, compromising the export goals and the sterilisation of excess reserves could pose major problems for monetary policy.

A crucial challenge for the Plan is the development of infrastructure. The two main areas of concern here are power and the rural infrastructure in the form of irrigation, roads and rural electrification that is necessary for revitalisng agriculture. The issue here is not just the resources but the managerial capacity to implement and operate this infrastructure efficiently.

The real test of feasibility for the Plan does not lie in the arcane algebra of growth accounting or inter-sectoral consistency but in the political economy of public policy choices and on that, some skepticism and caution is warranted because of the lack of political will to correct past distortions in policy. But there are strong growth impulses in the private sector. The main challenge for sustaining high growth is a public policy framework that ensures that this contributes to sustained growth by maintaining competitive pressures and pushing industry closer to technological frontiers, a matter dealt with later in this paper.

## International Comparisons

The sense that we are exceptional is perhaps unavoidable in any large country and a comparision with others may be considered irrelevant. However, it surely is worth finding out if countries similarly placed in some broad sense have done better or worse. Table 2.4 presents data on observed growth rates in developing countries aggregated by continent and a rank for where India would stand in the developing country growth rate league table in each period.

**Table 2.4**

*Growth Rates in a Global Perspective*

*(Average annual growth in GDP at PPP$ at 1990 prices)*

| | *1951-1964* | *1965-1979* | *1980-1990* | *1991-2001* |
|---|---|---|---|---|
| India | 4.11 | 2.95 | 5.76 | 5.63 |
| Asia less Japan | 4.76 | 5.60 | 5.37 | 5.61 |
| Latin America | 5.15 | 5.21 | -0.07 | 0.88 |
| Africa | 4.21 | 4.47 | 2.44 | 2.79 |
| Rank order of Indian growth | 68/108 | 87/108 | 13/108 | 16/108 |

*Note:* (1) The growth rates are for GDP calculated at purchasing power parity in 1990 $s.
(2) The rank order in the last row is the rank in the list of countries ordered by the average annual growth rate for the period indicated in the column. The three aggregated figures for 50 small countries were excluded from this ranking.

*Source:* Author's calculation based on data in Maddison (2003), basic tables 4b/5b/6b.

This table shows that the big difference between India and the rest of the developing world was in the 1965-1979 period. This difference cannot be attributed entirely to the droughts of 1965-66, 1972 and 1979 or to the political turbulence of the Emergency and the subsequent restoration of democracy. Nor can one blame the oil shocks of 1973-74 and 1979-80 which affected all oil importing developing countries. At least part of the blame must be laid at the door of the development strategy followed in the early seventies.

An interesting insight is provided by a comparison of growth rates in the South Asian region grouped by policy regimes that is presented in Table 2.5 drawn from the analysis presented by Dr. Kirit Parikh (2006).

**Table 2.5**

*Policy Regimes and Growth Rates of GDP in South Asia*

| *Policy Regimes* | *India* | *Pakistan* | *Bangladesh* | *Sri Lanka* | *Nepal* |
|---|---|---|---|---|---|
| Free market economy; Passive government | | | | 1947-1956<br>3.67% | |
| Import-substitution; Controlled economy | 1950-1967<br>3.4% | 1950-1957<br>3.1% | 1971-1981<br>2.7% | 1956-1965<br>3.4% | 1966-1980<br>2.3% |
| Import-substitution Rigid controls; Nationalisation | 1967-1980<br>3.8% | 1971-1977<br>4.7% | | 1970-1977<br>2.9% | |
| Export promotion regulated | | 1958-1970<br>6.6% | 1981-1989<br>3.9% | | |
| Deregulation; Import restriction | 1980-1990<br>5.6% | 1978-1988<br>6.1% | | | 1981-1990<br>4.9% |
| Liberalisation | 1992-1996<br>6.7%<br>1997-2000<br>5.4% | 1988-1999<br>4.4% | 1989-1992<br>6.7%<br>1992-2000<br>5.3% | 1977-2000<br>5.0% | 1991-2000<br>5.1% |

*Source:* Parikh (2006: Table 1.8).

The analysis presented in the table above suggest that GDP growth was correlated with the orientation of policy on two broad fronts—the stance towards the external economy and towards the domestic private sector. A shift towards export orientation and/or a reduction in controls on the domestic private sector increased the growth rate. When these are combined, as in the phases included in the last row which deals with liberalisation, the effects are not additive. The record since 2000, which shows a significant acceleration of growth in India and Pakistan since 2003-04, would tend to reinforce this concluson.

The views of planners and researchers on the strategies that can lead to high growth have also been shaped by the experiences of Japan, South Korea, Taiwan and China and the ASEAN countries. Sustained growth over long periods at the levels envisaged by Yojana Bhawan is not unprecedented. It was experienced by several economies in East Asia and elsewhere. Japan between 1950 and 1973, Korea and Taiwan between 1965 and 1990 and China since 1980 are some examples of high growth sustained over long periods.

The sources of East Asian growth have been the subject of extensive discussion amongst researchers. A seminal and much quoted article by Alwyn Young (1995) attributed the growth in non-agricultural output[12] to the increase in capital and labour inputs adjusted for quality with total factor productivity contributing only a modest amount. His estimates of the sources of growth in three East Asian countries and Singapore are presented in Table 2.6.

**Table 2.6**

*Sources of Growth in East Asia*

*(Growth per cent per annum)*

| *Country* | *Output* | *Aggregate Capital* | *Weighted Capital* | *Aggregate Labour* | *Weighted Labour* | *Total Factor Productivity* | *Memo: Labour Share* |
|---|---|---|---|---|---|---|---|
| S. Korea | 10.4 | 12.9 | 13.7 | 5.4 | 6.4 | 1.6 | 0.680 |
| Taiwan | 9.1 | 11.8 | 12.3 | 4.6 | 5.1 | 1.9 | 0.710 |
| Singapore | 8.5 | 10.8 | 11.5 | 4.5 | 5.7 | -0.3 | 0.470 |
| Hong Kong | 7.3 | 7.7 | 8.0 | 2.6 | 3.2 | 2.3 | 0.628 |

*Note:* The data are for non-agricultural output for South Korea and Taiwan and total output for Singapore and Hong Kong. The time period covered is 1966-1990 except Hong Kong where it is 1966-1991.

*Source:* Based on results reported in Young (1995).

12. Young (1995) estimates the sources of growth for four countries—Hong Kong, Singapore, South Korea and Taiwan. For the first two, no adjustment is made for agriculture as these are city states with a minimal agricultural sector. For the latter two, agricultural outputs and inputs are separated out and the sources of growth analysis is for non-agricultural output.

What this analysis shows is that the high growth was based primarily on high rates of factor accumulation. Rates of fixed investment, 30 per cent and over, drove a rapid accumulation of productive assets. There was also a large increase in the industrial labour force with substantial migration from rural to urban areas and an improvement in quality with spending on education and training increasing sharply. The rates of productivity growth seem quite modest in relation to the achieved growth rate.[13]

The sources of growth in China after the big policy changes that began with the Deng era are very similar. Calculations of total factor productivity for China in the pre- and post-Deng period are contained in Table 2.7 which shows that the sharp acceleration in the Chinese growth rate since 1978 is attributable to faster capital accumulation and to productivity growth roughly in the ratio of 1:3.

**Table 2.7**

*Sources of Growth in China*

| | *1952-1978* | *1978-1998* |
|---|---|---|
| **Average Exponential Annual Growth Rate** | | |
| GDP | 5.82 | 9.27 |
| Capital stock | 7.13 | 9.02 |
| Labour | 2.54 | 2.78 |
| Total factor productivity | 0.00 | 2.68 |

*Source:* Chow and Lin (2003).

High growth in East Asia and in South-East Asia was associated with an outward-oriented trade strategy with a strong export bias, based on undervalued exchange rates or export subsidisation. The degree of openness to foreign investment varied. Japan and Korea followed a very restrictive policy on foreign investment while Singapore and Hong Kong based their strategy on attracting foreign investment. Foreign aid may have helped Korea and Taiwan when they were making their transition to outward-oriented growth but not much after that. China and South-East Asia, who came later to the high growth game, are more open but even there the bulk of the investment has been domestic rather than foreign.

13. See Note 11 above on TFP.

The differences between the high growth Asians were less marked when it came to the induction of foreign technology. One characteristic of their high growth path was the high rate at which new products and processes were introduced in the economy. In fact, it has been argued that the production of new products for exports played an important role in stimulating capital accumulation. That is why the algebraic calculations of factor productivity may underestimate the actual pace of technological advance (Khan, 2006).

There are other dimensions to the East Asian experience which we need to understand. We tend to focus attention on what they did to promote industrialisation and exports. But they also put in a great effort at rural reconstruction-land reforms, agricultural development and rural infrastructure. All of them protected their agriculture sector from the opening of the economy.

The political origins of the East Asian high growth paths are rather special. Japan went through the huge trauma of war loss and occupation during which there was a major land reform and restructuring of the corporate sector. In South Korea and Taiwan too, there was an antecedent political upheaval before the new export-oriented policy was implemented. In these countries too, there was an element of US tutelage and support in the crucial early years of reform. In China, the new high growth era started after the political changes that took place with the death of Mao and the old guard and the emergence of Deng as the leader. All of the East Asian tigers had strong authoritarian governments or *de facto* one-party rule during the high growth period. These were systems that could extract high savings from the economy, hold down labour unrest and where government and industry saw eye to eye.

One point is worth emphasising. The East Asian miracle was a product of an interventionist state and that too a state which intervened not just to make markets work but to promote specific economic activities and even specific businesses. The archetype here was MITI (the Ministry of International Trade and Industry in Japan) which acted virtually like a super managing agency, including providing a safety net for business risks.

## Sustaining High Growth

There are many small lessons that one can learn from our own past policy regimes and their impact and from the experience of other high growth episodes. But there is one big lesson that is most important. Imitative development does not work. Each instance of high growth has been different in some essential respect from the other.[14] Even within a country certain policies succeed because of historically specific factors. For instance, one reason for the speed with which some of the East Asians built up domestic competencies in construction and South-East Asian economies started growing rapidly after the mid-sixties was a result of the large US spending in the region during the Vietnam war.

Even the mistakes that have been made sometimes turn out to be beneficial. Some of the "distorted" decisions taken in India during the years when an import-substituting strategy was pursued are today a source of comparative advantage. For instance, investments in aluminium in India were considered inefficient. But today India is a globally competitive producer of that metal.[15] The investments in chemical and petroleum process industries were also considered to be economically unjustifiable. But today, India is a competitive producer of these chemicals and a viable provider of process engineering skills. The auto industry is another example. When Maruti was set up it was widely criticised. But it led to the establishment of a viable component industry that is now a competitive global supplier (Luthra *et al.*, 2005). The establishment of domestic capacity for oil exploration and refining in the early sixties created ONGC which today is a commercially viable global player.

At any given point, a country's development strategy has to work with the competencies it has and the opportunities available. An acceleration of growth is possible as an economy that has been operating below its production frontier catches up and moves to this frontier. This is what may have happened in India in the eighties as the mild loosening of controls and the results of managerial capacity building led to improved project implementation and capacity utilisation. An acceleration is also possible

14. This is well demonstrated in Rodrik (2004).

15. A McKinsey study puts India's aluminium costs below Australia, North America, the energy-rich Middle East and Europe (Bhargava *et al.*, 2005).

with faster factor accumulation as an economy moves up its production function. These sources of acceleration are self-limiting as unused capacity gets used up and as diminishing returns set in with continued movement along a static production function. Sustaining high growth over long periods requires policies that lead to a continuous upward shift in the economy's production function.

In any growing economy, the input of primary factors will increase. A rapidly growing economy will have a high investment rate and the stock of capital will rise. Labour inputs may increase not just because of the increase in numbers but also changes in participation rates, rural-urban migration and most important of all, quality improvements because of better education and training. All of these can be thought of as necessary conditions for accelerating growth. But they are not sufficient for sustaining high growth over an extended period.[16] Judging from experience, the key to sustaining high growth lies in outward-oriented development policy and a continuous effort at maintaining global competitiveness, ensuring a steady shift in production functions that could be described as "technological dynamism" and institutional developments that allow markets to function efficiently.

## Outward Orientation

If growth has to be balanced in the sense that sectoral growth rates have to match the growth in domestic demand then the sector in which supply constraints bite the hardest defines the overall growth rate. This is an onerous restriction. Hence, high growth is almost always unbalanced in the sense that output growth rates across sectors vary more than implied by underlying differences in income elasticities of demand. Trade with other countries takes care of the imbalances in domestic supply and demand that emerge with growth.

The nature of the imbalance will vary with the type of strategy followed. Typically, import substitution policies with over-valued exchange rates and high levels of protection lead to growth in excess of demand across a large number of sectors. This is because they are often

16. The distinction between what is required to accelerate growth and to sustain high growth is a distinction that has been made in Rodrik (2004).

accompanied by a state-imposed capacity limits which prevent investments flooding into the most protected sectors.[17] An export-oriented strategy however works with world demand and capacity direction is hardly possible. Typically, the front of rapid growth is spread across a more limited number of sectors.

The link between the degree of openness to trade and growth has been a subject of extensive academic debate. At one level, the argument has been that trade theory has little to say on the subject beyond the standard case for the static gains from trade liberalisation, which also have been questioned on a variety of grounds.[18] At another level, cross-sectional regression equations linking growth with trade and other determining variables have been used by both sides in the debate.[19]

The more careful and nuanced studies done by OECD, NBER and World Bank have addressed this issue at the country level. The best known of these is the set of studies prepared under the supervision of Prof. Jagdish Bhagwati and Prof. Anne Kreuger.[20] The general conclusion of all of these more detailed studies was that export-oriented development strategies were more successful in promoting growth than import substituting strategies. There were several practical rather than theoretical considerations which could explain this.

- Export-promotion (EP) strategies were better for allocative efficiency because import-substitutions (IS) strategies involved capricious variations in effective rates of protection that distorted investment incentives.

---

17. Indian experience suggests that capacity direction by the government does not prevent a sequence of sectoral investment spurt as entrepreneurs flock to activities that appear most attractive at a given point in time. We have seen in India the rush of investments into sectors like synthetic fibres and mini-steel as entrepreneurs do not want to be left out of opportunities that suddenly seemed lucrative because of policy changes or changes in international prices. We have also seen how so many of these "investment rushes" turned out to be misguided and ultimately loss-making.

18. There is an extensive theoretical literature on trade and growth. In the standard neo-classical growth model of Solow, the steady state growth rate is set by the growth of the labour force in efficiency units and does not depend on trade possibilities at all. However, trade does matter in a Harrod-Domar or Feldman-Mahalanobis model with unused supplies of labour.

19. See Srinivasan and Bhagwati (1999) for a devastating critique of cross-country regression analysis of the link between openness and growth.

20. See Bhagwati (1978) and Kreuger (1978) for two seminal and influential studies.

- IS regimes with over-valued exchange rates went hand in hand with foreign exchange rationing, import controls and investment controls (licence-permit *raj*) and this led to rent-seeking behaviour by entrepreneurs rather than a focus on efficiency and productivity.
- Under IS regimes, tariff and trade barrier jumping foreign investments worsened the welfare losses of these regimes and were limited in amount by the scale of the domestic market.
- Not being limited by the size of the domestic market, EP regimes offered better prospects of scale economies and hence, may have generated a greater stimulus for investment thereby raising rates of capital accumulation.
- The need to compete in global markets may have led to a stronger incentive to absorb new technologies and to innovate.

These practical arguments are borne out by the fact that practically every major episode of high growth has been based on an export-oriented strategy with under-valued exchange rates and a high degree of public policy support for exporting activities.[21] Sustained high growth comes from a fuller exploitation of comparative advantage and goes with a high, and possibly growing degree of outward orientation, measured by the share of foreign trade in national income. Even more tellingly, the acceleration in growth in China and India came after they shifted their emphasis from import substitution to export promotion.

Such a conclusion in no way belittles the contribution made by the earlier IS strategy in building up domestic entrepreneurial and technological capacity. It only says that import substitution may be the way to capacity building and self-reliance but not to sustained high growth. In some ways, the academic dispute between IS and EP proponents misses the point. The important lesson from the EP approach is to recognise that the aim must always be to become globally competitive. The point of the IS strategy is that getting there may require some losses to be borne as competencies and capacities are built up. In fact, a type of infant industry protection may be required even when the ultimate aim is global competitiveness.

21. There are some exceptions like the episode of high growth in Brazil in the 1960s.

The Indian economy has become increasingly outward-oriented with the trade and foreign investment liberalisation after 1991. Exports as a percentage of GDP at market prices had increased slowly from the mid-seventies to reach 5.8 per cent in 1990-91. Since then, this percentage has gone up to 13.2 per cent in 2005-06. The import to GDP (at market prices) percentage rose in the seventies because of the oil price hike from 4 per cent to 9 per cent in 1980-81 and stayed at more or less the same level in 1990-91. Since then, with liberalisation the import ratio has shot up to 19.6 per cent in 2005-06. The story for net invisibles and foreign investment is even more dramatic. From near negligible levels in 1990-91, foreign investment inflows are now 2.5 per cent of GDP and net invisibles have risen from less than one per cent of GDP in 1991-92 to 5.1 per cent by 2005-06.[22]

An outward orientation could make an economy more vulnerable to external shocks. The main source of trade shocks have been the periodic flare up in oil prices which India could not avoid even with a more inward looking strategy as in the seventies. In fact, at that time the lack of an export base reduced the capacity to cope with the trade shock as India was not in a position to profit from the spending by oil rich countries, except through the remittances of expatriate workers. Trade shocks could also arise from business cycle fluctuations. Even here, the experience of the IT export sector suggests that the price competitiveness of sourcing in India could be an advantage when developed country companies are trying to cut costs to cope with an economic downturn.

The situation is rather different with capital account liberalisation. India has moved cautiously in this area and it is this caution which prevented the contagion from the financial crisis of 1997 spreading to India.

The global environment in the nineties has been very different from the preceding decades. The pace of globalisation has quickened as the new information and communication technologies have led to a rapid growth in service trade and financial flows across borders. India profited from it because of policy changes that reduced trade barriers and unleashed

22. The low net invisibles figure for 1990-91 is an aberration and hence, the comparison has been made with 1991-92.

entrepreneurial drive and because of the capacities that had been built up in earlier years in areas like IT services. Indian industry has also coped well with competition, at least in the organised sector, and restructured to thrive in the new policy environment.

India's strength in the global economy lies in skill-intensive manufactures and services. The IT boom rests on that. The same is now true of sectors like auto components. There is also a boom of sorts in the outsourcing of R&D to India. This is the comparative advantage that can continue to drive the growing outward orientation of the Indian economy. This skill-oriented internationalisation and the growing global ambitions of Indian entrepreneurs can help to integrate Indian industry into the world economy.

The dynamics of the global economy are changing and the recent financial crisis has perhaps accelerated the shift of dynamism to Asia. The world continues to depend on continuing growth in the USA; but Asia, including India, has also emerged as an important contributor as is shown in Table 2.8.

**Table 2.8**

*Share in Global Growth*

*(Percentage share in output increase)*

| | *1989-1995* | *1995-2000* | *2000-2004* |
|---|---|---|---|
| USA | 20.58 | 25.99 | 16.36 |
| China | 27.98 | 22.07 | 28.37 |
| India | 9.06 | 8.45 | 9.63 |
| Rest of developing Asia | 18.63 | 8.15 | 9.45 |
| Other regions | 23.75 | 35.34 | 36.19 |
| World | 100.00 | 100.00 | 100.00 |

*Source:* Jorgensen and Vu (2006).

These changes in global dynamics are to India's advantage as new markets and new opportunities develop closer to our shores. But to profit from this will require continuing competitive pressures and a capacity for technological dynamism.

## Technological Dynamism

Technological dynamism has to be thought of along several dimensions. One dimension is the familiar one of factor productivity—the efficiency with which primary factors like capital and labour are used. This is the dimension that we measure in calculations of total factor productivity. A closely related dimension is that of energy and material productivity. This is the dimension that we measure when we calculate changes in input-output coefficients over time.

These measurable dimensions of productivity dynamism are well known and understood. But sustained high growth requires us to look beyond these to the rate at which innovations in the form of new products, processes, business practices are introduced and the rate at which new markets are penetrated. This Schumpeterian dimension of productivity dynamism is perhaps the most important in the long run.

An outward-oriented development strategy generates pressures for technological dynamism in both senses—improvements in efficiency in established products and processes and the introduction of new activities, new products and new processes.

Export production depends much more on productivity management at the shop floor and enterprise level. International product and service markets operate within a quality band and a potential supplier has to be above a minimum quality threshold to be able to compete. Between this minimum and the global best practice, there is some scope for price competition, which can be assisted by an under-valued exchange rate. But below the quality minimum lower prices do not help. Hence, an export-oriented strategy generates pressures for quality improvement at the product level which, in turn often goes with productivity improvements, for instance in the form of a reduction in the proportion of defectives in production runs (Sutton, 2006).

Export production also requires that domestic suppliers who can pass the global quality threshold be price competitive. They have to operate in a market where other suppliers are continually improving their productivity and reducing costs. An under-valued exchange rate and export subsidies can give a one-time advantage but cannot help to cope with a continuous downward pressure on costs and upward pressure on product quality. Hence, an export-oriented strategy generates pressures for productivity dynamism in the exporting sectors.

High growth also involves the exploitation of scale economies and increasing returns. Increasing returns is difficult to accommodate within the framework of equilibrium economics and that is one reason why the standard version of neo-classical economics has always seemed implausible as a guide to policy makers in developing countries. Yet economies with increasing returns do operate within an essentially capitalist market economy and the recourse to governmental direction is an inadequate response to the problem. Market players respond to incentives and the real challenge is to design incentive compatible policy interventions that guide markets rather than direct producers so that the outcomes realise the gains from increasing returns.

Growth can be self-reinforcing. At the enterprise level, this can come from learning by doing as workers and managers hone their skills. It can also come from external economies. For instance, economies of agglomeration can arise as more and more enterprises enter a particular field of activity and input supply chains realise economies of scale, thereby reducing costs and improving reliability. These agglomeration economies are most often realised at specific locations resulting in a comparative advantage for that location and for the country.

The locational specialisation that comes from agglomeration economies can be seen in the skewed geographical spread of particular industries not just between regions but between cities and sometimes even within cities. This can lead to regional imbalances in overall development as the region or city which specialises in a fast growing industry wins out over others stuck with slow growing ones. In fact it has been argued that these microeconomic roots of growth inevitably lead to a worsening of regional imbalances during episodes of high growth (Aghion *et al.*, 2005).

Agglomeration economies are external economies because the cost benefits of an additional enterprise in the parent industry (that generates the external economies) accrue not just to that enterprise but to all. Hence, the private incentive to co-locate with others is less than the industry-level gain, which would justify a public policy that corrects the gap between private and social return. In India, closely linked agglomerations of linked firms come up almost inevitably because, with poor transport facilities, supplier firms try and locate close to the buyer firms. The link between entrepreneurship, caste and community amongst start-up entrepreneurs is another factor that works towards this. Public policy offering locational incentives must therefore work within the framework of a cluster approach.[23]

Technological dynamism and even factor accumulation is closely tied to the prospects and opportunities offered by evolving markets. When an opportunity opened up with the Y2K problem, large numbers of Indians went and acquired computer programming skills, often paying for it at commercial rates. In a sources of growth calculation, this will show up as an increase in labour supply in efficiency units and we would conclude that observed growth was a move along the production function rather than a shift of the function. That would be misleading as the skill acquisition is actually a product of the change in opportunities that leads to new activities appearing in the economy. A recent study treats sustained exports of new products as a proxy for this type of skill and technology acquisition and establishes its connection with investment (Khan, 2006).

The calculations of factor productivity presented earlier in Table 2.2 show a clear acceleration in productivity growth after 1980. Some estimates of factor productivity growth at the sectoral level are presented in Table 2.9. They should be treated as indicative since they rest on some heroic assumptions about factor use at the sectoral level. However, they do suggest a distinct acceleration in productivity growth in recent years.

The broader dimensions of technological dynamism are more difficult to measure. But there is some anecdotal evidence of a capacity for product and process engineering for innovation. Auto components are one area where technological dynamism is already evident. Around 80 per cent of Indian auto component suppliers have ISO 9000 certification.[24] There are examples of Indian firms re-engineering auto components like steering

23. This is being championed by the Foundation for MSME Clusters. More information is available at *www.smeclusters.org*

24. This is the international standard for quality management.

mechanisms, reducing manufacturing costs by lowering the level of automation and capital costs by refurbishing second-hand equipment. International auto makers like Toyota are investing in design development and manufacturing facilities in India. In fact in the auto sector, local content rules are becoming unnecessary as India is becoming a global supply source for most car manufacturers (Luthra *et al.*, 2005). The pharmaceutical industry is another one where domestic firms are graduating from reverse engineering already discovered compounds to new drug discovery.

**Table 2.9**

*Sectoral Growth in Factor Productivity*

*(Per cent per annum)*

| | *1950-51 to 1964-65* | *1965-66 to 1979-80* | *1980-81 to 1991-92* | *1992-93 to 2003-04* |
|---|---|---|---|---|
| Mining | -4.3 | -2.1 | -0.2 | 4.3 |
| Manufacturing | 0.4 | -0.8 | 1.3 | 2.4 |
| Electricity | -17.0 | 0.6 | 4.1 | 4.7 |
| Trans. & comm. | -2.1 | 1.5 | 2.8 | 4.9 |

*Source:* Virmani (2004b: Table 2.2).

Technological dynamism requires engineering skills and innovation needs investment in R&D. India started early on this track and some of the growth that we see today is a product of that foresight. However, it runs the risk of being left behind by countries like China which have expanded their system of higher education and raised quality standards rapidly. In civilian R&D investments also China is forging ahead. Hence, maintaining the edge that India has in skill based manufacturing and services will require a major effort to upgrade technical education and research capacity. Competitive pressures will do that in the private sector. But the world over corporate R&D needs the base of research in public institutions like universities and research laboratories.

## Promoting Competition

The major gains in productivity performance have come from the increase in competitive pressures on Indian industry. In the public sector, the shift away from budgetary financing to capital market-based financing has generated pressures to perform better. In the private sector, delicensing and tariff reduction have sharpened the edge of competition in the market place. Even in the infrastructure sector, the changes that we have seen in telecommunications are a product of competition.

A variety of policy changes have been made to make the economy not just business-friendly but also market-friendly.[25] The distinction between these two approaches is crucial. A business-friendly approach means a government which works closely with businesses, individually or collectively to promote preferred activities. It may take the form of directed credit, trade policy changes modulated to the needs of domestic producers, active help in foreign markets and so on. It quickly shades into what could be described as crony capitalism, a charge levied at the policy framework in some South-East Asian and even East Asian countries. The model for such an approach was provided by the Japanese MITI (Ministry of International Trade and Industry).[26]

A market-friendly approach, on the other hand focuses more on setting rules of the game and leveling the playing field for all producers and sectors. This means, for instance, that credit is not directed at specific borrowers or even to preferred sectors. A market-friendly credit policy works with measures like the interest rates at which the central bank will lend, prudential norms, disclosure requirements to protect consumers and so on. A market-friendly approach would also mean greater uniformity in indirect tax rates with differences being justified on objective social cost or benefit grounds. This is the liberal economic order that is beloved of economists and is the underlying philosophy of economic policy in countries like the USA and the UK.

A business-friendly policy system was possible in East Asia and South-East Asia in a political environment which was very different from the fractious and open political environment in India. Discrimination is possible in India at the sector level as the continuing support for small industry and backward area reservations and concessions shows. However, discrimination that goes much beyond this to promote "winners" in

25. See Kohli (2006) for a political scientist's view of this distinction and how it has played out in India.

26. The author recollects a strong interest amongst Indian policy makers in this model in the eighties.

specific sectors sooner or later degenerates into rent-seeking by politicians, bureaucrats and their business cronies. Even if it is a bona fide discrimination it will attract unfavourable political and media attention and soon become impossible. Hence, the MITI model is not the way to go as far as India is concerned.

India has to move towards a market-friendly, non-discriminatory mode of policy intervention. Some steps have been taken towards this end. In the fiscal sphere, the FRBM Acts, the changed procedures for government borrowing, the trend towards more standardised indirect tax rates are moves in this direction. In financial markets, the progress to a non-discriminatory rule-based regime is particularly striking. The changes include the replacement of discretionary controls exercised by the erstwhile CCI (Controller of Capital Issues) by SEBI, the establishment of the Insurance Regulator, the changes in the trading systems in the stock exchanges and the opening to private and foreign entrants which has sharpened the edge of competition for the benefit of consumers. Regulatory authorities have also been set up for power, telecommunications and other infrastructure sectors which have been also opened to competition from private and foreign suppliers.

The transition from planning to a market-friendly policy system is still work in progress. The objectives and modalities pursued by the independent regulators and the proposed Competition Commission have to be coherent. A market-friendly policy mode has to focus on ensuring freedom of entry, which is the best guarantor of competition, ensuring that market power is not abused and that consumers are protected. In pursuing these general objectives, each regulatory authority will have to ask more specific questions related to conditions in India.[27] Some of these are as follows:

- *Trade Competition*: Is the product tradeable/non-tradeable in principle and in practice? Does the size of the domestic market pose barriers to foreign competition?
- *Size Structure*: Are the units in the industry predominantly large/small/a mix of the two?

---

27. Academic research can play an important role in the evolution of a coherent approach to regulatory issues across sectors. Hence, the need for industrial and agricultural economics research will be even greater as we move to a market-friendly policy system.

- *Organisational Structure*: What is the public-private mix? What is the role of business houses (conglomerates)?
- *Market Integration*: How integrated is the domestic market as measured by price differentials? What is the degree of product differentiation?
- *Role of the Government*: What is the role of the government as purchaser? As controller of natural resources?
- *Entry Barriers*: Are their entry barriers because of the way upstream or downstream industries are organised or because of the nature of the distribution system?

A market-friendly policy does not rule out measures to assist producers. It only requires that such measures should be based on a sound analysis of market failure. For instance, it is plausible to argue that small producers who have the capacity to use credit well, do not have access to such credit because, given informational asymmetries and the small size of the loan transactions, large lending institutions do not meet their needs. This is a type of market failure in the market for small loans and can justify public intervention to promote micro finance, farm credit cooperatives and so on.

Making markets work involves more than interposing an independent regulator between the government and the producer or supplier. It also involves modernisation of trading practices and improved transport connectivity to connect markets better. There is some evidence that markets in India are becoming more integrated in the sense that price differentials for identical commodities are narrowing with the coefficient of variation across centres in different regions coming down (Virmani and Mittal, 2006). However, much more needs to be done to improve transport connectivity and to modernise trading systems for instance by bringing in screen-based trading for standard commodities the way it has been done for shares.

## What if We Succeed

The growth target of 9 per cent is clearly ambitious. But the evidence available suggests that a growth rate of 7 per cent or so is fully consistent with recent trends. The difference between these two is a measure of the challenge for policy. But it is also a measure of the distance India has travelled from the "Hindu Rate of Growth" of Raj Krishna.

What would India be like if the ambitions of the Approach Paper are realised and we have 9 per cent growth for say 15 years and in realising this, we do all of the things about outward orientation, technological dynamism, competition and regional balance that were stated as necessary conditions for this to happen?

There would clearly be a massive improvement in living conditions with per capita incomes tripling. But will the spread of income growth being more evenly spread between regions for if it is not, a political backlash can be expected. There is some evidence that regional disparities have widened after 1980s as growth rates of states have diverged (Rodrik and Subramaniam, 2004). Liberalisation tends to favour firms and regions that are closer to the production frontier and hence can widen disparity. That has happened since 1991 according to one study (Aghion *et al.*, 2003).

In India, the main challenge is to accelerate growth in the densely populated heartlands of the North and in the East. This is also where the growth in the labour force will be the largest. This part of the country needs labour-intensive non-agricultural employment. The impetus for this can come from the rising demand for consumer goods within the country, provided public investments in transport connects these regions to high growth regions reducing transit times to markets. This may be a more plausible route than labour-intensive export-production *a la* China. Of course, there are other things which will have to be done like labour training, power supply, and above all improved administration and law and order.

With 9 per cent growth, the structure of the economy would be very different so that agriculture would account for around 10 per cent of GDP as against its present share of 20-25 per cent. This structural change in the economy will also imply an India that is largely urbanised.

The occupational structure will also change. In the 2001 Census, there were about 400 million workers, 250 million in agriculture and household industry and 150 million in other sectors. By 2021, the total number of workers may be around 550 million on the assumption that the proportion of workers to the population in the 15-59 age group is around the same as in 2001.[28] If non-agricultural employment increases at 6 per cent per year,[29] as proposed in the Approach Paper, then the number of workers outside agriculture and household industry would be 440-480 million.[30] This would mean that agriculture would have 100 million or less workers by 2021.

The implications of such a structural change in output and employment are far-reaching. Non-agricultural work in India has always attracted workers from often distant parts of India even in pre-Independence days and even more so now. Hence, we can expect a high degree of mobility with many people living away from their home regions and practicing occupations quite different from their parents. The expansion of higher education and the rising proportion of young adults in the population will reinforce this tendency. What we are looking at is an India where many of the present divisions of caste, language and religion may become less relevant for determining a person's life chances or status in society. It is an India that will have to tolerate and even cherish diversity. There are of course strong ethical and political grounds for a culture of tolerance. The point in the context of this paper is that it is also an economic necessity in a booming economy where migration and mobility are absolutely essential.

An outwardly-oriented India will become a major player in the global economy with a GDP that would be the third largest in the world. Indian capital has already started going global and this internationalisation of Indian businesses would be reinforced by the search for energy and other materials and for markets. Technological dynamism would reinforce this trend.

A high growth development path based on outward orientation and the promotion of a competitive environment domestically leads clearly to a capitalist liberal economic order with a government that remains at arm's length from private decisions about investment, pricing, etc. Its role would

28. A rising proportion staying in higher education would tend to reduce the proportion, but an increase in the female participation rate may tend to increase it.

29. This would allow for a substantial increase in output per worker in non-agriculture given the Plan projections of growth in industry and services.

30. The range reflects the uncertainty about the extent of non-agricultural growth between 2001 and 2006.

be to set up the legislative and regulatory framework for protecting the public interest and maintaining competition. But would that be all?

The history of capitalist market-based development in a democratic environment suggests that the government may have to do more. For capitalist development to be accepted by the majority, who will be workers rather than owners, sooner or later, the state has had to accept certain social responsibilities. In the USA, it took the form of the new deal, in Europe it was the welfare state and the social market economy. The terminology varies but in all cases the state accepted a certain role in providing social protection.

India too will have to recognise this. The need for this will become greater as migration, urbanisation and occupational shifts take people away from traditional support structures. A predominantly non-agricultural urbanised workforce will need a safety net to cope with the ups and downs of business cycles. A growing population of older persons, separated from children who may have moved to new opportunities in a booming economy, will need pensions and other support. Social protection for an urban population is qualitatively different from the anti-poverty schemes that are today the dominant mode of redistributive intervention by Government in India. Sustaining high growth will require the establishment of a system of social security for which we are ill-prepared as of now.

There is another important role for governmental intervention and that is to protect the environment. This is necessary even now. In fact, the revival of agricultural dynamism will not be possible without addressing issues of externalities in land and water management that require social control and governmental support. But with urbanisation and industrialisation proceeding at a fast pace, there is a formidable challenge in establishing effective legislation and institutions from the municipal to the national level. There are also some long-term concerns, particularly in the area of energy and water, which are seldom reflected adequately in market signals. This is a case of missing markets or externalities and is perhaps the most important area for public intervention in a market economy.

Do we have the political process that is needed to realise the vision of development implied by a high growth path? The policy shifts required to sustain a high growth path are very substantial. They may resonate well in the few areas in the country that have done well in the new liberalised economy. But they command little support elsewhere though that seems to be changing with the states that have lagged behind aiming at duplicating the experience of leading states with a push to attract export industries and foreign investment. But we continue with a language of political discourse that seeks protection for sectional interests in public policy. The compulsions of electoral politics lead to decisions for short-term political gains. This is where the most serious doubts about the sustainability of high growth come in. We have an economy and a workforce that is capable of sustaining high growth. The real question is whether we have a political system that is capable of leading and directing us in that direction.

## References


Acharya, Shankar, Isher Judge Ahluwalia, K.L. Krishna and Ila Patnaik (2006). "Economic growth in India, 1950-2000", in Parikh, Kirit S. (ed.) *Explaining Growth in South Asia*. New Delhi: Oxford University Press.

Aghion, Philippe, Robin Burgess, Stephen Redding and Fabrizio Zilibotti (2005). "Entry liberalization and inequality in industrial performance", *Journal of the European Economic Association* 3(2-3): 291-302.

Bhagwati, Jagdish (1978). *Foreign Trade Regimes and Economic Development: Anatomy and Consequences of Exchange Control Regimes*. Cambridge, MA: Ballinger.

Bhalla, Surjit S. (2007). *Second Among Equals: The Middle Class Kingdoms of India and China*. Washington, DC: Institute for International Economics. (forthcoming)

Bhargava, Rajat, Rajat Gupta and Babar Khan (2005). "Unearthing India's mineral wealth", *The McKinsey Quarterly*, 2005 Special Edition.

Chow, Gregory and Anloh Lin (2003). "Accounting for economic growth in Taiwan and Mainland China: A comparative analysis", *http://129.3.20.41/eps/ge/papers/0306/0306003.pdf*

Hatekar, Neeraj and Amrish Dongre (2005). "Structural break's in India's growth", *Economic & Political Weekly* 40(14): 1432-35. Mumbai, India.

Jorgensen, Dale W. and Khuong Vu (2006). "Information technology and the world growth resurgence", Hitotsubashi University Research Unit for Statistical Analysis in the Social Sciences, *Discussion Paper* Series No. 181, Hitotsiubashi University, Tokyo.

Kelkar, Vijay (2006). "India: On the growth turnpike", in *The First Ten K.R. Narayanan Orations*, The Australian National University, Canberra: ANU E Press.

Khan, Faruk A. (2006). "New product technology, accumulation and growth", World Bank Policy Research", *Working Paper* No. 3846. Washington: World Bank.

Kohli, Atul (2006a). "Politics of economic growth in India, 1980-2005, Part I: The 1980s", *Economic & Political Weekly* 40(14): 1432-35, Mumbai, India.

———. (2006b). "Politics of economic growth in India, 1980-2005, Part II: The 1990s and Beyond", *Economic & Political Weekly* 40(14): 1432-35, Mumbai, India.

Kreuger, Anne (1978). *Foreign Trade Regimes and Economic Development: Liberalization Attempts and Consequences*. Cambridge, MA: Ballinger.

Luthra, Shashank, Ramesh Mangaleswran and Asutosh Padhi (2005). "When to make India a manufacturing base", *The McKinsey Quarterly*, 2005 Special Edition.

Maddison, Angus (2003). *The World Economy: Historical Statistics*. Paris: Development Centre, OECD.

Nagaraj, R. (2000). "Indian economy since 1980: Virtuous growth or polarisation", *Economic and Political Weekly*, pp. 2831-39. August 5.

———. (2003). "Industrial policy and performance since 1980: Which way now?", *Economic and Political Weekly* 38(35): 3707-15. August 30.

Nayyar, Deepak (2006). "India's unfinished journey transforming growth into development", *Modern Asian Studies* 40(3): 797–832. Cambridge, UK: Cambridge University Press.

Parikh, Kirit S. (2006). "Overview of South Asian countries: Case studies", in Parikh, Kirit S. (ed.), *Explaining Growth in South Asia*. New Delhi: Oxford University Press.

Rodrik, Dani (2004). "Growth strategies", Kennedy School of Government; *http://www.ksg.harvard.edu/rodrik/*

Rodrik, Dani and Arvind Subramaniam (2004). "From 'Hindu Growth' to productivity surge: The mystery of the Indian growth transition", IMF Staff Papers.

Sivasubramaniam, S. (2000). *The National Income of India during the Twentieth Century*. Delhi: Oxford University Press.

Srinivasan, T.N. and Jagdish Bhagwati (1999). "Outward-orientation and development: Are revisionists right?", Center *Discussion Paper* No. 806, Economic Growth Center, Yale University.

Sutton, John (2006). "The globalization process: Auto-component supply chains in China and India", London School of Economics, available at *http://personal.lse.ac.uk/sutton/auto_component_printroom_version3.pdf*

Virmani, Arvind and Surabhi Mittal (2006). "Domestic market integration", ICRIER *Working Paper* 183. New Delhi: ICRIER.

Virmani, Arvind (2004a). "India's economic growth: From socialist rate of growth to bharatiya rate of growth", *Working Paper* No. 122, ICRIER, February. *www.icrier.org/wp122.pdf*

———. (2004b). "Sources of India's economic growth: Trends in total factor productivity", *Working Paper* No. 131, ICRIER, May. *www.icrier.org/wp131.pdf*

Young, Alwyn (1995). "The tyranny of numbers: Confronting the reality of east asian growth experience", *Quarterly Journal of Economics*, August.

# 3 Transparency in Macroeconomic Policy

Indira Rajaraman*

## Introduction

Vijay Kelkar was the Chairman of the Thirteenth Finance Commission, which was appointed to a two-year term in November 2007. Of the other four members, I was the only one who had no prior experience of having worked with him. During the two-year tenure of the Commission, I could see his deep commitment to fiscal reform, and in particular, his convictions about the configuration that the goods and services tax (GST) should take for it to be maximally facilitative of a common market, and minimally distortionary of resource allocation.

I myself had just completed my membership of the Transparency Advisory Panel of the Committee on Financial Sector Assessment (the report of the Committee was published with a lag, in 2009). I was keen that the recommendations of the Finance Commission should, among other things, enhance the transparency of the fiscal system in India, and Chairman Kelkar was willing to accommodate that concern. This essay expands further on those discussions, which were limited to the fiscal sphere.

Fiscal transparency finds very wide support in general. More, and better, information about public expenditure and revenue intent is sought by both market-friendly reformers and supporters of the role of the state. The case for fiscal transparency is atheoretic. It is not shaped by theory, nor constrained by issues other than the need to protect the identity of individual taxpayers, and perhaps national security considerations.

---

* This paper is based on a presentation by the author at an IPD Task Force Meeting on *Governance, Transparency and Accountability* at Columbia University, 27-28 April 2009.

Monetary policy, on the other hand, relies on the control of levers affecting private market players. The issue of what should be revealed therefore becomes amenable to theorising on the reactions of market players to information. Present-day prescriptions for monetary policy transparency are based on stylised models. This essay argues that the standards beamed at developing countries, for what constitutes transparent functioning and accountability in the conduct of monetary and regulatory policy, carry some components that are diagnostically flawed, and unsuited to the economic structures and political economy pressures found in these countries.

The case of the Reserve Bank of India (RBI) is used to illustrate this issue. A widely cited assessment of 100 central banks over the period 1998-2006 by Nergiz Dincer and Barry Eichengreen (2009), based on an index developed by Petra Geraats (2002), gives the RBI among the lowest ratings for monetary policy transparency. This essay argues that the low rating is a consequence of the term "transparency" having been subverted in the Geraats calibration to mean rigidity in adherence to certain pre-announced targets, in particular the inflation rate in the market for goods and services, sanctioned by stylised models which do not factor in the long-term structural damage that can occur in the intervals between comparative static equilibria.

The actions taken by the RBI, in the face of the quadrupling of capital inflows over 2004-2008, are examined as a case in point. It is not the burden of this essay to defend the particular policy choices made during that episode. The purpose instead is to argue that the freedom to choose targets, in a context-specific manner, cannot be judged on a transparency dimension.

Transparency correctly defined remains of paramount importance, but it should be correctly defined to mean full disclosure of policy decisions, prior to effective dates, with pre-announced finite (or indefinite) durations, and full disclosure *post facto* of interventions by the central bank as a buyer or seller in any market of relevance to its role as defined under its statutes. There is a massive literature on what that role should be, which is not covered in this essay. The limited purpose here is to argue that that role, whatever it may be, is not amenable to rating on a transparency scale.

Other transparency messages beamed at developing countries, such as that state ownership of commercial banks is in and of itself an obstruction to transparency in the financial system, are not examined here, because they have been effectively challenged by the role of privately owned banks in precipitating the global financial crisis.

## Received Stylised Monetary Policy Models

In the stylised monetary policy model that underpins the Geraats transparency index (Geraats, 2002), the central bank maximises the objective function:

$$W = -\tfrac{1}{2}\alpha\,(\pi - \tau)^2 - \tfrac{1}{2}(1 - \alpha)\,(y - \kappa)^2$$

Inflation target : $\tau$ (actual inflation is $\pi$)

Output gap target : $\kappa$ (actual output gap is y)

The actual output gap y is impacted by the rate of interest, r, and unanticipated demand shocks, d, thus:

$$y = -r + d$$

The economy is defined by the following expectations–augmented Phillips equation, which accommodates unanticipated supply shocks, s, thus:

$$\pi = \pi^e + y + s$$

The optimal (policy) rate of interest in such a system will be given by the first order condition for maximisation of the objective function W of the central bank with respect to r, thus (given $\pi^e$):

$$r = \alpha\,(\pi^e - \tau) - (1 - \alpha)\,\kappa + \alpha s + d$$

If there is a credible inflation target to which inflationary expectations in the economy get equated, so that the first term in the above equation disappears, that leaves (for unchanged output targets) a rate of interest that needs to be changed only for adjustment to unanticipated supply and demand shocks. It is this first order condition which underlies the diktat that credible prior disclosure of $\tau$, the inflation target, should be the core component of monetary policy transparency. By setting inflationary expectations, the policy rate of interest is free to target adjustments to supply and demand shocks to the system, and therefore reduce output volatility. Note that the transparency definition so obtained is not an end in itself, but is justified because it subserves the larger cause of macroeconomic stability.

The problem with this formulation of course is that the exogenous shocks s and d in the equation are all real shocks, and inflation stability refers uniquely to prices of real goods and services. Exogenous developments in the financial sector do not have any play in this model. An example of the kind of exogenous financial shock that could destabilise the real system might be, say, a capital inflow surge, in a world of free capital flows. In the face of such a surge, the single-minded pursuit of stable (inflation in) prices of goods and services could lead to disastrous volatility in another price, the exchange rate of the domestic currency. An appreciation spike in the exchange rate could then lead to a follow-on negative real (external) demand shock, d, which will be endogenous to policy pursuit of the inflation target. In a friction-free world, the directionality of correction would of course be perfectly aligned with what it should be to restore the system to the pre-surge equilibrium. The interest rate r will be lowered to correct the negative external demand shock, and it will reinforce the exchange rate appreciation to choke off the capital inflow surge which caused the problem in the first place.

The central problem is that in the world as we know it, which is not friction-free, this process of adjustment will not be instantaneous. If it ruptures links between exporters and buyers which cannot quickly get restored, there could be a long-term demand shock which does not get corrected with lower interest rates. The extent to which this is likely would be a function of the concentration of products and destinations in the export basket; the importance of exports in aggregate demand; and whether the export production vector is aligned with the domestic demand vector. Developing countries are in general far more vulnerable than developed countries on all three counts. There could arise situations in which large-scale defaults by exporters could seriously destabilise the banking system. Single-minded pursuit of price stability could result in disastrous instability, both real and financial.

Although the objective function maximised in the model allows two goals, the analysis in the paper takes each of these targets sequentially, holding the other constant, and the advantages of prior disclosure apply unambiguously in the case of $\tau$ alone. Indeed, the paper shows that prior disclosure of $\kappa$ alone, without prior disclosure of $\tau$, would mean that inflationary expectations are not anchored, and could require movements in the rate of interest opposite in direction to that required to correct the output gap.

## Rating Central Banks on Transparency

The monetary policy transparency index advanced by Geraats (2002), based on the model outlined above, provides for a rating of Central Banks on a scale of 0-15. The index has five constituents, each carrying three sub-components with a maximum score of one. The five constituents are: political; economic; procedural; policy; and operational transparency respectively.

Political transparency is defined as "...a formal statement of objectives, including an explicit prioritisation in case of multiple goals, (and) a quantification of the primary objective(s)..." This component of the Geraats index requires, for multiple goals, quantified disclosure of each. In the simple two-goal monetary policy objective function used in the Geraats paper, this calls for disclosure of both $\tau$ and $\kappa$, and further prioritisation of these (the parameter alpha in the model). As described earlier, the only unambiguous prescription flowing from the model applies to the disclosure of the inflation target alone. The impact of disclosure of multiple objectives is not addressed, and clearly the quantification of both could in practice raise serious issues of mutual compatibility.

Economic transparency is defined as "disclosing data, policy models and forecasts", procedural transparency as "release of minutes and votes", and policy transparency as "prompt announcement and comprehensive explanation of policy decisions". Disregarding for the moment issues of overlap between these categories, transparency so defined reduces the central bank to a mechanically predictable player in financial markets, a dangerous reduction in autonomy for a policy function. The final requirement of operational transparency, calling for "release of information about disturbances and control errors", removes the last trace of judgement from the monetary policy function.

The Geraats index therefore subverts the term "transparency" to mean:

- adherence to a preferably single objective like stability of price levels in the market for goods and services, with admissibility of other objectives if there is quantification of both the targets themselves as well as their relative priority with respect to price stability, when what developing countries (and arguably developed countries as well) need is macroeconomic stability, where the components of that objective are not possible to prioritise *a priori*, independently of context;
- rigidity in central bank objectives, when flexibility is needed to respond to unforeseen eventualities as developing countries open up; and
- predictability in central bank actions, and full exposure of the basis for those actions, which denies discretionary actions towards ensuring real and financial stability.

Finally, by posing an index for the measurement of monetary policy transparency alone, the regulatory function is ignored, where this could be an even more important lever by which to ensure financial stability, as the global crisis of 2008 so clearly demonstrates.

The exercise by Dincer and Eichengreen assigns transparency scores to 100 central banks using the Geraats index, for each year of the eight-year period 1998-2006. The average score across all of them rose from 3.4 in 1998 to 5.4 in 2006. The Reserve Bank of India (RBI) scored 2 in 1998 and stayed there, among the lowest scores in the whole set, and the lowest in South Asia. In the section which follows, the actions of this particular central bank, rated by D-G as hopelessly non-transparent, during an episode of capital inflow surge, are examined.

## Price Stability and Financial Stability

India witnessed an unprecedented quadrupling of capital inflows over the period 2004-2008. In the year 2007-08 alone, net capital inflows amounted to 108 billion dollars (9.2 per cent of GDP), at a time when the current account deficit amounted to only 17 billion dollars (1.5 per cent of GDP).

Clearly, the conjunction of the two posed heavy appreciation pressure on the Indian currency. This was resisted by the central bank through sterilised purchase of dollars. Figure 3.1 shows the outcomes in terms of capital inflows, external reserves, and the nominal effective exchange rate of the rupee.

By having pursued multiple objectives which were unquantified and not prioritised, the bank lost all hope of improving its Dincer-Eichengreen transparency score, but in the words of the Report of the (Raghuram Rajan) Committee on Financial Sector Reforms (Planning Commission, Government of India, 2009): "...monetary policy (did manage to) strike a balance between managing inflation and stabilising the nominal exchange rate" (pp.28-29). The report hastens to add: "...this Committee believes it is neither possible nor advisable to manage the external value of the rupee". In its overall recommendations, the report says: "The RBI should formally have a single objective...a low inflation number...and move steadily to a single instrument, the short-term interest rate...... to achieve it."

**Figure 3.1**

*Capital Inflows, Reserves and NER*

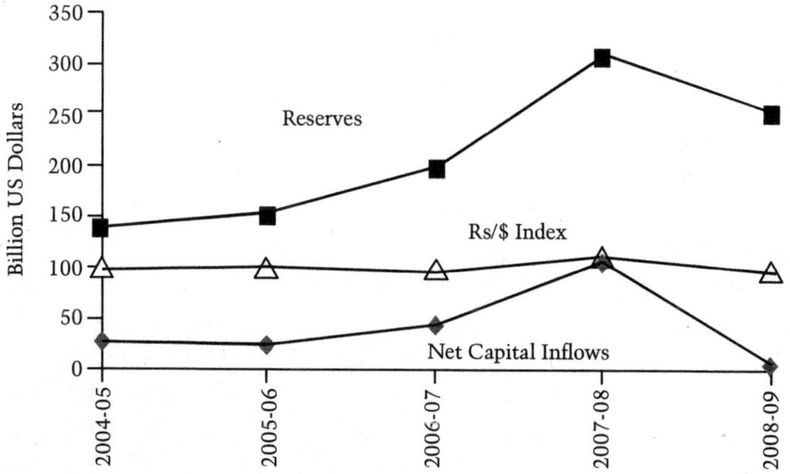


*Note:* NER - Nominal Exchange Rate.

*Source:* *Reserve Bank of India Bulletin*, assorted issues.

The issue here is not that of whether the actions taken were correct in quantum or direction. There may still be analysts who would argue that the best option at the time would have been to allow some appreciation of the rupee. What is at issue is whether the RBI should have been free to determine its course of action in response to contingencies as they arose, in this case an unparalleled and unpredicted capital inflow surge, or whether it should have had its hands tied by a prior quantified commitment to price stability. Surely there would have been a severe loss of monetary policy effectiveness if instead of retaining the option of a variety of instruments, there had been an unavoidable choice of instrument dictated by a prior commitment. Monetary policy cannot be reduced to a mechanical element in the policy structure, with no judgemental discretion left with which to handle external shocks. The impact on exports of a volatile exchange rate driven by capital inflows over 2004-2008 would have led to widespread exporter defaults, and thereby destabilised the banking system. The retention of multiple options in monetary policy was arguably more reassuring to markets than a policy straitjacket that ruled out some options altogether. That policy straitjacket, as was clear from the model, is not lacking in internal consistency or coherence. The element missing is that the comparative statics of the model do not factor in the time intervals between equilibria, and the economic (and possibly political) turbulence during those intervals.

## Bubbles and Regulation

In a bid to regulate the housing bubble building up over 2005-2008, concomitant with the capital inflow surge, the RBI took pre-emptive action on two fronts. Risk weights on commercial real estate loans were raised starting July 2005 in stages to a peak of 150 per cent by May 2006, and provisioning requirements were raised starting May 2006, also in stages. Both were lowered back to pre-existing levels in November 2008. These hikes did not affect housing loans to individuals; indeed, at the same time as the risk weight hikes for commercial real estate, those applying to individual housing loans were actually reduced for some classes of borrowers as a function of the loan to value ratio. However, provisioning requirements were raised for individual loans along with those for commercial real estate, although not to the same levels. Other interventions included a notification in March 2006, restricting loan disbursement to commercial real estate borrowers only when all prior government clearances for the project had been obtained.

The second was the issue of *Guidelines on Securitisation of Standard Assets* in February 2006, as a safeguard against the abuse of originate-to-distribute practices, which were at the heart of the global financial collapse of 2008. These actions were critically important in containing the build-up of a real estate bubble in India.

The document on *Securitisation of Standard Assets* is an exemplary prudential document, which can with advantage serve as a model for the world. It is not reproduced here, but the distinctive features which served the financial market well was the careful distinction drawn between "true sale" of a housing loan, under which the originator would not be required to maintain any capital against the value of assets transferred out, and transactions where the originator carried first and second loss credit enhancement facilities so as to give comfort to the buyer. Both of these facilities were to be deducted from Tier I and Tier II capital of the originating bank, at the amounts the bank would have been required to hold for the full value of the assets, had they not been securitised. Detailed provisions applied also to liquidity and underwriting facilities.

Both these actions fall in the regulatory sphere, not strictly monetary policy of the core kind rated by Dincer and Eichengreen. Nevertheless, it is interesting to examine them on the kinds of considerations which go into that rating. The enhanced risk weights and provisioning requirements were promptly disclosed, but without substantiation, in the absence of a good property price index. The episode generated awareness of the need for such an index, one of the many lacunae in the database on the Indian economy. But by the standards of the transparency rating, the price index should have been developed first, so as to provide the justification for policy action. Without that, the bubble remained a suspicion, rather than a proven fact.

Emerging economies suffer from many infirmities, chief of which is a poor database. There is a political economy aspect to this as well. Data carry low priority in economies where so many other tasks make a prior claim on public expenditure. Exactly as in the case of the asset build-up, databases get constructed in response to a crisis, rather than as prior platforms on the basis of which the policy response to a crisis can be calibrated.

Asset market prices are not among those recommended by conventional wisdom to be on the watch list of a central bank, whether for monetary policy or regulatory purposes. Differentiated risk weight enhancements are not supported by conventional wisdom on bank regulation, on the grounds that monitoring end-use of a loan is intrusive and easily violated. However, Pillar 2 of the Basel II norms, which sets rules for supervisory review of capital adequacy, includes the freedom for the regulator to set supplementary levels of minimum regulatory capital for risks not covered, or inadequately covered, under Pillar 1. It might be added that the move to Basel II norms was scheduled for completion by the end of March 2009.

Rated as non-transparent by the Geraats index, the RBI effectively protected the Indian economy from the financial and real diseases unleashed globally in 2008, providing the very stability that the transparency measure was designed to serve. The rate of growth of the Indian economy was 6.7 per cent in 2008-09, lower than the 9 per cent recorded in 2007-08, but not disastrously so. The gross non-performing assets in the Indian banking system actually declined from 2.5 per cent of gross advances at the end of 2006-07 to 2.3 per cent at the end of 2007-08, and remained at that level in 2008-09.

## Transparency Redefined

Transparency in macroeconomic policy assumed prominence after the Asian crisis of 1997, when it was identified as a necessary preventive to such crises. Full (public) disclosure was elevated to an entitlement for (private) market players.

The global crash of 2008 demonstrates the equivalent need for disclosure by private market players.

The case for macroeconomic policy transparency on the part of government, as an important player in financial markets, remains paramount. Unlike fiscal transparency, however, monetary policy transparency poses some definitional issues. Monetary policy transparency should not be so defined as to require rigidity in central bank targets and instruments. A central bank cannot, in pursuit of a good transparency reputation, be reduced to a predictable and mechanical element in the policy structure, with no range of instruments with which to handle unforeseen eventualities that could threaten macroeconomic stability. This is endorsed by the Code of Good Practices on Transparency in Monetary and Financial Policies of the International Monetary Fund, which does not envisage any particular objective for monetary policy. Transparency should not require that a central bank should watch prices only in the market for goods and services, and not in any other markets. The central bank may in particular situations choose to so limit itself, but that limitation should be a choice rather than a compulsion. Nor should transparency require disclosure of internal forecasting models used by central banks, or votes in internal meetings. These requirements destroy the willingness to dissent, on the basis of which alone robust policy actions can emerge.

Transparency correctly defined should require full prior disclosure of policy decisions, with effective dates, and pre-announced finite, or indefinite, durations, and full *post facto* disclosure of all interventions in any market. It should permit the full range of supervisory discretion under Pillar 2 of Basel II. At the end of the day, the credibility of a central bank is a function of the financial stability it is able to deliver, not a function of prior straitjackets adopted.

## References

Committee on Financial Sector Assessment (2009). *Report of the Advisory Panel on Transparency Standards*, Vol VI of *India's Financial Sector: An Assessment.* Mumbai: Foundation Books for Reserve Bank of India.

Dincer, Nergiz and Barry Eichengreen (2009). "Central bank transparency: Causes, consequences and updates", *mimeo*, February. *http://www.nber.org/papers/w14791*

Geraats, P.M. (2002). "Central bank transparency", *Economic Journal* 112(483): F532-F565.

Planning Commission, Government of India (2009). *A Hundred Small Steps: Report of the (Raghuram Rajan) Committee on Financial Sector Reforms.* Delhi: Sage.

Reserve Bank of India (Various dates). *Reserve Bank of India Bulletin.* Assorted issues.

# 4 Consistency of Fiscal, Monetary and External Sector Policies for Sustained Macroeconomic Growth

S.S. Tarapore

As Amartya Sen has pithily described, we, as a nation are "argumentative" and "talkative" and this applies with even greater force to Indian economists. Dr. Vijay Kelkar is a unique example of an Indian economist who cannot be classified under Amartya Sen's appellations. Despite his significant achievements, Dr. Vijay Kelkar stands out as a self-effacing and modest personality who consistently refuses to brandish his outstanding achievements. A unique feature of Dr. Kelkar's personality is to listen to what others have to say and only after deep reflection does he air his views. Had more economists in India imbibed Dr. Kelkar's characteristics, the quality of Indian economic thought would have been greatly enriched.

When we look at Dr. Kelkar's achievements one is faced with a time warp. He became Economic Advisor, Ministry of Commerce, at the young age of 35 and then rose to the highest posts in the government. He is in many ways unique in that after his retirement, both the public and private sectors vie for his services and he floats effortlessly too and fro between the two sectors. As such, Dr. Kelkar is a role model for future generations of public sector and private sector honchos. It is indeed a privilege to be associated with this Festschrift to honour Dr. Vijay Kelkar.

This paper attempts to discuss some of the more enduring issues in Indian macroeconomic management and emphasises the need for consistency in fiscal, monetary and external sector policies so as to enable the country to achieve sustained growth.

## Macroeconomic Policy Issues

### Determinants of Growth

The Indian economy witnessed an unprecedented GDP growth of an average of 9.4 per cent in the three years ended 2007-08 and it was only in the context of the global slowdown that the growth rate declined to 6.7 per cent in 2008-09 and a projected 7.5 per cent in 2009-10. Although there is a distinct slowdown of growth during the past two years, in an international context, India's growth rate is the second highest in the world. Quite clearly, India has arrived on the international economic scene and the world looks to India for a lead in many areas. While these are the positives, it is essential, that for sustained macroeconomic growth viable policies are pursued.

It is legitimate, especially for an emerging market economy (EME), to endeavour to grow at a faster rate, but the crucial issue is whether the economy can sustain the higher rate of growth. The ratio of gross domestic savings to GDP of 37.7 per cent and gross capital formation of 39.1 per cent in 2007-08 and a capital-output ratio of say 4.5, puts a cap on the overall growth of a little less than 9 per cent. In 2007-08, capital inflows rose to a level as much as 9 per cent of GDP.

There is a strong view that if the capital inflows are as high as 9 per cent of GDP, we should be able to absorb this inflow and instead of piling up forex reserves, we should be able to step up investments. Why cannot the Indian economy attain a higher investment rate and hence a higher growth rate? The higher capital inflows can result in raising the overall growth rate only if the current account deficit (CAD) in the balance of payments rises from the present level of around 2 per cent to 9 per cent of GDP. As our recent experience has shown, large capital inflows, particularly portfolio flows, can be fickle and there can be large capital outflows. Again, if India were to take recourse to a CAD of say 8-9 per cent of GDP we can be sure that there will be a loss of confidence by the international community and there would be a severe dislocation of the Indian economy. It is just not possible to recklessly raise the CAD sharply when capital inflows come in and drastically reduce the CAD when capital outflows take place. Thus, during periods of rapid capital inflows, India necessarily has to build up forex reserves, and far from reflecting poor macroeconomic management it is reflective of prudent policies.

When an economy stretches at the leash, it invariably gets reflected in the build-up of inflationary pressures and distortions emerge in the distribution of income. It is not without force that it is often argued that we should be more efficient and reduce the capital-output ratio. This is easier said than done. First, as the economy becomes more sophisticated, the capital intensity of output rises. Secondly, over the years there has been a neglect of the infrastructure and there is a need to step up infrastructure investment, particularly in the social sector. As infrastructure development has a long gestation lag, it tends to push up the capital-output ratio.

## Business Cycles

With the inception of planning, we, in India, developed an erroneous view that business cycles are irrelevant for India. In fact, with the sophistication in the pattern of output, inter-sectoral imbalances develop and mal-investment comes to the fore. There could be shortages of investment in some sectors and excess investment in other sectors and as inter-connectivity among sectors becomes more intense—large tracts of output are inputs into other sectors—the ugly face of business cycles emerges strongly in the Indian economy. Again, as we have discovered to our discomfort, slowdown in the rest of the world impacts adversely on Indian exports. Thus, it is not a question of poor macroeconomic management, but the sheer vagaries of international developments having an adverse impact on the Indian economy.

It is indeed strange that even after the reforms and liberalisation, it was recognised that the business cycle was not given adequate attention. We have been, for far too long, fed on the well-entrenched view that slowdowns are attributable to under-investment i.e., expenditure on capital goods being too low in relation to savings; this then calls for pump-priming by the authorities. It is this insidious approach which led to two generations of economic policy makers in India to believe in the virtues of pump-priming and kick-starting the economy. In this approach what is ignored is the dislocation of the economic system following from monetary inflation. In other words, there is over-investment, with expenditure on capital goods well in excess of savings. It is the shortage of savings which brings about the downturn in growth. The excessive monetary expansion fuels wrong expectations resulting in inappropriate allocation of productive resources and as expectations are belied, there is an inevitable collapse of output.

In the euphoria of recent years, there is a real danger of our ignoring the hard facts of economic life. When we attain high growth rates, as in the three years ended 2007-08, the amber lights should have been out that various sectors must be stretched to the hilt and bottlenecks and maladjustments were bound to be on the anvil. Unfortunately, success generates its own elixir and cheer squads call for even higher rates of growth.

## Ceiling on Growth

On many occasions it has been explained that there are clear limits to growth. While in the short-run it is possible to achieve somewhat higher rates of growth, as more is eked out from an already strained infrastructure, any artificial attempts to further step up the overall growth rate not only gets aborted but in fact carries the danger of the economy going into a tail-spin. It is in this context that we need to examine the concept of a 'ceiling on growth'. Each time an economy recovers from a low point of growth, euphoria is generated that higher and higher rates of growth are possible and once the sustainable level of growth is exceeded, a dislocation of the system is bound to occur. Kick-starting an economy when growth is historically below trend is one thing and experimenting with a kick-start when the engines of growth are at full throttle is quite another as it can only assure a sharp slump down the line. There have been, admittedly, significant changes in the Indian economy and profound changes are in train to make the economy more efficient, and there is some merit in the argument that the sustainable rate of growth could be higher than what could have been envisaged a few years ago, but it would be imprudent to believe that there is no limit to growth.

It is sometimes argued that a little inflation is desirable as it acts as a stimulus for growth by bringing down real rates of interest and raising profitability. It is also argued that demand could be stimulated by public spending. Looking at inflation as a panacea to achieving lower real rates of interest is a dangerous policy as it could deepen the downturn. Larger public spending could result in larger monetisation which would only fuel inflation and raise nominal rates of interest. Money creation is quite clearly not the way out of an impending slowdown.

## Overheating of the Economy

As we progress down the reform path, it is essential that we accept the concept of 'overheating' of the economy. It is necessary to assess the 'output gap' i.e., the 'actual' growth rate of the economy and its 'potential growth'. This is, admittedly difficult to determine but the historical trend rate of growth adjusted for any structural changes is a proxy for the potential rate of growth. Thus, as the growth rate starts rising above the potential, it is desirable to apply corrective brakes to ensure that the economy does not get overheated and degenerate into an acceleration of inflation-delayed policy response after the downturn starts which merely results in a sharper downturn.

Now how does China deal with 'overheating'? The authorities often make explicit statements on overheating. For instance, the National Statistical Bureau, periodically, warns that unless some sectors are constrained, the economy would suffer from overheating. Top officials are often candid in admitting that the brakes have failed and that urgent corrective action is required. The central bank is vigorous in its warning about overheating. What tops all this is that the Chinese Premier Wen Jiabao has, on occasions, forcefully warned that China's growth rate is unsustainable, that investment is rising too rapidly, that there are too many factories and that there is excess liquidity. Inflation is the after-effect of overheating. If warning signals of overheating are picked up and early remedial measures are taken, these measures will be less harsh than if measures are taken after inflation gathers momentum.

It is indeed sad that despite all the sophistication in our economy, any talk about overheating of the economy and the need to slowdown is taboo and those who talk about it are treated as heretics. The price for such taboos is far too heavy. The time has come to recognise that there are phases in the business cycle when there are advantages in actively cooling the economy. We must avoid the temptation of populist policies calling for higher and higher growth rates. We need to develop techniques for correct and timely assessment of the limit to growth. The art of skillful macro-management would be to 'creep along the ceiling of growth' as long as possible. If early attention is given to overheating of the economy, the medium and long-term growth rate will be much higher than if the economy grows in fits and starts with very high unsustainable growth rates punctuated by slumps.

## The Scourge of Inflation

There is a real danger in excessive policy emphasis on growth with insufficient attention to the fallout of a high growth rate in terms of inflation. While it is argued, not without force, that a higher growth rate is essential, if large tracts of poverty are to be alleviated, there is the danger that growth can be skewed against the lower income groups. The seductive doctrine that we should tolerate inflation in the interest of growth is indeed dangerous. The experience, the world over, is that moderate inflation can easily degenerate into a spiral which eats into the vitals of the economy. To ensure that inflation does not dislocate the economy's progress, it can on occasions require a moderation of growth. Macro policy makers have to bear in mind Prime Minister Dr. Manmohan Singh's dictum, set out many years ago, that there can be no better anti-poverty programme than the control of inflation.

India has a history of strong policy action when inflation crosses tolerance levels. All along India took pride in being one of the emerging market economies (EMEs) with the lowest inflation rate. It is disconcerting that, in the recent period, sufficiently strong action has not been taken to douse inflationary fires. There is sterile debate about the appropriate price index—wholesale, food inflation or consumer price inflation. This is totally otiose. The consumer price indices (CPI) towards the end of 2009 indicate a year-on-year increase ranging between 13.5-17.2 per cent. The annual year-on-year inflation for food articles is well over 17 per cent. The world over it is consumer prices which is used as an indicator of inflation. In India, there has been excessive emphasis on the wholesale price index (WPI). Proponents of growth made shrill noises that a few months ago the WPI was in negative territory. It is now widely accepted that by the end of March 2010, the WPI will show an increase of around 8.5 per cent and unofficial forecasts are that the WPI would enter into double digits by the end of March 2010; this is way beyond the established comfort zone of 5 per cent set out by the RBI. This conclusively shows that inflation control ought to be the topmost priority for policy makers.

There is a very powerful lobby which argues that the current inflation is a supply-side phenomenon and that this cannot be tackled by monetary policy and only real sector policies to ease supply constraints can break the bottlenecks. What is alarming is that this view is gaining all pervasive support. It is one thing to talk about supply-side inflation when there is a steep price rise in one commodity, say onions, and quite another when inflation cuts across a wide array of commodities. Commodity inflation invariably degenerates into generalised inflation, requiring strong, unswerving, anti-inflationary monetary-fiscal policies. The more policy action is delayed, the harsher would be the measures which would be needed to douse inflation.

The rest of this paper endeavours to present a consistent framework of fiscal, monetary and external sector policies.

## Ingredients of a Sound Fiscal Policy

### Changing Definition of the Fiscal Deficit and Transparency

India has been afflicted by a fisc which has been out of control for the good part of 50 years. Rather like Robert Bruce, the fisc periodically claws back the deficit only to fall back once again.

Till the early 1990s, there was a narrow and unrealistic concept of the budget deficit *viz.*, changes in cash balances and ad hoc Treasury Bills. This meant that the entire borrowing of the government showed up as an above the line receipt item. With the recasting of the fiscal accounts, there was a move to the concept of the gross fiscal deficit which was more reflective of the actual deficit. With the historic Supplemental Agreements between government and the Reserve Bank of India (RBI) of 1994 and 1997, the ad hoc Treasury Bill as an instrument was extinguished. This was followed by the Fiscal Responsibility and Budget Management (FRBM) Act, 2003 and the acceptance of the need for greater fiscal transparency. With more stringent prescriptions on limits for the revenue deficit and the gross fiscal deficit, it is a matter of distress that a new animal *viz.*, the quasi-fiscal deficit emerged which is merely fiscal expenditure kept outside the budget.

This put paid to the entire fiscal consolidation process. It is time that this charade is put to an end and the practice of recording expenditures outside the budget should be stopped forthwith and a proper and transparent presentation made of the fiscal accounts and any fiscal fudge should be strictly *verboten*.

## Impact of the Fiscal Deficit

To the extent that the fisc runs a large deficit, created money inevitably puts a pressure on prices and interest rates. There is a well articulated school of thought which claims that the fiscal deficit has no relationship to inflation and that the fisc does not crowd out the commercial sector. A single resource cannot do double duty and crowding out is a fact of life—this would no doubt be challenged by a number of Indian economists. The belief that there are "good deficits" and "bad deficits" is akin to believing in "good sins" and "bad sins" and with the fervent hope that "good sins" would lead us to paradise. It is time we got rid of such illusions.

Subsequent to the FRBM the combined gross fiscal deficit of the Centre and States came down to 4.2 per cent of GDP in 2007-08, but this rose to 8.9 per cent of GDP in 2008-09 and is estimated to rise further to 10.2 per cent of GDP in 2009-10. The quasi-fiscal deficit, some time back, was estimated at 3 per cent of GDP. It is imperative that the government comes clean in the ensuing period and shows the quasi-fiscal deficit as part of the gross fiscal deficit.

It was to prevent such subterfuge that some Committees had recommended that the fiscal deficit should follow the standard public sector borrowing requirement (PSBR), but this concept has not found favour not only with the government but also independent economists.

The Y.V. Reddy-E.A.S. Sarma Group which did the preparatory work for the FRBM Act had articulated the need for an ongoing independent assessment of the implementation of the Act. In the final enactment this clause was dropped, which then provided loopholes for deviating from the trajectory. The market borrowing of the Centre as per the Budget Estimate (BE) for 2008-09 was Rs. 99,000 crore but as per the Revised Estimate (RE) it turned out at Rs. 266,539 crore. For 2009-10, the market borrowing is expected to be around Rs. 450,000 crore. The gross fiscal deficit of the

Centre for 2009-10 is expected to be 6.8 per cent of GDP. Thus, for all practical purposes the FRBM has been torn to shreds. The loss of fiscal control cannot be attributed entirely to aftermath of the international financial crisis. It is indeed sad that the hard earned fiscal rectification of past years has been lost at one stroke.

The government has sought a relaxation of the FRBM targets for the gross fiscal deficit which is now placed at 5.5 per cent of GDP in 2010-11 and 4.0 per cent of GDP in 2011-12. The Thirteenth Finance Commission, headed by Dr. Vijay Kelkar has been entrusted with the task of redrawing the entire roadmap for fiscal correction.

## Reorientation of Fiscal Expenditures

The government has to ensure that weaker sections of society are protected. Hence, despite the large fiscal deficit the government is right to step up the various anti-poverty programmes which have been vastly improved in terms of delivery. How should such expenditure be met? It is here that Dr. Vijay Kelkar has provided a lead by suggesting that government should withdraw from certain sectors where government's presence is not indispensable and divert the resources to sectors where government presence is imperative. This important recommendation by Dr. Kelkar should be given serious attention.

## Public Sector Divestment

There is the important issue as to what should be done with the proceeds of public sector divestment. To make such divestment meaningful, such divestment proceeds should be used to reduce the government's liability. The family silver should not be used to meet consumption needs. Unfortunately, there do not seem to be any takers for this viewpoint. The likelihood is that the divestment proceeds would be used merely to show a lower deficit. Such reduction in the deficit is a violation of the spirit of the FRBM. Parliament should approve divestment only if the proceeds are used to reduce government's liabilities. The strong argument against prudence is that in either case the government liability will go up as the deficit would be wider. It is precisely such kinds of arguments which make the deficit rectification opaque.

## Repayment of Government Debt

Many years ago, reports of successive Finance Commissions, Comptroller and Auditor General and the RBI warned about the rising internal debt and the need to work out a viable scheme of debt repayment. Up to the 1960s, there was a system of a Consolidated Sinking Fund to which contributions were being made by government to enable smooth repayment of the government debt. It is unfortunate that in the context of rising fiscal deficits the government abandoned this salutary scheme. The RBI, in the 1990s worked out a comprehensive scheme for setting up a Consolidated Sinking Fund. The scheme was ostensibly rejected by the government as the already large deficit would have swelled further. There was fatigue on the part of proponents of a Sinking Fund and more recent Finance Commissions have just side-stepped this issue. It was argued that once the primary deficit was wiped out, the problem of excessive government debt would go away. Facts have belied such wishful thinking as the primary deficit has widened and the internal debt is assuming critical proportions.

There is an erroneous view that there is no inter-generational debt burden. This ignores the fact that those generating the debt are not those who have to repay it and in this sense there can be no free lunch.

The insidious nature of internal debt is that, unlike external debt, the explosion does not come after critical warnings; rather the internal debt suddenly explodes. The French experience in the 1950s and the Italian experience in the 1970s points to this danger. It is surprising that sometimes everyone sees the danger but there is a paralysis of policy. The debt-GDP ratio is now around 80 per cent of GDP and we take comfort that other countries have higher debt-GDP ratios. There is need for early action before the situation gets totally out of hand and the country lands in an irretrievable situation.

## Iniquity in Taxation

It is well known that indirect taxes are generally regressive while direct taxes are meant to be progressive. What is disconcerting is that over the past 25 years the direct tax system has tilted in favour of the upper income groups and distinctly against the lower income groups. With the abolition of the estate duty, the virtual abolition of the wealth tax on financial assets, abolition of capital gains tax on stock market transactions and the unlimited exemption of gifts to relatives, these taxes have been diluted; simultaneously, the erstwhile steep income tax rates have been moderated. In the upshot, the Indian direct tax regime is one of the most liberal in the world and comes close to tax havens. There is a pressing need for a rectification of the direct tax system.

C.A. Yandle, a retired senior official and fiscal expert of the International Monetary Fund, in an unpublished briefing paper on *Tax Policy Consideration* (2003) sets out three well accepted principles of tax system design *viz.*, efficiency, equity and administrative simplicity. First, for a tax to be efficient it should bring about the least possible change to individual incentives and decisions. Secondly, from an equity (fairness) standpoint, taxpayers who are similarly situated or have the same ability to pay should be equally taxed. Those with equal income should pay the same amount of tax. Thirdly, taxes should be administratively simple.

The total exemption of dividends from income tax in India violates all three canons of taxation and is quite clearly a fiscal atrocity. The unlimited exemption of dividends from companies and mutual funds, while interest from bonds, bank deposits and post office savings schemes are subject to income tax is unconscionable. The ostensible reason for removing the tax on individual dividend income, and substituting it by a dividend distribution tax, is that it would help the small recipients who have to go through arduous procedures for obtaining refunds. In the upshot, small and large dividend recipients pay the same rate of tax through the dividend distribution tax. It is unbecoming of a country which claims to be working towards a just and equitable financial system to undertake such a crude subterfuge to blatantly support high net worth individuals at the cost of vast tracts of persons with modest incomes. This is plutocracy at its worst. The appropriate step would be to restore the *status quo ante* under which dividends are taxed in the hands of individuals and the dividend distribution tax could be abolished. To the extent the government is concerned about evasion of tax, the tax deduction at source on dividends should be the maximum tax on income with tax vouchers given to dividend recipients. Of course, the tax refunds system, which is cruel towards small income taxpayers, should be streamlined and refunds should be paid automatically within six months of the filing of tax return. If the government is unable to implement this because of the extremely powerful lobby for tax-free dividends, it should make all interest incomes on financial assets exempt from income tax. To continue the present system would mean that the government subscribes to the Thrasymachus principle in Plato's *Republic* that "justice is the interest of the stronger".

Yet another fiscal atrocity on the anvil is the ill-conceived idea of adding to income the entire corpus of retirement savings at the time of maturity to the income in the year in which the retirement benefit accrues. There is no social security worth the name in India and to deprive retirees 30 per cent of their corpus is a cruel joke. The best thing would be to remove any tax deduction for contributions at the time they are made.

There is much merit in a senior citizen bond under which the individual is assured of a very low real rate of interest of say 2 per cent, but compensated for inflation erosion of the real rate of interest as also the capital. It is unconscionable to argue that a modicum of inflation protection to senior citizens would result in the whole economy being indexed. There could be modest limits for investments in such bonds.

### Urgency for Fiscal Correction

The weakness of the Indian fisc is the biggest threat to long-term macroeconomic stability. While undertaking the fiscal rectification, the government would do well to accept the sagacious advice of Dr. Vijay Kelkar to redirect fiscal expenditures towards socio-economic sectors which cannot be handled by the commercial sector.

## Monetary Policy Objectives, Instruments and Transparency in Formulation

### Recent Monetary Policy Initiatives

Monetary policy is part of overall macroeconomic policy. While there are various vital policy objectives, it is important that monetary policy is assigned the task best suited to it which is ensuring price stability. The history of the past 60 years has been that monetary policy has to bear a disproportionate burden and assigning too many nebulous and conflicting objectives attenuates the effectiveness of monetary policy. While conflict in central bank-government relations is a universal phenomenon, there is a need for a transparent and equitable framework for resolving these issues. It is unfortunate that, in India, the monetary policy framework of decision taking is totally unsatisfactory as there are no rules of the game. This brings to the fore, the issue of central bank autonomy. Autonomy is never given, it is earned and taken.

A former Governor of the RBI Mr. L.K. Jha, 40 years ago summed up the monetary-fiscal policy dilemma when he said that someone else (the government) jams the accelerator and the monetary policy task is to brake as hard as it can. During the recent global crisis, the RBI jammed the monetary accelerator and the government jammed the fiscal accelerator, resulting in an unprecedented swelling of liquidity in the system. The liquidity release (including potential liquidity) by the RBI was a staggering Rs. 540,000 crore, equivalent to 9 per cent of GDP. The fiscal stimulus was equivalent to 3 per cent of GDP.

While *prima facie* the clawing back of the monetary stimulus appears to be daunting, it is pertinent to note that the bulk of the monetary stimulus was in the form of potential liquidity and with the withdrawal undertaken in October 2009, such potential liquidity would be fully withdrawn by the end of March 2010. The actual release of liquidity was in terms of the 4 percentage point reduction in the cash reserve ratio (CRR) amounting to Rs. 160,000 crore; of this withdrawal of Rs. 36,000 crore, by way of a CRR increase of 0.75 percentage point, was announced on January 29, 2010. The clawing back of the remaining 3.25 per cent of the CRR (the actual claw back would depend on the evolving situation) had best be completed by the end of September 2010. The RBI needs to use every window of opportunity to claw back the CRR and it should never give any assurances that it is unlikely to act during the inter-policy review period. It would be best to undertake a non-disruptive calibrated withdrawal of the excess liquidity. Of coursc, if capital inflows surge, as they threaten to do, the pace of clawing back of liquidity will have to be accelerated. *Per contra*, if the government's borrowing programme is way beyond the RBI's expectations, the withdrawal of the monetary stimulus would need to be recalibrated.

The sequencing of the liquidity withdrawal before hiking policy interest rates appears to be a prudent policy. In the absence of curtailment of liquidity, policy interest rate increases would be ineffective. A fear expressed is whether, in a scenario of a curtailment of liquidity, a larger than expected borrowing programme and moderate capital inflows, banks would access the RBI repo window. In such a situation it would be only appropriate that the liquidity withdrawal be so calibrated that the banks nibble at the repo window at somewhat higher interest rates than the prevailing rate of 4.75 per cent. The reverse repo rate of 3.25 repo should not be raised and in fact at some stage the reverse repo facility could be abolished. In the current scenario, banks taking recourse to the reverse repo facility is indicative of the fact that the pace of clawing back of excess liquidity by the RBI needs to be stepped up.

## Monetary Policy Objectives

The RBI's monetary policy objective should primarily be on inflation control. Over the past year, inflation rates in India have been intolerably high and the RBI's policies should not be swayed by talk about inflation being a supply-side phenomenon, that inflation is essentially in food items and that the WPI shows a relatively lower increase than the CPI. The RBI's WPI projection for March 2010 of 8.5 per cent is clearly above the tolerance level. The RBI's *dharma* is inflation control and it should treat other objectives as subsidiary.

## Process of Monetary Policy Formulation and Government's Role

The whole gamut of issues relating to the formulation of monetary policy, transparency and the all pervasive government roles in the formulation and execution of monetary policy need to be given greater attention than hitherto. At the present time, the RBI and government dialogue and the assignment of responsibility and accountability is totally opaque. Again, there is a breakdown of the unwritten code of the government not airing in the public domain, what it deems the appropriate monetary policy action. It is unfortunate that in contrast to the international practice of clear delineation of government-central bank responsibilities, the present status of these arrangements in India are, to say the least, totally unsatisfactory. There is a pressing need to undertake a complete overhaul of the present arrangements.

## Formulation of Monetary Policy

It would be unrealistic to expect total autonomy for the RBI, but it would be legitimate to expect that the RBI would have enough headroom to operate monetary policy consistent with clearly laid out objectives. The RBI Advisory Group on Transparency of Monetary Policy and Other Financial Policies chaired by Mr. M. Narasimham (2000) had set out a comprehensive scheme for the formulation and execution of monetary policies but it is unfortunate that neither the RBI nor the government saw merit in the proposal.

## Agreement between RBI and Government

The Advisory Group recommended that the objectives of monetary policy should be clearly set out in an agreement between government and RBI and the agreement should be put in the public domain. While the central objective should be in terms of a medium-term inflation target, there could also be other objectives but with a clear ordering of priorities. To the extent the government wishes to change the objectives, this should be done transparently and put in the public domain.

## Autonomy for RBI on Use of Monetary Policy Instruments

Once the government sets out the objectives, the RBI should have instrument freedom to attain the objectives. The RBI would then be accountable for the deployment of its instruments. To the extent the fall-out of the use of instruments is not acceptable to government, it can change the objectives, but transparently and put in the public domain.

## Monetary Policy Committee

The Advisory Group recommended the setting up of a Monetary Policy Committee consisting of the governor, the deputy governors and external members. To give decision taking powers to such a Committee would require extensive legislative changes. There would also be the question of the external members getting involved with the decision-making process and there could be conflicts between the RBI top management and the external members, as has occurred in Korea. Such external members could conceivably need to give up a good part of their activities and the present system of remuneration would be inadequate to attract the best talent.

The RBI, in a pragmatic move in 2005, set up a Technical Advisory Committee on Monetary Policy, with the governor, four deputy governors, two board members and five external members. The Committee meets four times a year and being advisory there is no procedure of voting by members. There is merit in increasing the number of meetings to say six and the record of discussion could be put in the public domain, albeit with an appropriate lag. Eventually the RBI Act needs to be totally overhauled, as has been done in a number of countries and explicit powers should be assigned by legislation to the RBI in the conduct of monetary policy. *Inter alia,* the revamped Act could have a provision for setting up a formal MPC with specific powers. The revamped RBI Act needs to explicitly set out the powers of the government and the powers of the RBI.

## External Sector Policies

### Current Account

The external sector is the one area in which it could be claimed that the economic reforms have been an unqualified success. The current account of the balance of payments was liberalised in quick steps and by 1994, we attained *de jure* current account convertibility. Even in 2008-09, a year of international turmoil, the current account deficit was 2.5 per cent of GDP and the debt service ratio was as low as 5 per cent.

### Capital Account Liberalisation

On the capital account, convertibility was always available to non-residents but residents were subject to draconian controls. Over the past 15 years there has been a process of a gradual well-calibrated liberalisation of the capital account. While there were initially fears of large outflows, on the contrary, the liberalisation has resulted in even larger capital inflows. The liberalisation on the capital account was first for corporates, then banks and lastly individuals. There were intense fears in some policy circles that if individuals were granted even a modicum of capital account convertibility, there would be a large exodus of capital which could dislocate the economy. When ultimately resident individuals were given a sizeable degree of capital convertibility (US $ 200,000 per annum), the fears did not materialise. On the capital account there are still limits for different sectors, but with some element of confidence it could be said that these sectors enjoy capital convertibility. These limits need to be judged from the point of 'reasonableness', with reasonableness being assessed by the user seeking to take out capital. Thus, for all practical purposes we have arrived at capital account convertibility without knowing it!

The international experience over a long period of time has been that after bouts of large capital inflows there are large bouts of capital outflows. In 2008-09, India experienced large capital outflows and it is to the credit of the authorities that these outflows were handled smoothly and without any restrictions. This is recognised by the international community and would, in the near future, result in large inflows.

There are some rumblings in policy circles as to how to manage large capital inflows. It would be best not to reintroduce any direct controls but it would be quite legitimate to improve the quality of capital inflows. In this connection, a few measures could be considered.

## Participatory Notes (PNs)

Participatory notes are, indeed an enervating issue and the matter come up from time to time. The use of this instrument reflects opaque practices. Earlier, it was felt that because of tardy registration procedures for FII sub-accounts PNs provided a convenient instrument. The major drawback of this instrument is that the name of the investor is not known to the authorities and shady investments can enter India. The false fears were that if there was a ban on PNs, fresh inflows would slowdown and there could be even large outflows. As President Kennedy said, the time to repair the roof is when the sun is shining and at the present time the sun is shining brightly on India. If the authorities have the slightest concern about large capital flows, the time is apposite to totally ban PNs.

## Foreign Currency Non-Resident (Banks) Scheme (FCNRB)

Under the FCNRB deposit scheme, non-resident Indians are allowed to place deposits with Indian banks in foreign currency and the interest is also free from tax. This is a vestige of times when India was scrounging for foreign exchange. In the changed milieu, it is demeaning to continue this scheme. NRIs are welcome to place deposits with Indian banks in the Non-

Resident External Rupee Accounts scheme. The time has come for us to close the FNCRB scheme by not allowing fresh deposits under this scheme and outstanding deposits can be repaid on the due date of maturity. To the extent Indian banks wish to raise foreign exchange resources, this should be done through the wholesale market and not depend on retail deposits with tax concessions.

## Exchange Rate Management

India's exchange rate management has been exemplary though the articulation of the policy has been unnecessarily apologetic. The *leit motiv* of the RBI has been for many years that it is only concerned about volatility and that it does not have any "appropriate" exchange rate in mind and that the exchange rate is "market determined". This contrasts with the pre-1997 position in which the RBI openly stated that it used the real effective exchange rate (REER) as the lodestar. In the post-1997 period, the RBI seemed to fear that if it declared its position that it was following the REER, there would be speculative attacks which would, so to say, "break the bank". When there are very large capital flows the RBI does intervene in the forex market and mops up the excess foreign currency, and then mops up the surplus liquidity via the CRR, the LAF and MSS Bonds.

There are concerns about the impossible trinity that a country should not try to have an open capital account, a managed exchange rate and yet have control over monetary policy and that one of these objectives needs to be given up. In terms of practical policy, there can be a second best solution where a country tries to come as close as possible to the three corners. In other words, a country may not find it feasible to totally abjure from one of the three objectives of policy. Since monetary control is an overriding priority and a role back of capital liberalisation is not feasible, it is concluded that the exchange rate has to be market determined. The actual forex management of the RBI is totally faultless. Surely, the RBI cannot let the exchange rate depreciate wildly, to say US $1=Rs. 60 and also let it appreciate, to say US $1=Rs. 30. Such wild oscillations would disrupt the real sectors and the RBI is right not to let the rupee fluctuate wildly as it could without RBI intervention. The RBI would no doubt be using some kind of indicator and the six country REER (1993-94=100) is as good a proxy as any other. The RBI, if it so chooses need not swear by the REER but equally it should not be defensive and claim that it is only concerned with volatility. While volatility is a concern, levels also have to be a concern.

There is an insidious articulation that the RBI should allow an appreciation of the rupee when there are heavy inflows and also when there are inflationary pressures. It is one thing for a country with a large and persistent current account surplus to allow an appreciation and quite another for a country with a persistent, albeit small, current account deficit to allow its currency to appreciate (in real effective exchange rate terms). It would be suicidal to allow an appreciation in the latter case. The Indian authorities have done well not to be enticed into undertaking such imprudent policies as exports would become uncompetitive, imports would be stimulated and the CAD would widen to an unsustainable level. At the margin, it is perhaps better to have a slightly undervalued currency rather than a slightly overvalued currency.

## Managing Excessive Capital Inflows

Finally, there is the question of excessive capital flows. In the ensuing period there would, in all probability, be excessive capital inflows. What sort of measures should the authorities consider? Quantitative controls are not optimal as they could work in an arbitrary manner and controls beget further controls. Again, the much talked about Tobin tax to be efficient would need to be very small and levied on all foreign exchange transactions and would need to be adopted by all major countries simultaneously. A Brazil type of tax on capital inflows, say at a rate of 1-2 per cent of the capital inflows, is problematic as the need to dispense with the tax once capital inflows abate may not coincide with the government's ability to forego the tax revenue.

To the extent the excess capital flows are moderate, it is best handled with internal measures like what India had done earlier by way of burden sharing by banks (CRR and incremental CRR), the RBI (LAF) and the government (MSS Bonds). If the capital inflows are far too excessive, the authorities can consider an unremunerated reserve requirement on all capital inflows (other than FDI) of say 10 per cent of the inflow which could be impounded for a period of one year.

## Concluding Observations

Reflecting the sound macroeconomic management of the economy, India has become a force to reckon with in the international community. It is important that we preserve these hard earned gains and progressively move to even more sustainable macroeconomic management. The reform process must continue and fiscal, monetary and external sector policies must be mutually consistent to ensure sustained growth. Given the vast income disparities and large tracts of deprivation, the socio-economic objectives and distributive justice have to be given pride of place in the firmament of Indian macroeconomic policies. Ultimately it is people like Dr. Vijay Kelkar, among others, who have contributed to this achievement. Let us salute Dr. Vijay Kelkar.

# 5 Preventing and Responding to the Crisis of 2018

Arvind Subramanian*

## Introduction

Vijay Kelkar has been, in my view, one of India's most creative and thoughtful policy intellectuals over the last several decades. He has made genuine intellectual contributions to the policy debate in a way that few have. As an intellectual practitioner, he remains unsurpassed. Whether it has been in articulating a vision for the role of markets and government, for the importance of a sound public sector balance sheet, for tax reform, for fiscal federalism or simply for the process of policymaking and generating consensus for ideas, his contributions will long endure. India has been blessed with many high quality intellectual practitioners. Many of them have been wise and sensible. Vijay has been visionary.

What would Vijay Kelkar have made of the recent global financial crisis? This essay tries to answer that question.

Policy makers should be rattled enough by the crisis to attempt to draw lessons, albeit provisional/interim, from it in thinking about preventing and responding to the next crisis—the crisis of 2018.

What has come as a genuine surprise is the impact on India—on the financial side—of this crisis compared with that of the Asian financial crisis (AFC) of the late 1990s. Stock prices have declined by nearly 40 per cent and the exchange rate decline of about 25 per cent would have been considerably greater but for intervention by the RBI. This differential financial contagion has stemmed from the simple fact that India has

* This is a revised version of an essay that appeared in the *Economic and Political Weekly* in January 2009. I am grateful to Josh Felman, Olivier Jeanne, Vijay Kelkar, Dani Rodrik and John Williamson for helpful discussions.

become much more integrated in international capital markets. Net capital inflows reached a peak of over 10 per cent of GDP compared with relatively negligible amounts leading up to the AFC. India may still be relatively closed in policy terms but that has not deterred substantial inflows. In *de facto* terms, India is no longer a closed economy from the perspective of financial integration.

There was surprise on two scores. First, policy makers and market participants under-estimated the extent of India's financial integration: while they were or must have been aware of cumulative non-resident investments in rupee assets, they did not fully grasp the magnitude of foreign funding (liabilities) of Indian financial institutions and corporates, especially those that had borrowed abroad to finance their mergers and acquisitions in the last few years.

Second, and perhaps more importantly, they assigned relatively low probabilities to the perfect storm of foreign exchange pressures emanating from so many fronts, all related to the financial crisis in industrial countries. Deleveraging led to non-resident flight from rupee assets while tightening credit markets abroad forced Indian corporates to turn to the Indian banking system for credit and for rolling over their foreign funding. In the ultimate analysis, this sharply increased demand for foreign exchange—manifested in part and in the first instance as a demand for credit from the Indian banking system—placed considerable pressure on the rupee and the RBI's foreign exchange reserves. What appeared to be a very comfortable reserve position at the start of the crisis, seemed a little less robust in light of the magnitude of reversal of capital flows. In the event, the rupee depreciated by about 20-25 per cent and the RBI lost about $40-50 billion in reserves over the space of two months.

Looking ahead, the big macroeconomic policy question for India is the following: in light of the crisis, should India's strategy emphasise greater self-insurance, with a necessarily more cautious approach to capital market integration, or does the crisis point to an even more enthusiastic embrace of foreign capital? There are also other questions relating to fiscal and monetary policies as well as financial sector development that this note will address.

## Self-Insurance and Macroeoconomic Policy

Self-insurance is not a new idea or policy objective. Implicitly or overtly, and to varying degrees, the East Asian countries made self-insurance an important policy objective after the AFC. But India did not do so in the aftermath of the AFC because it was not seriously affected by it. In terms of highlighting the importance of self-insurance, this crisis has done (or should do) to India what the AFC did to the East Asian countries.

While the impact of the crisis has been greater than expected, it is undeniable that India's foreign exchange reserves helped in limiting this impact. If India had gone into the crisis with $100 or even $150 billion of reserves instead of $300 billion, confidence would have been vastly more difficult to manage, in part because foreign exchange intervention could not have been deployed to the same extent. As important, the ability to use counter-cyclical monetary policy would have been severely constrained if the external situation had been less robust.

So, one lesson seems to be that self-insurance is a prudent and even necessary strategy to limit the impact of financial crises. This would, of course, have to be qualified if international collective arrangements—regional and multilateral—can provide liquidity during crises. There have been some encouraging developments in the recent crisis: the IMF has now a quick disbursing facility and the Fed provided dollar liquidity under swap arrangements with four emerging market countries. India should as a responsible member of the international community work hard toward building these arrangements, but for the foreseeable future, liquidity provision under them is unlikely to become a full or adequate substitute for domestic self-insurance.

Moreover, the contrasting experience of China—which experienced limited financial contagion because of its staggeringly large foreign reserves—and the others, even those with large amounts of reserves (such as Russia, Brazil, Korea and India) must give pause. China's relative immunity seems to lend support to a stronger version of self-insurance, a kind of Powell doctrine (a description that Vijay Kelkar approved of) for financial crises: a financial crisis like war requires vast firepower to mount an effective response so that the battle is won even before it begins. If this is true, being prepared for, or minimising the impact of the next crisis requires large amounts of reserves, perhaps even more than India had at the beginning of this crisis.

So, what does Powellian self-insurance imply? In its most extreme form, it implies a counter-cyclical macroeconomic strategy of moderate/ serious mercantilism with a country aiming to run current account surpluses in order to accumulate reserves steadily and thereby also keeping its net foreign indebtedness manageably small. It certainly means avoiding currency appreciation.

Two distinctions are necessary. First, self-insurance and building up reserves relate to net flows but vulnerability to crises depends on gross inflows, in fact on gross liabilities. India in this crisis has found itself somewhere between Korea and China. China self-insured with a vengeance ($2 trillion dollars of reserves) and restricted capital inflows. India and Korea had broadly similar and lower levels of self-insurance. India, however, had larger levels of gross inflows than China but smaller than those of Korea.

The second distinction is between mercantilism and the associated reliance on a competitive exchange rate as development strategy (on which there is a lot of debate) and mercantilism as counter-cyclical macroeconomic policy. A self-insurance objective would argue for a certain approach to the capital account and exchange rate to accumulate reserves during good times, with these reserves being used up during times of crisis.

## How much Self-Insurance?

This crisis will re-kindle debate about how much is adequate self-insurance. The old rules, including the Guidotti rule that reserves should be as much as debt falling due within a year needs to be revisited. A starting point would be to ask: what are the total gross foreign liabilities of all financial and corporates falling due within a 12-18 month period. The recent experience suggests that any funding by Indian corporates in foreign capital markets (such as those of TATA or even Arcelor Mittal) should be included in thinking of the optimal size of the war chest.

The problem is that one cannot stop there. In the recent crisis, non-resident investments in the equity market were also prone to sudden withdrawal. In fact, in the recent crisis, the reversal of these flows were as important as debt rollovers in putting pressures on the currency. It is not obvious why reserves should not cushion against this kind of sudden stop as well. To be sure, there is one difference between foreign portfolio investments in the domestic stock market and foreign currency-denominated debt. Withdrawals of portfolio investments have a self-limiting aspect to them: prices adjust to moderate outflows. But the recent crisis shows that even if they are self-limiting, the process can easily play itself out enough to create significant pressures on the currency, especially if there have been sizeable cumulative inflows.

One could go even further. If there are no capital controls on residents, crises could also lead to pressure on foreign exchange reserves from residents fleeing rupees directly or indirectly through trade channels. Of course, it is not possible for the government to self-insure against all these sources of pressure on foreign exchange but prudence would require taking a broader view of vulnerability to crisis: vulnerability stems not just from foreign-denominated contractual liabilities (i.e., debt instruments) but from a much broader class of capital flows.

Two conclusions follow: first, effective self-insurance might require *a la* the Powell doctrine a sizeable war chest of reserves. To change metaphors a little, one might say that the Chinese experience shows that one should not just save for the rainy day but that to prepare for the deluge, one should build nothing less than Noah's ark. Second, the size of the chest will depend directly on how much the country opens itself to capital—gross capital—flows. The more open the capital account, the greater the likely deluge and the bigger the required ark.

Two clear reservations to a strategy of self-insurance must be noted. First, there is a fallacy of composition issue. Mercantilism might work for a few countries but mercantilism by all would lead to beggar-thy-neigbour outcomes and international frictions. The first-best of course is the creation of pooled liquidity at international level that could be made easily and quickly available to some or many countries in crisis. If that option is not seriously on the cards—and nothing about the recent crisis will engender confidence that option is on the horizon—the pursuit of self-insurance by some or many countries will be an unavoidable second-best option, and for countries such as India even a necessary option.

The second reservation is at the country level. Self-insurance and the associated mercantilism protects against financial contagion. But this strategy will also increase reliance on exports and foreign markets for sustaining growth. Export-to-GDP ratios will increase. A consequence of this is greater vulnerability to trade contagion. If the economies of the US and EU head into recession, China is more susceptible to a cyclical slow-down because of its greater reliance on exports. So, what a country gains on the swings (protection against financial contagion), it loses partly on the roundabouts (vulnerability to trade contagion). Policy makers will have to trade-off these benefits and costs. One argument, of course, is that this susceptibility to a slowdown from declining foreign demand can be offset by offsetting policies to boost domestic demand, which China has sought recourse to. But this requires a strong sovereign balance sheet.

## Strengthening the Sovereign Balance Sheet: Vijay Kelkar's Obsession

The one safe conclusion to draw from this crisis is that there will be other crises of similar magnitude in the not-too-distant future. True, it will probably not take the same form, but that there will be a crisis is inevitable. So, what other mitigating strategy apart from self-insurance on the external side can a country deploy?

Crises such as these show that the lender/guarantor of last/ultimate resort is the government. This is a point that Vijay Kelkar has made and far ahead of most commentators. Governments have to take over often substantial amounts of private sector liabilities in crises and governments have to implement counter-cyclical fiscal policy during steep downturns. The US demonstrated the former; and the Chinese with the huge fiscal effort announced recently have implemented the latter. India has, sadly, not been in a position to easily do either because its sovereign balance sheet is shaky (it has been noteworthy that during this crisis, the brunt of the burden of providing macroeconomic stimulus has been forced upon monetary policy because fiscal policy has been hamstrung by the state of the public finances).

For the future, therefore, India should aim for a balance sheet that is robust and sound enough to be able to increase public liabilities by large amounts within a short space of time: say, up to 10-20 per cent of GDP. The implication is that it is imperative to have India's debt, during the phase of rapid growth, to come down to levels from which ramping up of the orders mentioned above will be feasible. This implies a debt-to-GDP ratio in good times of no greater than 30-40 per cent of GDP. Medium-term fiscal consolidation involving a substantial reduction of public sector indebtedness is an urgent task for the future, once the crisis has passed (during the crisis, some fiscal expansion, taking advantage of oil price declines, should not be ruled out).

## Foreign Capital

Before the Asian financial crisis, the orthodoxy (Mark I) was to aim for capital account liberalisation. After that crisis, the revised orthodoxy (Mark II) was that countries that had already opened up to capital flows should not reverse policies but that closed or semi-open countries such as India should proceed cautiously on the path of capital account opening especially short-term debt flows. But one can detect the emergence of a new view that has not yet attained the status of orthodoxy (Mark III) but is garnering more adherents. On this view, not only should those not already open be cautious but even countries that are open should think of careful and prudent ways of managing, even dampening, inflows through policy actions.

In the last few years, India has been moving from Mark II to Mark I. It is undeniable that this development—India's rapid integration in world capital markets—has been one of the principal reasons for the surprisingly large magnitude of the impact of the crisis on India.

Does this impact necessitate a re-think of capital account convertibility? What should India aim for?

Capital account convertibility (CAC) has been a hotly debated topic in India and the subject of three officially-sponsored reports: Tarapore II, Mistry and Rajan. One can argue that all of these need to be revisited in light of the crisis for one simple reason: none of them addressed directly the question of whether self-insurance against financial crises should be a macroeconomic policy objective guiding CAC. In other words, the issue here is not whether foreign capital is good or bad for India's growth from a development perspective; rather, it is whether the introduction of a self-insurance objective into policy—arguably one of the lessons of this crisis for India—should alter in any way the current macroeconomic policy toward CAC.

What follows assumes that self-insurance should be an important future objective because that is one of the lessons of the crisis. If that is so, looking ahead, India faces three options.

The first option is to continue the current policy of continuing and accelerating the move toward CAC as argued in the Mistry, and more guardedly in the Rajan Committee, report. It is a necessary consequence of pursuing this option that it would not allow for any serious self-insurance and therefore, would be based on a relatively sanguine view about the vulnerability to sudden stops and their consequences. This view will necessarily lead to large and sharp swings in asset prices including exchange rates.

The second option assumes that sudden stops create large costs and that there is need for substantial self-insurance. This requires preventing the exchange rate from sharp swings, especially appreciation, and which in turn requires being extremely cautious about further CAC and perhaps also requires consideration of prudent, transparent, probably price-based and possibly short-term measures to dampen incremental inflows. The essential logic of this view is that self-insurance requires managing the exchange rate which becomes progressively difficult the greater the capital flows. Put more starkly, this view sees full capital account openness as both increasing the vulnerability to crises (the more the capital that comes in, the more that can exit) and also reducing the ability to respond to crises because openness limits the ability to maintain competitive exchange rates and hence, build up reserves through current account surpluses. China is very much the model for this option.

There is a third view. This view favours capital account opening but also deems self-insurance as important. This is the it-is-possible-to-keep-the-baby-without-the-bathwater view. The challenge for this view is to show how self-insurance and capital account opening can be kept compatible for the duration that is necessary to build up reserves. Or, how can exchange rates be managed and prevented from over-appreciating over long enough periods of time with open capital accounts?

Proponents of this view would argue that there is a policy arsenal—comprising sterilisation and counter-cyclical fiscal policy—that can keep CAC compatible with self-insurance. But consider each of these policy measures.

Can sterilisation or rather sterilised intervention be effective for managing the exchange rate for long periods of time? China cannot be invoked as the model because China has managed to sustain sterilisation only because it has been carried out in the context of a relatively closed capital account (that makes sterilisation less self-perpetuating) and financial repression (that makes sterilisation less costly fiscally because of the low interest rates). India cannot and should not revert to financial repression. With that constraint, sterilisation becomes unviable with an open capital account because sterilisation by keeping interest rates high perpetuates the inflows, requiring more sterilisation and so on.

The other option is to have a fiscal policy that: (i) can be tightened and (ii) tightened quickly enough when the economy overheats from capital inflows and appreciating exchange rates. The Indian experience with fiscal policy, especially with all the complications arising from fiscal federalism, does not offer much comfort that fiscal policy can be an effective counter-cyclical policy tool. What finance minister can raise taxes or cut expenditures at a time when foreigners are willing to lend so much to a country?

In previous episodes of currency appreciation, many have called for structural reform as a competitiveness enhancing measure. Structural reforms are desirable in themselves but they cannot become a tool of counter-cyclical monetary or macroeconomic management.

Is this discussion of self-insurance and CAC relevant for India? The answer is an emphatic yes. Consider, the likely outlook for reserves, capital flows and the exchange rate, once the crisis has passed.

India will emerge from the crisis with about $200 billion in reserves. If self-insurance is an important new objective, what target level of reserves should India be aiming for say 5 or 10 years ahead? This question must be faced.

Similarly, while currency pressures have been the most significant manifestation of the crisis, the collateral benefit has been to bequeath to India a hyper-competitive exchange rate for after the crisis. At Rs. 50 to the dollar, Indian exports will be hyper-competitive, and Indian growth prospects restored to close to pre-crisis levels of 8-9 per cent. At that stage, it is highly probable, given significantly higher returns in India compared to elsewhere that capital will once again come pouring in to India. This outcome is close to inevitable. That is the point at which all the issues raised here of self-insurance, mercantilism and capital account openness will become relevant. What should India do when the rupee finds itself once again soaring from Rs. 50 to Rs. 40 to the dollar within a short space of time? Should India allow that to happen especially if it is aiming for self-insurance reserve levels of say $500 billion or even $1 trillion a few years ahead? That will be the next big policy challenge.

## Finance

India is still under-intermediated and the Indian financial system is in considerable need of improvement. There are many important issues relating to financial sector reform such as inclusiveness; market and product development; the international dimension of financial sector reforms; and controlling leverage.

But it is the international dimension of some aspects of financial sector reform that is most central to the policy questions raised in this paper. Take the case of developing the Indian domestic government and corporate bond markets which is an important objective, especially to facilitate the financing of infrastructure. The difficult choice would arise if bond market development were to entail a surge in capital inflows. These flows could create the same consequences for exchange rate appreciation/self-insurance and be prone to the same sudden stops phenomenon as other portfolio inflows (say in equity markets). Bond market development may well have positive benefits in terms of mobilising savings and better allocating capital. But if it is associated with significant net inflows (which is likely given higher growth prospects in India), the attendant consequences for vulnerability to crises and attenuated ability to self-insure must also be taken into account. Will these costs be worth the benefits?

This cost-benefit calculus has to be freshly examined in light of the lessons of the current financial crisis.

Careful re-assessment could spur the search for intermediate solutions. For example, can India allow foreign players to participate in domestic bond markets (FDI) without necessarily leading to a flood of foreign capital? Or, if foreign capital were allowed freely into domestic bond markets, could there be requirements that they be invested for a minimum period of time (as with say hedge fund investments) or that there be price-based incentives/taxes to prevent large swings in these flows? Recognising that financial development that leads to surges in foreign capital flows is not unambiguously beneficial from a self-insurance perspective is key to the more nuanced and pragmatic thinking that the crisis should motivate.

Two final points on CAC. Even those who see the importance of self-insurance and the need to manage inflows argue that technological change and trade integration make capital flows increasingly difficult to control. Surely, some leakage is inevitable but the difficulty of controlling flows is sometimes overstated: in its extreme form it suggests that opening to capital flows will have no effect on actual flows because controls have already been evaded (for example, it is difficult to believe that liberalising bond markets in India and opening them to portfolio inflows will have no effect on actual flows). Even if regulations are difficult to maintain for long periods of time, this should not preclude careful assessment of benefits and costs, taking account of the implementation difficulties.

Second, will a cautious approach to CAC send the wrong signals to foreign investors? The zeitgeist has changed, and the intellectual climate is shifting away from a no-questions-asked-embrace of financial globalisation. In this climate, sensible and pragmatic policies are unlikely to send the wrong signals.

Moreover, to the extent that this concern is valid, India can easily counter it by moving faster on opening up its markets to foreign direct investment. The message will be that India is not moving back in terms of its attitude to foreign capital; rather it will be that India recognises, like most countries, that distinctions need to be made between different forms of capital flows based on the experience among others of the recent crisis.

## Monetary Policy and Asset Prices

We have learnt yet again that asset prices—of stocks, bonds, housing and exchange rates—that rise very sharply over short periods of time must be carefully watched and responded to. For countries such as India, it is especially important to avoid rapidly appreciating currencies.

The stock market bubble of the late 1990s and the housing bubble that led to the current crisis provoked a fierce debate about the appropriateness of policy—monetary and financial—to respond to sharp asset price increases. Alan Greenspan famously persuaded the world that bubbles could not be easily identified, and hence pricked, *ex ante*. Far better to pick up the pieces after the bubble had burst. It is fair to say that this asymmetric policy response—the Greenspan put—is being seriously questioned if not discredited.

Monetary and financial authorities must be vigilant when asset prices rise sharply, and deviate from some broadly sensible norm; and depending on context, must use monetary policies and/or prudential policies to, yes, prick them. If sharp increases in asset prices are concentrated in some sectors, directed prudential policies (greater provisioning, higher margins, tighter capital adequacy standards etc.) will be called for. If, however, increases in asset prices are more broad-based and related to credit expansion more generally, tightening monetary policies should remain an option.

Central bankers should abundantly combine paranoia and puritanism: paranoia about any sharp increases in asset prices and puritanism in taking away the punch-bowl (by tightening prudential and monetary policies) to prevent the bubble from becoming intoxicating. Policy should strive to be as anti-cyclical as good judgement and common sense will allow, and hence more symmetric than Alan Greenspan argued for. He wanted to focus on addressing the hangover. The crisis suggests that his successors should also strive to limit drunkenness.

## Inflation Targeting

A related consequence for monetary policy is in the area of inflation targeting. There are calls in India for the RBI to focus on inflation as a near-exclusive objective. This is not the time to debate the merits of inflation targeting. But the crisis has thrown up a new reality. In the presence of a crisis, the US Fed has behaved as if it has not one (inflation), not two (inflation and growth) but three mandates (inflation, growth and financial stability). Stephen Roach of Morgan Stanley has called for an explicit codification of this triple mandate for the US Fed. Indeed, in the current crisis, deflation-cum-financial-distress is nudging central banks toward a "credibly irresponsible" abandonment of the traditional inflation objective.

It is inevitable that preserving financial sector stability will be an important objective for India too. Setting up a legal framework with a formal, and somewhat rigid, adherence to one objective seems to run counter to the sensible behaviour—including focusing on asset prices—that central bankers have exhibited during the recent crisis. Moreover, if the crisis leads to self-insurance becoming an important objective of economic policy, it will be hard for monetary policy not to keep an eye on the exchange rate as it strives to facilitate the amassing of the required levels of reserves in the future.

The crisis has shown that leverage is perhaps the original sin of finance. India is still under-intermediated but leverage in the financial and non-financial sectors should be closely monitored and regulated, with a particularly watchful eye on rapid increases in leverage. For banks, and all financial institutions, there should be direct limits on leverage in addition to any future Basel II-type capital adequacy requirements.

## Conclusions

India did not focus on self-insurance after the Asian financial crisis of the 1990s because it was then closed to capital and hence, relatively unaffected by that crisis. This crisis has been very different. Its serious adverse impact should awaken India to the need for effective self-insurance in the future. If self-insurance becomes an important policy objective, India will need to revisit macroeconomic policy, including exchange rate management and capital account convertibility. Put starkly, self-insurance calls for counter-cyclical policy—dampening flows and keeping the currency competitive—so that reserves can be built up during good times.

More broadly, on a host of issues, from capital account convertibility, exchange rate flexibility, financial sector development and inflation targeting, the intellectual climate in India was increasingly characterised by market fundamentalism and finance fetishism. The crisis has now allowed a long overdue pushback to these developments, a pushback that would otherwise have been derided as Luddite and dirigiste. It is not that finance is unimportant or that markets should be spurned. It is rather that the ardour of the influential devotees of finance and markets should be replaced by Talleyrand's counsel: *pas trop de zele*. This is a counsel that Vijay Kelkar may not completely share but would certainly appreciate.

# 6 Stabilising the Indian Business Cycle

Ajay Shah and Ila Patnaik*

## Setting

### The New Indian Business Cycle

In the India of old, good times and bad times were primarily about weather. A good year was one with a good monsoon and vice versa. The business cycle analysis in standard economics textbooks—involving an interplay of expectations, inventories and private investment—did not substantially matter in India. In addition, the domination of government in investment implied a high stability of investment demand, since year-to-year fluctuations in government investment do not take place based on forward-looking expectations.

In the following years, these features of the economy have changed dramatically (Patnaik and Sharma, 2002; Shah, 2008). The share of agriculture in GDP has dropped sharply from 40 to 17 per cent in the three decades from 1979 to 2009. Alongside this decline of agriculture to 17 per cent, there has been a new rise of private corporate investment. Figure 6.1 shows the time-series of private corporate investment, expressed as per cent of GDP. All the way till the early 1980s, this stayed below 5 per cent. In this period, the fluctuations in corporate investment would have had little to do with overall macroeconomic conditions.

After 1980, private corporate investment has achieved big values. It has also been strongly linked to business cycle conditions. The two great expansions in India—the mid-1990s and the post-2002—were each

* We are grateful to Nachiket Mor, Vijay Kelkar and Josh Felman for numerous insightful discussions on these issues.

associated with very large expansions of private corporate investment. A change in private corporate investment of as large as 10 percentage points was observed in the recent expansion.

**Figure 6.1**

*Private Corporate Investment (Per cent to GDP)*

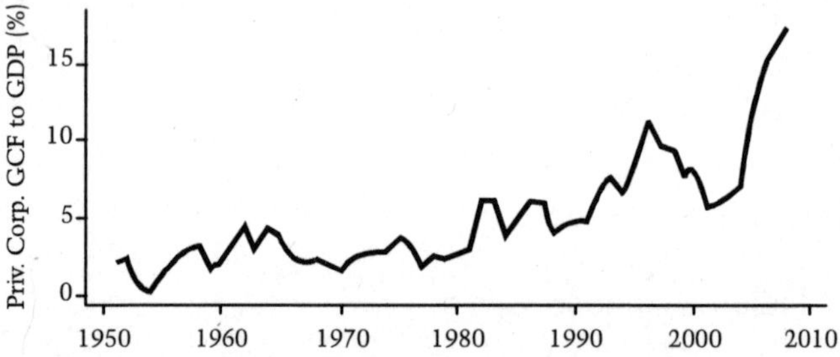


Figure 6.2 turns to GDP volatility. Each point in this graph is the standard deviation of the latest 10 values for annual GDP growth. Vijay Kelkar has emphasised that India's growth acceleration, from 1979 onwards, was accompanied by a decline in GDP volatility (Kelkar, 2004; 2005). This is clearly visible in the graph, where this standard deviation declined from values such as three to four percentage points to values such as one to two percentage points in the period after 1990. The first point in the graph (standard deviation over 1951-1961) was 2.71 per cent. The last point in the graph (standard deviation over 1999-2009) was 2.08 per cent, showing a sharp decline of 63 basis points.

**Figure 6.2**

*Volatility of GDP Growth*

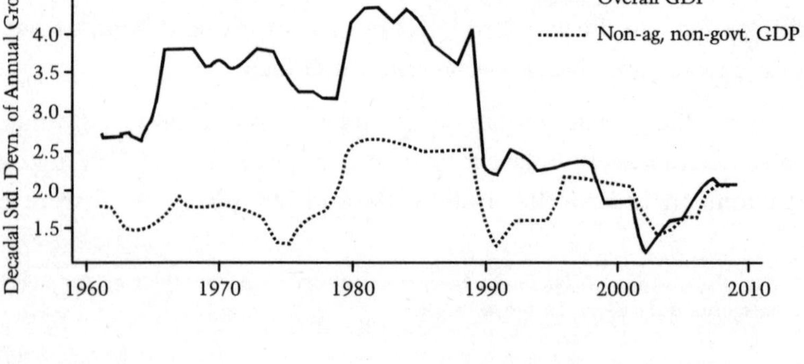

*Prima facie*, this would suggest that India does not have a big problem of macroeconomic stabilisation. Both growth and stability got better, despite no significant change in macroeconomic policy institutions. However, the cause of this decline in GDP growth volatility is primarily the decline in the volatility of agriculture, the share of agriculture in GDP and the linkages (covariances) between agriculture and other parts of the economy. Figure 6.2 also shows a dashed line which is the volatility of non-agriculture and non-government GDP. This shows a broadly stable pattern from the early 1960s onwards. The first point in the graph (standard deviation over 1951-1961) was 1.8 per cent. The last point in the graph (standard deviation over 1999-2009) was 1.96 per cent, a worsening of 16 basis points.

The decline in volatility of overall GDP, despite the minimal extent of institutional reform on macroeconomic policy, might make us complacent that for reasons that we might not be able to fathom, macroeconomic volatility is declining on its own. However, once agriculture and government is removed from the picture, the story changes to one where the minimal extent of institutional reform on macroeconomic policy was (unsurprisingly) associated with a slight worsening of GDP volatility.

## The New Problem of Macroeconomic Stabilisation

Macroeconomic stabilisation, or business cycles, have not been prominent in Indian economic policy thinking in previous decades. However, several arguments motivate a greater interest in these issues:

- Higher GDP volatility is likely to induce greater idiosyncratic variation of individual stock returns. If capital controls or incomplete markets inhibit full diversification and hedging of portfolios, then there is a possibility that the cost of capital required for investing in India could be higher when GDP volatility is higher. Through this, macroeconomic stabilisation could deliver a reduced cost of capital and thus higher investment.
- Greater stability of consumption could directly improve welfare of citizens.[1] The presence of non-linearities such as bankruptcy costs—

1. However, this proposition needs to contend with the argument from Lucas (1987) that these gains are small. In the standard modern DSGE models, the bulk of the welfare gains from stabilisation come from reducing price volatility. It is hard to reconcile this with the strong interest of politicians in smoothing GDP fuctuations.

which are likely to be bigger in a developing country—give another argument in favour of a smoother trajectory for output.

- Whether economists think stabilisation is important or not, politicians in a democracy are unlikely to stand aside when a downturn comes. As an example, in 2007-2009, when the business cycle downturn came, politicians in India tried to come out with impromptu responses. The choice that India faces is not one of a framework for stabilisation *versus* the absence of such a framework. The choice that India faces is one of stabilisation as hectic crisis responses *versus* stabilisation as a well-planned framework, grounded in law and well understood and anticipated by the private sector.[2]

  This is related to the rules *versus* discretion theme in economic policy analysis (Barro and Gordon, 1983; Kydland and Prescott, 1977). While a government might not promise to sharply enlarge the deficit in a harsh downturn, the market might know that in the absence of a well-enforced fiscal rule, such a deficit enlargement is going to take place anyway. If a rules-based environment could be constructed, it would reduce uncertainty, improve responses in a downturn through better planning as opposed to crisis management, and stabilise expectations.

In India, the framework of fiscal and monetary policy was established before the business cycle fluctuations of a market economy came about. In the new setting, it is important to carefully design the legal and institutional frameworks for fiscal and monetary policy so as to reduce the extent of business cycle fluctuations.[3]

---

2. An analogy is found in the field of deposit insurance, where it is said that democracies are unable to cope with large bank failures. The choice, then, is not one between having or not having deposit insurance. The choice is one of impromptu crisis response as opposed to sophisticated institutional machinery that is grounded in transparency and law and fully understood by the private sector ahead of time, thus reducing uncertainty.
3. A more complete treatment would examine the mechanisms through which financial sector policy also induces procyclicality (or can be modified to reduce procyclicality). In addition, there are intimate linkages between fiscal, financial and monetary policy, as examplified in the issues surrounding the establishment of the Debt Management Office (DMO) (Aziz, 2008). In this paper, we restrict ourselves to a treatment of fiscal and monetary policy frameworks.

A natural point of departure for such a discourse is the theoretical analysis and real-world experience with fiscal and monetary policy institutions in OECD countries. In the last 30 years, a considerable body of work has come together, which has guided a fundamental transformation of rules and institutions (Chari and Kehoe, 2006; Taylor, 2005; Mishkin, 2007).

Erstwhile developing countries like Korea have graduated into OECD membership and are increasingly aligning their institutional architecture to the best practices found amongst OECD countries. As India becomes more of an open economy and a market economy, there is undoubtedly a lot to learn by going along this path. At the same time, there are certain unique features of India which are likely to be with us for a decade or two. These unique features have a significant influence on strategic thinking in India about the monetary and fiscal policy frameworks that will be the most useful. The remainder of this paper seeks to achieve a judicious blend of sound ideas from theory and OECD practice, attenuated by the critical aspects where the Indian reality suggests first order modifications.

## Stabilisation through Monetary Policy

### The Monetary Policy Transmission (Or Lack Thereof)

In advanced economies, when the central bank changes the short-term interest rate, the financial system induces changes in a broad swathe of interest rates in the economy, across a diverse array of maturity and credit quality. Through this, changes in the short-term rate influence aggregate demand and thus output and prices. In many countries, central banks use this capability to stabilise the economy by focusing on achieving low and stable inflation.

When the financial system is weak, the monetary policy transmission is relatively ineffective. An illiquid and inefficient bond market implies that changes in the short rate do not transmit to a diverse array of interest rates. When there is a lack of competition in the banking system, changes in the cost of funds at the short end do not rapidly turn into changes in the cost of borrowing from banks.

In an underdeveloped banking system, the magnitude of borrowing (expressed as per cent of GDP) is small, so that changes in the policy rate have a small impact upon borrowers. As an example, in India, 'non-food credit' at the end of calendar 2009 stood at Rs. 29 trillion, or roughly half of GDP. When the financial system is underdeveloped (Mistry, 2007; Rajan, 2008; Patil, 2005; Thomas, 2006; Shah *et al.*, 2008), changes in the policy rate do relatively little in terms of altering aggregate demand. In other words, countries with a weak financial system tend to have a feeble monetary policy transmission.

The monetary policy transmission is critically about the capability of the banking system and the bond market. These are areas where India is relatively weak. As an example, the World Federation of Exchanges shows NSE and BSE at 3rd and 5th rank in the world, by number of transactions. There is no ranking of banking or bond market characteristics where India or an Indian entity is in the top 25 in the world.

In terms of empirical evidence of the impact of short-term monetary conditions upon the Index of Industrial Production or upon prices, Bhattacharya *et al.* (2010) find that after controlling for the exchange rate channel, the null hypothesis of no-effect cannot be rejected. This is consistent with the idea that the Indian bond market and banking system are so highly undeveloped that, for all practical purposes, they do not deliver a monetary policy transmission. Even if monetary policy in India desired a role in stabilisation, this is (at present) infeasible.

### Implications of a Large Informal Sector

The formal financial system in India is relatively small. A substantial part of the economy works through what is termed the 'informal' financial system. This includes equity financing from friends and family, borrowing from moneylenders, indigenous methods of trade financing, etc.

In recent years, there has been a considerable focus on the problem of 'financial exclusion', which is defined as the class of individuals or firms who are not part of the formal financial system. Concerns about financial exclusion are primarily motivated by a sense that the lives of these individuals would be improved if they could also connect to the formal financial system.

For the present discussion, the persistence of a large informal sector in India accentuates the ineffectiveness of the monetary policy transmission. When RBI raises the short-term interest rate, this can (at best) influence the price charged by the banking system and the bond market to formal sector borrowers. It is likely to have little impact upon the cost of capital in the informal sector.

The focus on financial inclusion has traditionally been motivated by the agenda of poverty reduction. However, financial inclusion, and the full integration between the formal financial system and the world of informal finance, should legitimately be a part of the policy agenda for building an effective monetary policy transmission. Recent innovations in financial engineering connected with informal finance, such as linking up micro finance institutions to the wholesale bond market through securitisation, would help improve integration between formal finance and informal finance, and thus help further this agenda of creating a meaningful monetary policy transmission.

## Exchange Rate Flexibility: A Tool for Stabilisation

As argued above, in countries where financial sector reforms have made little progress, we get problems such as a weak bond market and banking system, low levels of private debt to GDP, and a large informal financial system which is poorly integrated into formal finance. This generates a weak monetary policy transmission.

In many countries afflicted with weaknesses in financial sector reform, however, the process of trade reform has made considerable headway. When goods arbitrage takes place, 'exchange rate pass-through' is observed, where fluctuations in the exchange rate influence local prices.

This yields a channel for influence for monetary policy. Changes in the policy rate influence the exchange rate (though *de facto* capital account openness) and thus influence prices. Raising interest rates would lead to capital coming into the country, which would lead to an exchange rate appreciation, and thus, lower domestic prices. Even though changes in the policy rate may have a limited impact upon aggregate demand, changes in the policy rate could be a useful tool for targeting inflation, through the impact upon the exchange rate and thence the exchange rate pass-through.

When capital flows come into the country, on one hand it is expansionary since this is generally associated with increased investment demand. But at the same time, with a flexible exchange rate regime, an exchange rate appreciation would be obtained. This would reduce profitability and thus, investment demand in the tradeables sector. While the empirical magnitudes need to be determined, there is an element of stabilisation that is in-built, when shocks to capital flows are allowed to influence the exchange rate.

The exchange rate is the only monetary tool for stabilisation where significant effects are empirically visible in India today. A proper configuration of monetary policy in India should hence involve exchange rate appreciation in good times. When times are good, capital flows (which tend to be procyclical) would come into the country; the exchange rate would appreciate; this would crimp the profitability and thus investment demand of the tradeables sector. When times are bad, capital flows would leave the country; the exchange rate would depreciate; thus augmenting the profitability and investment demand of the tradeables sector.

Volatility of the exchange rate (and stability of reserves) is the path to stabilisation of the business cycle. Conversely, instability of reserves and a stable exchange rate generate enhanced business cycle fluctuations. The idea that the central bank should buy reserves at a time of increased capital inflows (and thus achieve an invariant exchange rate) is synonymous with giving up the only tool for stabilisation—the exchange rate—which the central bank in India possesses (Patnaik, 2005).

These insights put a new perspective on the evolution of monetary policy in India. In a closed economy with a fixed exchange rate, and without a sophisticated financial system, monetary policy is largely ineffective. It is ironic that RBI's efforts, in preventing a capable bond market and banking system from coming about, have implied that RBI as a central bank is relatively ineffective. Exchange rate flexibility and capital account openness gives a first avenue through which stabilisation can take place.

## Short-term Strategy

In the short term, the long-standing weaknesses of financial sector policy cannot be changed. In the short run, the bond market cannot be brought to life; an efficient and competitive banking system cannot come about.

Hence, in the short term, the only tool for stabilisation is the exchange rate coupled with an open capital account. Capital flows are inherently procyclical. In good times, money would come into the country, the exchange rate would appreciate, inflation would be curtailed, profitability and thus investment demand of the tradeables sector would be crimped. All these things would operate in reverse in recessions.

The traditional monetary policy transmission requires sophisticated institution-building: on financial sector policy and on monetary policy. In contrast, exchange rate flexibility only requires inaction on the part of the central bank. It does not require a sophisticated institutional machinery in order to deliver useful stabilisation.

### Medium-term Strategy

In the medium term, the long-standing weaknesses of the financial system can and should be addressed. This involves attacking the problems of the bond market, the banking system and financial inclusion. The technical roadmap for this has been defined by a series of committee reports (Mistry, 2007; Rajan, 2008; Patil, 2005; Aziz, 2008).

Once a monetary policy transmission has been achieved, a strong monetary policy process is also required, based on the key principles of independence, accountability and transparency. Through this, changes in the short-term interest rate would be an important tool for stabilisation of the economy. This can, however, only happen in the medium term, since it requires a sophisticated financial system and a new RBI Act.

## Stabilisation through Fiscal Policy

### Generic Difficulties of Discretionary Fiscal Policy

From the 1960s onwards, the use of discretionary fiscal policy in business cycle stabilisation has come under increasing criticism. Two major constraints that have been identified are: speed and politicisation.

In the National Bureau of Economic Research (NBER) data for US business cycles, in the 10 downturns from 1945 to 2001, the average recession lasted 10 months. This short duration is hard to reconcile with the real world delays of fiscal policy. For discretionary fiscal policy to come into play, the following delays are encountered:

1. The first delay is the time taken for the statistical system to discern a recession. As an example, we now know that the three month moving average growth of seasonally adjusted IIP peaked (at 20%) in late 2006.[4] But till the end of 2007, most analysts had not understood that IIP growth had peaked in the previous year.[5]
2. Substantial responses by the government—e.g. an expansion of the deficit by more than 0.5 per cent of GDP—can only happen through a budget. This generally induces a delay between the date that a downturn is seen and the date of the budget. Conversely, in February, when a budget is being formed (and when data about the previous December has not yet come in), relatively little is known about business cycle conditions in the year that is to start from the coming April.
3. Large changes in a budget made in February typically do not generate modified expenditures until June.

Hence, under ideal conditions and assuming no mistakes are made, a downturn in September would be clearly visible by February; it would induce a response on the part of discretionary fiscal policy which would hit the economy by the coming June. This is a delay of nine months. This shortest delay is possible for a recession that begins in September. For all other starting dates of a recession, the delay for discretionary fiscal policy would be larger.

If, as in the US, recessions are a year long (on average), then these delays make discretionary fiscal policy ill-suited for the task of stabilisation.

The second problem with discretionary fiscal policy is its politicisation. Prior to an election, it is likely that politicians will favour expansionary fiscal policy, thus inducing election cycles exactly as is the case with central banks that lack independence. Further, the design of taxation or expenditure

4. *Source: http://www.mayin.org/cycle.in*
5. This problem is not unique to India. As an example from the US, the NBER dating committee made the announcement that December 2007 had been a peak in December 2008, i.e., a full year later.

programmes as part of a fiscal stimulus, in a crisis environment, can lead to favours being given out to marginal constituencies.[6]

The research literature has shown sombre empirical results about discretionary fiscal policy. It is found that GDP volatility is higher in countries where there is more discretion in fiscal policy. Countries which put more constraints on fiscal policy fare better. Further, these effects are stronger with poor countries. These conceptual arguments and evidence suggest that India should avoid utilising discretionary fiscal policy responses to a downturn.

## Unique Indian Features of Discretionary Fiscal Policy

These arguments, about the delays and politicisation of fiscal policy, and thus the optimality of avoiding discretionary fiscal policy, have been widely accepted worldwide. When we think about India, there are some unique features of the Indian economy which need to be taken into account.

India has an unhappy history of chronic fiscal indiscipline. In the 31 years from 1979-80 onwards, the median value for the gross fiscal deficit of the Centre was 6.26 per cent of GDP. Large primary surpluses are the hallmark of a period where a country achieves fiscal consolidation. It is only in the brief period from 2003-04 till 2007-08 that India ran small primary surpluses. The overall picture is one where the median primary surplus was -2.19 per cent. Owing to this failure to achieve primary surpluses, in these three decades, India has never had a period where the debt/GDP was paid down significantly, in the fashion seen in many other countries.

In the period after 1990-91, the median value of the Central government's debt/GDP ratio was 57.13 and the latest value (for 2009-10) was 63.83 per cent. This is a worrisome level of indebtedness, when we consider that government debt was below 60 per cent of GDP in most

6. Other consequences of the use of discretionary fiscal policy include an increase in uncertainty for the private sector. The ideal tax system is one in which there is long-term stability of tax rates. Once major reforms of the tax system are finished, and India is on a framework that emphasises the personal income tax and the GST, the aim should be to have at most one change to one of these rates per decade. This stability will assist the ability of the private sector to undertake long-term planning in confidence. Year-to-year fluctuations in tax rates damage plans of the private sector.

episodes of default by governments in emerging economies in recent years (Reinhart *et al.*, 2003).

In this setting, of fiscal fragility as the normal condition, suppose discretionary fiscal policy is used to achieve stabilisation when a downturn comes along. This has important negative ramifications. Fiscal fragility is worsened, which exacerbates the downturn in various ways. As an example, the cost of borrowing of private firms abroad goes up in a downturn since the credit rating of the sovereign gets downgraded.

Indian-style chronic fiscal distress thus involves a new channel for procyclicality through increased fiscal fragility when discretionary fiscal policy is used in a downturn.

## Procyclicality of the Fiscal Balance in India

The other channel for fiscal procyclicality lies in the budget constraints faced by the government. When a country has weak fiscal institutions, and deficits and debt have reached uncomfortable levels, in bad times or in normal times, finance ministers are cautious about spending. In booms, the pressure of deficits and debt appears to be alleviated owing to automatic stabilisers (the response of tax revenues to good times, and the smaller expenses that some existing programmes incur in good times). In such times, finance ministers feel comfortable about the fiscal situation, and governments embark on enlargement of spending programmes.

Conversely, when there is a business cycle downturn, deficits and debt achieve uncomfortable values, and governments embark on austerity drive.

Such behaviour yields procyclical fiscal policy. When times are good, government expenditure makes them better. When times are bad, government tightens its belt, making things worse.

Figure 6.3 illustrates this problem in India's Central government finances. It shows that on an average, the growth in expenditure in 2010-2011 is likely to be bigger by 0.3786 percentage points for each percentage point of growth in gross tax revenues in 2009-10 (and vice versa). A government making a budget in January and February is likely to spend more in the coming year when growth in gross tax revenues in the current year has been better (and vice versa). Through this, government spends

**Figure 6.3**

*Central Government Spends More in Year t when Gross Tax Revenues Grew Well in Year t–1*

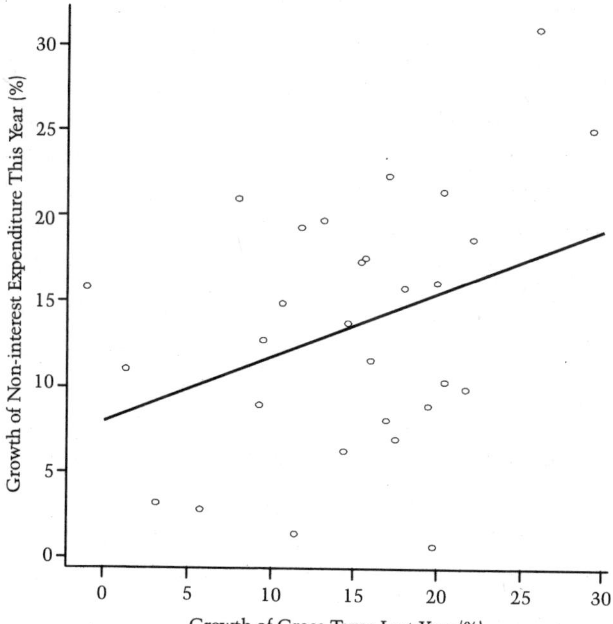


*Note:* The x axis of this graph shows the growth in gross taxes in the year (in per cent), using data from 1980 onwards. The y axis shows the growth in non-interest expenditures (in per cent) of the Central government in the next year. It highlights the idea that in February 2010, when a budget is being prepared, a strong performance on gross tax revenues in 2009-10 generates a bigger bias in favour of expansion of expenditure for 2010-11.

The coefficient of the regression line is 0.3786 (with a t-statistic of 1.983). On average, a 1 percentage point improvement in gross tax revenue growth in year t yields bigger non-interest expenditure growth, of 0.3786 percentage points, in year t+1.

more when business cycle conditions are buoyant and vice versa, inducing procyclicality.

The other dimension of fiscal policy and stabilisation pertains to rare and catastrophic events. When a country has healthy values for debt and deficits under ordinary times, this creates the space through which the rare use of discretionary fiscal policy can help the economy in rare and extreme events. The deeper consequence of this fiscal space is that the private sector feels more confident in the outlook for the country, knowing that the State has the capability to marshal remarkable responses when extreme situations arise once or twice a century. This confidence induces bigger investments in financial and human capital.

### Looking Forward

In this difficult situation, how can India's fiscal policy framework best cater to stabilisation? The three key ideas appear to be:

1. Fiscal consolidation needs to be the first area of focus. The channels of procyclicality described above are critically related to fiscal fragility. India needs to cap the consolidated debt/GDP ratio (of Centre and states) at 60 per cent and credibly ensure that it will not rise above 60 per cent even in a sharp downturn.
2. Discretionary fiscal policy induces many problems. In terms of fiscal policy, the sensible path would involve expansion of programmes such as NREG, which are automatic stabilisers. That is, they yield bigger deficits in bad times and smaller deficits in good times, without discretionary action by the government. The fiscal space for these programmes can be made by shrinking expenditures of the government which yield little by way of public goods such as subsidies, and existing programmes on health and education.

   As with the analysis of informal finance above, this emphasis on the safety net (through programmes such as NREG) is another area where the poverty alleviation agenda is consistent with institution building for India as a mature market economy. While the NREG is desirable from the viewpoint of poverty alleviation, it is also desirable from the viewpoint of business cycle stabilisation through non-discretionary fiscal policy.
3. Progress on monetary policy reform will yield a new mechanism of stabilisation, which will reduce the pressure upon politicians to engage in discretionary fiscal policy when faced with a downturn.

## Economic Reforms as a Tool for Stabilisation

Economists generally think in terms of counteracting business cycle fluctuations using fiscal policy and monetary policy. But in India, both fiscal policy and monetary policy institutions are relatively feeble. They do not have the capability to make a substantial difference if the challenge that is posed to them is counteracting a decline in private corporate investment of 10 per cent of GDP or Rs. 550,000 crore a year.

In coming years, India must build up high quality fiscal, financial and monetary policy institutions. This will give the institutional capability through which stabilisation can be done. This is a desirable goal and should be undertaken. In the short term, when faced with a storm, the institutional capabilities required for stabilisation are largely absent. If the challenge is a potential decline of investment by Rs. 550,000 crore a year, fiscal policy and monetary policy are mere spectators.

In a downturn, the private sector tends to be concerned about the outlook for Indian GDP growth. The private sector needs to be persuaded that India is serious about economic policy reform, so as to get back to an optimistic environment where India is on the move, growth expectations are strong and investment gets going again.

The will to invest of the private sector is thus shaped by 'animal spirits' of private corporations. Accelerating broad-based economic reforms is an important tool for stabilisation. In a downturn, it can induce greater optimism about India, and yield increased private corporate investment. The magnitudes involved here are larger than those which can be mustered through monetary or fiscal policy.

## Conclusion

Drawing together the key ideas of this paper, the policy directions emphasised in this paper, in order to achieve macroeconomic stabilisation in India, may be summarised as follows:

- Fiscal consolidation needs to be the first area of focus. The channels of procyclicality described in the paper are critically related to fiscal fragility. India needs to cap the consolidated debt/GDP ratio (of Centre and states) at 60 per cent and credibly ensure that it will not rise above 60 per cent even in a sharp downturn.
- Discretionary fiscal policy induces many problems. In terms of fiscal policy, the sensible path would involve expansion of programmes such as NREG, which are automatic stabilisers. That is, they yield bigger deficits in bad times and smaller deficits in good times, without discretionary action by the government. The fiscal space for

these programmes can be made by shrinking expenditures of the government which yield little by way of public goods such as subsidies, and existing programmes on health and education.

- Progress on monetary policy reform will yield a new mechanism of stabilisation, which will reduce the pressure upon politicians to engage in discretionary fiscal policy when faced with a downturn.
- In the short term, business cycle stabilisation through the short-term interest rate is largely ineffectual, owing to shortcomings of both financial sector policy and monetary policy.
- In the short term, exchange rate flexibility is a tool through which stabilisation can be obtained. A rupee appreciation reduces inflation, reduces profits of the tradeables sector and thus, the investment demand of the tradeables sector. Through this, a rupee appreciation is contractionary (and vice versa).
- In the medium term, the implementation of the four major committee reports on financial sector reforms will yield a financial system with a meaningful monetary policy transmission. This would need to be accompanied by commensurate reform of monetary policy arrangements.
- In the short term, structural economic reform is a tool for stoking investment demand in a downturn, by increasing optimism about India.

## References

Aziz, J. (2008). *Report of the Internal Working Group on Debt Management in India*. Ministry of Finance.

Barro, R.J. and D.B. Gordon (1983). "Rules, discretion and reputation in a model of monetary policy", *Journal of Monetary Economics*.

Bhattacharya, R., I. Patnaik and A. Shah (2010). "Monetary policy with a weak monetary policy transmission", *Discussion paper*, NIPFP.

Chari, V.V. and P.J. Kehoe (2006). "Modern macroeconomics in practice: How theory is shaping policy", *Discussion paper*, NBER.

Kelkar, V. (2004): "India: On the growth turnpike", *Discussion paper*, K.R. Narayanan Memorial Lecture, Australian National University.

———. (2005). "India's economic future: Moving beyond state capitalism", *Discussion paper*, Gadgil Memorial Lecture.

Kydland, F. and E. Prescott (1977). "Rules rather than discretion: The inconsistency of optimal plans", *Journal of Political Economy* 85: 473-490.

Lucas, R.E. (1987). *Models of Business Cycles*. Oxford.

Mishkin, F.S. (2007). *Monetary Policy Strategy*. MIT Press.

Mistry, P. (2007). "Making Mumbai an international financial centre", *Committee Report*, Sage Publishing and Ministry of Finance, Government of India.

Patil, R.H. (2005). *Report of High Level Expert Committee on Corporate Bonds and Securitisation*. Ministry of Finance.

Patnaik, I. (2005). "India's experience with a pegged exchange rate", in Bery, S., B. Bosworth and A. Panagariya (eds.) *The India Policy Forum 2004*. Brookings Institution Press and NCAER. pp. 189-226.

Patnaik, I. and R. Sharma (2002). "Business cycles in the Indian economy", *Margin* 35(1): 71-79.

Rajan, R. (2008). *Committee for Financial Sector Reforms*. New Delhi: Planning Commission, Government of India.

Reinhart, C.M., K.S. Rogoff and M.A. Savastano (2003). "Addicted to dollars", *Working Paper* 10015, National Bureau of Economic Research.

Shah, A. (2008). "New issues in macroeconomic policy", in Ninan, T.N. (ed.), *Business Standard India*, Chap. 2. Business Standard Books. pp. 26-54.

Shah, A., S. Thomas and M. Gorham (2008). *India's Financial Markets: An Insider's Guide to How the Markets Work*. Elsevier.

Taylor, J.B. (2005). "Thirty five years of model building for monetary policy evaluation: Breakthroughs, dark ages and a renaissance", *Discussion paper*, Stanford University.

Thomas, S. (2006). "How the financial sector in India was reformed", in Narayan, S. (ed.), *Documenting reforms: Case studies from India*. New Delhi: Macmillan India. pp. 171-210.

# 7 Tax Compliance and Tax Rates

*India 1996-2010*

Surjit S. Bhalla

## Introduction

It is a privilege to be invited to write this essay honouring Vijay Kelkar. I have known him as a friend, and as a senior policy economist, for the last two decades. He has been at the forefront of economic policymaking and in this essay, I would like to talk about his contribution to thinking about tax issues. As India embarks on implementing some radical changes in direct and indirect taxes, it owes an enormous debt of gratitude to Kelkar's thinking and research for the better part of the last decade.

There is another issue of policy in which Vijay was far ahead of the curve, and where his recommendations have had far-reaching effects on Indian economic policy and economic growth. The growth acceleration in the Indian economy is up from a level of 5.5 per cent annual GDP growth to the now emerging normal of double-digit growth. After the pioneering 1991 reforms and the 1997 tax cut (about which more later), the Indian policy cupboard had been left somewhat bare and the economy and industry was suffering under the yoke of very high real interest rates. In the Budget Speech of February 1999, Finance Minister Yashwant Sinha announced a 50 basis point cut in the interest rate that "small savers" received, as government largesse, and policy, on their deposits. The cut was from truly a princely level of 12.5 per cent. Inflation for several years had been in the 3 to 4 per cent range, so the real interest rate, on deposits with a government authorised and mandated "small savings" scheme was upwards of 8 per cent. Seventy-five per cent of the money gathered by this scheme went to the state governments. These governments were *de facto*, not able to borrow from the Reserve Bank of India nor from  the market (no state bonds please). This easy access to borrowing, facilitated by the guarantee of the Central government, allowed states to operate a Ponzi scheme—keep borrowing from the people and pay interest to old borrowers from investments of new borrowers.

The importance of this cut in interest rates (I called it "The Most Kindest Cut" in my review of the Budget) can be appreciated by understanding the "mindset" of most politicians, policy makers and economists at that time. Even today, most economists in India are shy of admitting to an important role of interest rates in affecting economic decisions. The belief remains that it is animal spirits and other factors that determine investments, rather than monetary policy. But not so Vijay. It was his influence that guided Mr. Sinha towards reducing the small savings rate. Over the next few years, Mr. Sinha went on to reduce this rate to 8 per cent; in 2003, this policy got the approval of even the conservative RBI, which agreed that the rates on small savings should not be much different from other government borrowing i.e., small savings interest rates should be market determined. The kindest cut led to rates on all government borrowings to drop, and real interest rates in the economy fell by as much as 500 to 600 basis points between 1999 and 2003. The Indian economy changed its growth path; the new Hindu rate of growth became 8 to 9 per cent. (See Bhalla, 2010 for a detailed discussion about India's growth performance, 1950-2008 and particularly, 2003 onwards.)

The major reforms in the next few years will be with regard to public finance. And Vijay has had a deep involvement with the suggested reforms. Once the proposed new direct and indirect tax codes (GST) become policy, the economy will move to a more efficient growth path. This essay examines the economics, and the likely impact of the proposed new direct tax code. The results suggest that not only will tax collections be revenue neutral in the face of a large tax cut, they will be revenue enhancing as well.

## The Laffer Logic of Tax Reforms

In 2002-03, as Economic Advisor to Finance Minister Yashwant Sinha, Mr. Kelkar published two separate task force documents on taxes—one pertained to indirect taxes, and the other to direct taxes. The proposed new tax codes owe an intellectual debt to these documents. The proposed reduction in the average tax rate for 2010 onwards is about 3.7 percentage points, a large cut by any reckoning, but smaller than the less talked about 2008-09 tax cut (reduction in average tax rate from 15.7 to 9.7 per cent) and the 1997 tax cut (reduction from 16.8 to 10.2 per cent). By the time the 2008-09 tax cut came about, tax drift had caused average tax rates to match their pre-1997 levels. With that context, the 2008-09 tax cut was large in absolute terms but not relative to the past. This tax cut has not been commented upon much by the fiscal cognoscenti perhaps because this tax reform was geared towards the lower end of the tax paying distribution.

Many economists question the efficacy of the Laffer curve, a proposition that states that tax revenues will increase with a decline in tax rates. The math behind the proposition is very simple—at zero tax rate, the government receives no revenue; ditto at a 100 per cent tax rate. If any tax revenue is collected at any tax rate between 0 and 100, then the Laffer curve exists. Its importance in advanced economies may be questioned; in such economies, everyone is in the tax net, and tax administration is not lax, or subject to much corruption. In developing economies like India, it is another story. Here, tax administrators gain from high tax rates (and the country loses). Why? Because tax compliance is a matter of negotiation. Under-declaration of income is a trade-off for a lower tax rate. The "rent" from this exchange does not accrue to the government. Hence, the likelihood of a Laffer curve successfully operating in a country like India is very large.

No one suggests that continually increasing the tax rate will lead to an increase in tax revenue; all admit that beyond a point, an increase in the tax rate will be counter-productive. What the inflection peak tax rate is, is a matter of debate and research. So when economists question a decline in tax rates, they are implicitly asserting that the tax rate is far from the maximising tax revenue level; when others (like Vijay and myself) assert that a tax cut is needed, they are contending that the present level of rates are higher than the peak maximum revenue level. The divergence in views should not be a matter of ideology; it should be a matter of research. This paper attempts to provide some research on this important policy subject.

Central to the success of any proposed tax cut is the assumption of an increase in tax compliance. Tax compliance is defined simply as the number of people paying taxes within a tax bracket (or overall) as a percentage of the people who are theoretically in that bracket. The reform proposes to reduce tax rates for all income classes; the new tax schedule is as follows: No taxation for incomes below Rs. 1.6 lakh; between Rs. 1.6 lakh and Rs. 10 lakh a 10 per cent tax rate; for incomes ranging from Rs. 10 to Rs. 25 lakh a 20 per cent tax rate and for incomes exceeding 25 lakh, a 30 per cent tax rate. At present, the highest tax rate of 30 per cent begins at Rs. 10 lakh.

Table 7.1 documents the tax schedule for 2007-08, 2008-09 and the proposed new tax schedule; the average effective tax rate in each schedule is also reported, as well as the average tax rate of the tax paying population. The proposed direct tax code reduces the effective tax rate by 3.7 percentage points—from 9.7 per cent to 6 per cent.

**Table 7.1**

*Tax Codes for 2007-08, 2008-09, 2009-10 and Proposed New Code*

| *For 2007-08* | | *For 2008-09* | |
|---|---|---|---|
| *Individual Income (in Rs. lakh)* | *Tax Rate (%)* | *Individual Income (in Rs. lakh)* | *Tax Rate (%)* |
| 0-1.1 | 0 | 0-1.5 | 0 |
| 1.1-1.5 | 10 | 1.5-3 | 10 |
| 1.5-2.5 | 20 | 3.0-5.0 | 20 |
| 2.5-10 | 30 | 5.0-10 | 30 |
| >10 | 30 | >10 | 30 |
| Effective tax rate | 15.7 | | 9.1 |
| *Individual Income (in Rs. lakh)* | *Existing Rate 2009-10 (%)* | *Proposed New Tax Rate (%)* | |
| 0-1.6 | 0 | 0 | |
| 1.6-3.0 | 10 | 10 | |
| 3.0-5.0 | 20 | 10 | |
| 5.0-10.0 | 30 | 10 | |
| 10.0-25.0 | 30 | 20 | |
| >25.0 | 30 | 30 | |
| Effective tax rate | 9.7 | 6.0 | |

*Note:* The effective tax rate is the average tax rate of those who pay some tax.
*Source:* Ministry of Finance, Tax Schedule.

The new tax code does not change the tax rate for those earning between Rs. 1.6 to Rs. 3 lakh or those earning more than Rs. 25 lakh. For the former, there was a large tax cut in the 2008-09 tax reform. Overall, the new tax code will imply a reduction in the tax rate (of those whose tax obligations are greater than zero) of 3.7 percentage points, a not insignificant amount by any standards. Consequently, some fiscal experts (e.g. Rao and Rao, 2009) have questioned the economic basis of the proposed direct tax reform. The worry is that the reduction in tax rates will lead to a reduction in tax revenue, a prospect that the country can ill-afford at any time, and especially when the economy is operating with large fiscal deficits. "By any reckoning this is a massive reduction in the tax rates involving substantial loss of revenue...At a time when it is necessary to garner higher revenues to return to the path of fiscal consolidation, such a massive giveaway may only make fiscal adjustment process that much more difficult. Such a liberal giveaway does not serve the cause of vertical equity either. For a country with per capita income of Rs. 25,500 (sic), levying the 10 per cent tax up to Rs. 10 lakh income is tantamount to throwing the baby out with the bathwater" (Rao and Rao, 2009: 36-37). As the analysis below shows, what Rao and Rao are ignoring is the compliance inducing effects of the tax cut—something that has happened with every tax cut in India, and something that happened as recently as 2008-09.

Somewhat unnoticed by the tax experts (especially outside of the Ministry of Finance), the Indian economy has gone through a major structural transformation over the last decade—a transformation which suggests that the proposed direct tax code is the appropriate tax code for the Indian economy of 2010. Nominal incomes per worker have grown at an average rate of 10.2 per cent per annum since the last major tax reform in 1997; for the five years ending in 2008, the growth rate is close to 12 per cent. Tax schedules are in nominal terms and this means there has been a substantial shift in incomes towards the higher tax brackets; thus, more nominal income and more real tax revenues are available from each tax bracket. The impressive gain in tax collections is both a function of this rightward movement in the income distribution and an increase in tax compliance. What tax reform should do is increase compliance (whether income compliance i.e., a more accurate statement of incomes, or return compliance i.e., a larger fraction filing tax returns). Both compliance ratios have risen impressively from the year prior to the first major tax reform of 1997—from below 30 per cent to above 50 per cent.

Both income and return compliance in 2008-09 are around the 50 to 60 per cent mark. This means that while a considerable portion of the low hanging fruit has been harvested, a lot of fruit still remains to be plucked. Kelkar referred to the "missing middle" in his discussion of direct taxes in the 2002 task force report. The missing middle is most likely composed of professionals and the self-employed. They need to be targeted for revenue enhancement. The proposed tax changes is aimed at this group. It should allow compliance levels to proceed upwards of 80 per cent i.e., almost developed country standards.

## Data and Methods

This section documents the data and methodology used to estimate compliance and the effects of tax changes on tax revenue. Tax return data, according to broad income slabs, are available, from two sources: till 1996-1997, from an All India Tax Statistics or AITS publication. This publication documents, for each tax slab, the number of returns, the gross income, net income and taxes paid. For the years 1997-98 to 2007-08, the Comptroller Auditor General (CAG) of India reports contain data on the returns filed across different income classifications (0-Rs. 50,000, Rs. 50,000-Rs.1 lakh, etc.). These data are also reported on the CAG website (*http://www.cag.gov.in/html/unionaudit.html*). In addition, for only the year 2001-02, detailed data on tax returns based on a large 1 million sample of actual tax returns are available (see Kelkar, 2002: 186-187). The Kelkar Task Force (KTF) provides an estimate of tax returns separately for salaried and non-salaried taxpayers for 2001-02.[1] The total returns filed in this year are 23.5 million, or about 10 per cent higher than obtained from the reduced sample used by the AITS publication.[2] While the KTF has more accurate data for a single year, the CAG source has the advantage that the

1. On page 185 of the report, the number of returns filed are reported for the fiscal year (2002-03) or assessment year (2003-04). This number is an estimate and represents a 15 per cent increase over the "actuals" reported in the survey.
2. In page 73 of the KTF report, the number of taxpayers for 2001-02 are reported as 28.7 million; the reconciliation of the different data series is beyond the scope of this paper; the fact remains that all of them show the same exploding trend after the tax reforms of 1997.

data are available for a large number of years. Hence, it is the CAG data that are used in the analysis. (The results are unaffected by source of data.)

The CAG tax return data is a quasi-distribution of income of those filing returns and with incomes as stated by the individuals. This distribution contains within it the two compliance errors—people not present in the tax distribution because they avoided paying tax altogether, and people present but with understated income. If the "true" distribution of incomes were known, then one could assess the magnitude and therefore importance, of the compliance errors. This paper generates such a distribution for all the years 1996-97 to 2010-11.

## Earner Distribution

The National Council for Applied Economic Research (NCAER) is the only organisation in India that has systematically (since the mid-sixties) collected and tabulated data on household incomes. The organisation has conducted three important income distribution surveys: the 2004-05 household income and expenditure survey, the 1994-95 Micro Impact Macro Adjustment Policies (MIMAP) survey and the 1975-76 income distribution survey. The 2004-05 survey has all the information needed on incomes for all classes of households—cultivators, self-employed, wage and salary earners. For purposes of our study, the NCAER data have two drawbacks: the sample size is not very large, 63,000 households or about half the size of the National Sample Surveys (NSS), and the fact that the distribution of income is available at a household level, rather than an earner level. It is the latter which is necessary for construction of an earner distribution.

In contrast, almost every five years, the NSS has conducted employment and unemployment surveys. These surveys contain estimates of earnings for those deriving income from wages and salaries. These data are available (125,000 households or approximately 400,000 earners) for each of the years 1983, 1987-88, 1993-94, 1999-2000 and 2004-05. Each of these surveys describes the work, education and wage activity of the earners. The only drawback to this large wealth of information is that earnings data are not reported for self-employed households (these constitute about half of the total workforce).

Part of this drawback does not affect our analysis because by Indian law, the self-employed cultivators are not eligible to pay tax. So the only worker set for which earnings data are missing in the NSS survey are the self-employed non-agricultural workers. However, analysis of distribution of income in the NCAER survey shows that the distribution of self-employed is virtually the same as the wage and salary earners. Hence, an overall tax earner distribution is obtained by using the NSS distribution of wage and salary income and using the non-cultivator population in the economy as "weights".

Two problems remain. First, the distribution can change over time. However, the Gini coefficient of earners has stayed near constant at around 0.55 since 1993-94 (per capita consumption Gini is at a much lower level of 0.35). The second problem arises from lack of survey capture i.e., the NSS survey mean income per worker is considerably lower than the mean according to national accounts (the latter is the income the tax administrator sees!). If the assumption is made that individual income distribution has stayed approximately constant at the 1999-2000 level, one has an earner distribution for all the years 1996-97 to 2010-11. The distribution remains the same as 1999-2000; the mean changes according to mean private income per worker. Private income is obtained from national account statistics; the non-cultivator worker population is obtained from NSS data 1993-94 to 2004-05. Since 2004-05, the worker population is assumed to grow at 2.5 per cent per annum. With these assumptions, all the data required for constructing a theoretical tax distribution for each year are available—an income level, the number of earners at that level, and the applicable tax rate for that income. This theoretical distribution is then compared to the actual taxpayer distribution (the AITS data) and estimates of compliance obtained.

## The Distribution of Earnings, 1996-2010

The per-earner distribution for 1999-2000 and 2009-10 is reported in Table 7.2. (The two are identical distributions but with means equal to per worker private income in the two years; Figure 7.1 shows the distribution for three years.) The incomes are in current rupees. This estimate of the distribution suggests that only 16 per cent of the earner population (from the 85$^{th}$ percentile onwards) was eligible to pay taxes in 1999-2000. The mean gross income of the 84th percentile in 1999-2000 (not shown in the table) was Rs. 73,000; the standard deduction (one-third or Rs. 25,000, whichever is lower) for this individual would be Rs. 24,333. Given the exemption for the first Rs. 50,000 of taxable income, this individual does not belong in the tax bracket.

A decade later, almost the same fraction of people were paying taxes. There is a popular observation of taxes in India—too few people pay taxes. Newspapers and academic articles are filled with statements like the following: something has to be done about the tax system because too few people in India pay taxes; only 3 per cent of people in India pay taxes. True. But the data contained in Table 7.3 illustrates that not much more should be expected!

**Table 7.2**

*Taxable Income Distribution and Taxes (in Rs.)—1999 and 2009*

| | *1999* | | *2009* | |
|---|---|---|---|---|
| *Percentile* | *Income* | *Implied Tax* | *Income* | *Implied Tax* |
| 43 | | | 51718 | |
| 45 | | | 55549 | |
| 50 | | | 63027 | |
| 55 | | | 66112 | |
| 60 | | | 78994 | |
| 65 | | | 81010 | |
| 70 | | | 97212 | |
| 75 | | | 114569 | |
| 80 | | | 140250 | |
| 85 | 51915 | 194 | 190457 | 3137 |
| 90 | 89665 | 6048 | 271623 | 11497 |
| 95 | 129848 | 13610 | 371149 | 29077 |
| 96 | 147373 | 16686 | 414556 | 38018 |
| 97 | 166767 | 20695 | 462591 | 47914 |
| 98 | 195535 | 28750 | 533844 | 66307 |
| 99 | 253965 | 45110 | 678565 | 110797 |
| 100 | 481216 | 108741 | 1233172 | 282170 |

*Note:* Derived from the NSS Employment-Unemployment Survey for 1999-2000. See text for details.

The breakdown of the reasoning is as follows. First, the worker population is about 40 per cent of the total population. Second, the non-

**Table 7.3**

*Indian Population and Taxpayer Characteristics, 1996-2010*

| Year | Population | Level of (in millions) | | | | Fraction of (%) | | | |
|---|---|---|---|---|---|---|---|---|---|
| | | Workers | Workers Non-Cultivators | Population That Should Pay Tax | Population Paying Tax | Workers | Workers Non-Cultivators | Population That Should Pay Tax | Population Paying Tax |
| 1996 | 930 | 350 | 250 | 37 | 9 | 37.6 | 26.9 | 4 | 0.9 |
| 1997 | 950 | 360 | 260 | 39 | 11 | 37.4 | 26.9 | 4.1 | 1.2 |
| 1998 | 970 | 340 | 240 | 36 | 15 | 34.8 | 24.4 | 3.7 | 1.5 |
| 1999 | 990 | 370 | 270 | 41 | 17 | 37.3 | 27.1 | 4.1 | 1.7 |
| 2000 | 1000 | 380 | 280 | 45 | 23 | 37.6 | 27.6 | 4.5 | 2.3 |
| 2001 | 1000 | 390 | 290 | 49 | 26 | 37.8 | 28 | 4.9 | 2.6 |
| 2002 | 1000 | 400 | 300 | 52 | 28 | 38.1 | 28.5 | 5.2 | 2.8 |
| 2003 | 1100 | 410 | 310 | 58 | 29 | 38.5 | 29 | 5.3 | 2.6 |
| 2004 | 1100 | 420 | 320 | 63 | 27 | 38.8 | 29.5 | 5.7 | 2.5 |
| 2005 | 1100 | 430 | 330 | 61 | 29 | 39.2 | 30 | 5.5 | 2.6 |
| 2006 | 1100 | 440 | 340 | 67 | 31 | 39.5 | 30.5 | 6.1 | 2.8 |
| 2007 | 1100 | 450 | 350 | 74 | 33 | 39.9 | 31 | 6.7 | 3 |
| 2008 | 1100 | 460 | 360 | 62 | 36 | 40.3 | 31.5 | 5.6 | 3.3 |
| 2009 | 1200 | 470 | 370 | 69 | 39 | 40.8 | 32.1 | 5.8 | 3.3 |

*Note:* Population that should pay tax is obtained via matching of income distribution and tax schedules; see text. 1996 refers to the 1996-97 fiscal year etc.

cultivator population, i.e., the population in the tax net, is even smaller. The farmer population (cultivators and farmers outside of food grains) has been steadily declining from about 120 million in the late 1990s. For our simulation purposes, we have taken 100 million as the cultivator population. This brings the population theoretically subject to tax to an average of 30 per cent of the population (27 per cent in 1996 and 33 per cent in 2009). Given that not everybody who earns income is required to pay tax (there is a minimum exemption, which for the fiscal year 2009-10, is Rs. 1.6 lakh per earner), the number of people in the taxable bracket goes down still further.

The fraction of people eligible to pay tax has increased from about 4 per cent of the overall population in 1996 to close to 6 per cent today. In 2007-08, the last year for which returns data are available, about 33 million workers filed tax returns while 74 million "should" have filed returns giving an overall compliance level of 45 per cent. While it is true that only 3.3 per cent of the population is paying taxes, it is equally true that only 5.8 per cent of the population should be paying taxes. This simple fact is often ignored by those who argue that Indian workers are taxed "too little" or have low compliance. As will be shown later, the compliance ratio is most effectively raised by lowering tax rates, not raising them.

There is some interest in the number of individual taxpayers in the 'above Rs. 10 lakh a year' class. It is estimated that there are approximately 1.1 million such individuals today, up from only 65,000 in 1996 and 286,000 in 2001. The sudden increase in this group is the result of a shift in the distribution to the right. Figure 7.1 documents this shift.

## Tax Compliance in India, 1996-2010

Official data suggests that there were 9 million individuals filing tax returns in 1996-97, 17 million on 1999-2000, and 33 million in 2007-08 (the last year for which official CAG return data are available). There is a marked acceleration in the growth rate of tax returns after the 1996 tax reforms. However, this acceleration cannot be taken as indicative of an increase in compliance; because of nominal income drift into higher tax brackets, one would "artificially" obtain more taxable workers over time. Compliance reflects the increase in returns adjusted for the fact that because of income drift into higher slabs, there are more taxpayers in each slab.

**Figure 7.1**

*Income Distribution of Taxpayers in India*

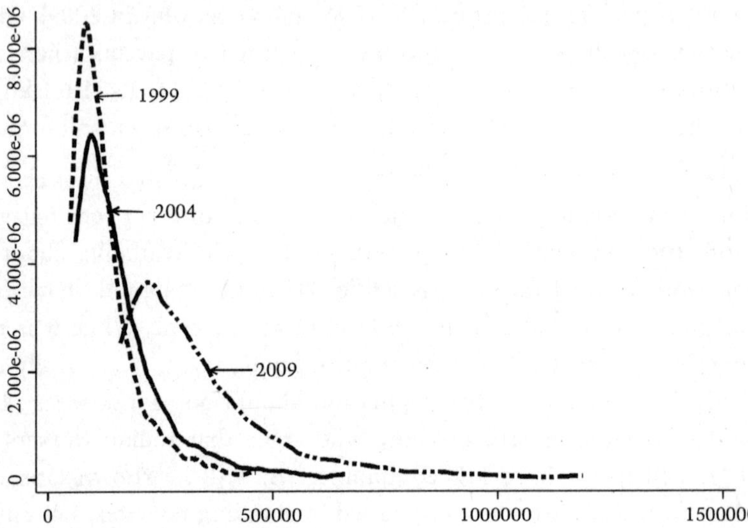


*Note:* The distribution is obtained from the NSSO Employment-Unemployment Survey, 1999-2000; the starting point of each distribution is the income level at which taxation begins. See text for details.

Table 7.4 shows the compliance percentages for the two definitions: return (based on the filing of returns) and income (based on how much income is "admitted" to). In both cases, the comparator is what is given by the theoretical income distribution. Prior to the major tax reforms of 1997-1998, return compliance was only 24 per cent. Since then, return compliance has more than doubled and in 2008-09, was at its peak value of 58 per cent. Income compliance defined as the ratio of tax collected to what should have been collected if everyone declared income correctly, has also markedly increased—from 30 per cent in 1996 to 64 per cent in 2008-09. Also reported in Table 7.4 is the average rate of taxation. The effect of the 1997 tax reforms is clearly reflected in the data. The average tax rate was close to 17 per cent in 1996-97; this declined by about 7 percentage points with the 1997 reforms. Compliance increased markedly, doubling in the space of a few years.

**Table 7.4**

*Compliance and Average Tax Rates, 1999-2010*

| *Year* | *Return Compliance (%)* | *Average Tax Rate (%)* | *Income Compliance (%)* |
|---|---|---|---|
| 1996-97 | 23.8 | 16.8 | 30.2 |
| 1997-98 | 27.6 | 10.2 | 53.4 |
| 1998-99 | 40.8 | 11.6 | 38.8 |
| 1999-2000 | 41.6 | 12.1 | 42.1 |
| 2000-01 | 50.5 | 12.4 | 31.7 |
| 2001-02 | 52.9 | 12.1 | 28 |
| 2002-03 | 53.9 | 13.1 | 29.4 |
| 2003-04 | 50 | 13.5 | 27.1 |
| 2004-05 | 42.6 | 15 | 23.8 |
| 2005-06 | 47.5 | 12.9 | 26.4 |
| 2006-07 | 45.8 | 14.3 | 37.9 |
| 2007-08 | 44.9 | 15.7 | 40.4 |
| 2008-09 | 57.5 | 9.7 | 64.1 |
| 2009-10 | | 9.1 | |
| 2010-11 (old) | | 9.7 | |
| 2010-11 (new) | | 6.0 | |

*Note:* Return compliance is the fraction of people paying tax as a ratio of people who should pay tax; income compliance is a parallel ratio for incomes.

A formal relationship between tax compliance and tax rates is explored for the time period 1989 to 2007 (Table 7.5). A dummy variable is inserted for 1997. The dependent variable is the ratio of those paying taxes (obtained from CAG tax return data) to those that should be paying taxes (obtained from the fitted income distribution data for each year and the tax schedule for each year). The independent variable, average tax rate, is obtained as a weighted average tax rate "theoretically" paid by the simulated income and tax distribution. A surprisingly good fit is obtained for the entire period; the coefficient on the tax rate is -6.2, with a t-statistic of -8.4. This implies that for each 1 percentage point cut in the average tax rate, compliance increases by over 6 percentage points. A back of the envelope calculation suggests that this fits the 1997 experience rather well. That reform reduced the average tax rate by 5.3 percentage points, so the average compliance level should have increased by 35 percentage points, which is almost exactly the increase observed between 1996 (the year before the reforms) and 2008-09 (last year for which tax return data are available).

**Table 7.5**

*Tax Compliance in India, 1989-2009*

| *Dependent Variable* | *Constant* | *1997 Dummy* | *Avg. Tax Rate* | *Time Period* | *R2* |
|---|---|---|---|---|---|
| Return compliance | 125<br>(10.8) | -34.6<br>(-7.6) | -6.2<br>(-8.4) | 1989-2007 | 0.71 |
| Income compliance | 77.6<br>(5.9) | 6.8<br>(1.4) | -3.0<br>(-3.7) | 1989-2009 | 0.59 |

*Note:* 1) Return compliance is the per cent of people who file tax returns as a fraction of those who should be filing taxes.
2) Income compliance is the per cent of income on which tax is paid as a fraction of income on which tax should be paid.
3) The average tax rate is the tax rate for only those whose incomes are above the minimum level (Rs.1.60 lakh in 2009-10) and who are required to file income tax (e.g. farmers are exempt).

A partial regression plot clearly illustrates the importance of tax cuts for return compliance. If ever there was confirmation needed that the Laffer curve exists, it is provided by Figure 7.2.

**Figure 7.2**

*Inverse Relationship between Tax Compliance and Average Tax Rates*

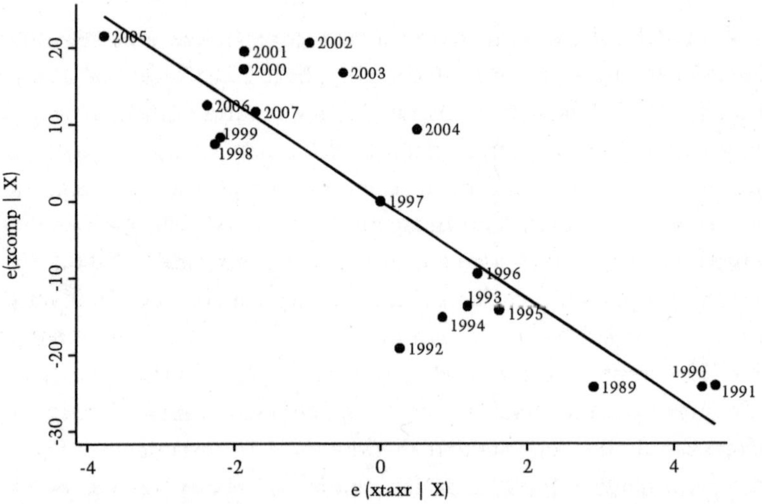


*Note:* coef = -6.387803, (robust.) se = .55563834, t = -11.5.

Note the tight fit (the reason that 1997 is on the line is because that year is not included in the estimation). Also notable is how the years 2000 to 2004 are above the predicted line i.e., tax returns were of a larger magnitude than that indicated by average tax rates.

While steepness of the tax schedule is an important determinant of compliance, there are other determinants that could be confounding the results reported above. In particular, other policies like the compulsory TDS payments and/or the one-in-six scheme adopted by the Government of India (i.e., ownership of consumption items like telephone, TVs etc.) are believed to have had a major impact on compliance. Both these suggested determinants came into prominence after the tax cut of 1997-98 with the one-in-six scheme being introduced in 1998-99. This most likely is the effect of improvements in tax administration and the increased use of deduction of tax at source.

Table 7.5 also reports the regression for "income compliance". The results are equally strong and the coefficient on the average tax rate suggests that each 1 percentage point decline in the average tax rate should increase income compliance by almost 3 percentage point.

How well the model performs can be seen from its forecasts for the 2008-09 tax cut. In that year, as noted earlier, tax rates for the low income taxpayers were drastically reduced. The minimum level at which a tax was applied was raised from 1.1 lakh to 1.5 lakh (Table 7.1); the second slab was enlarged and included taxpayers from Rs. 1.5 to Rs. 3 lakh; previously, the range for the 20 per cent tax bracket was the narrow range Rs. 1.5 to Rs. 2.5 lakh; this was now enlarged to the range Rs. 3 to Rs. 5 lakh. The change in the tax slabs led to a decline in the effective tax rate of 6 percentage points. With no change in compliance, this would have meant a decline in personal income tax collections of about 25 per cent. However, the income compliance equation would predict an increase in the compliance rate of 6 times 3.0 or 18 percentage points. In 2007-08, the average rate of income compliance was 40 per cent; an increase of 18 percentage points would lead one to predict a compliance level of 58 per cent; actual income compliance level observed—64 per cent. The actual reality because of the tax cut—personal income taxes increased by 3.6 per cent.

## Evaluating the Tax Revenue Implications of the Proposed New Tax Code

The above equations relating compliance to tax changes can also be used to forecast the revenue effects of the new tax code. Simulation of old and new tax rates for incomes during 2010-11 reveal the following. First, the tax reduction for the average taxpayer is 3.7 percentage points—from 9.7 per cent expected during 2010-11 to the 6 per cent proposed level. With no change in compliance, this tax cut is expected to lead to a 13 per cent decline in tax revenue. This is comparable to the 25 per cent decline in tax revenue that was expected after the previous 2008-09 tax cut. As noted above, instead of declining, tax revenues actually increased in 2008-09; most likely the increase would have even been higher if 2008-09 was not a global, and local, recession year.

What is the likelihood of no increase in compliance? Given the 2008-2009 experience, very little. Table 7.6 documents the trend in actual tax collections, theoretical tax collections and related data. The ratio of the first two is income compliance. First, a forecast for the 2009-10 tax revenue data. At a 64 per cent compliance level, tax returns for 2009-10 should be around Rs. 138,000 crore; this is given by the knowledge that expected theoretical returns for the year is Rs. 215,000 crore. Income growth, and drift into higher tax rates suggests that the theoretical revenue should increase from Rs. 215,000 crore in 2009-10 to Rs. 265,000 crore in 2010-11. The predicted income compliance level with the new tax code is 3.7 (the tax cut) times 3.0 (coefficient in regression) or 11.1 percentage points above the observed 2008-09 income compliance level of 64 per cent i.e., 75.1 per cent.

If the new lower tax code becomes operational, theoretical tax revenues in 2010-11 drop from Rs. 265,000 crore to Rs.164,000 crore. At a 75 per cent compliance rate, tax revenues are projected to be Rs. 123,000 crores. With no new tax code, actual collections are predicted to be 0.485 (obtained from the income compliance equation with an average tax rate of 9.7 per cent and the dummy variable for 1997 equal to zero) times 265,000 or Rs. 129,000 crores. i.e. not much revenue loss or gain. In addition, as has been observed with previous tax cuts, increases in compliance continue to occur after the tax cut. Thus a few years hence, one should not be surprised to see income compliance nearer the 90 per cent mark, a level seen in developed economies.

**Table 7.6**

*Tax Collections, GDP and Related Data: India 1996-2010*

*Level of (in '000 crore)*

| *Year* | *GDP* | *Private Income* | *Private Taxable Income* | *Personal Income Tax Collections* | *Theoretical Tax Collections* | *GDP Per Capita (in Rs.)* | *GDP Per Worker (in Rs.)* |
|---|---|---|---|---|---|---|---|
| 1996 | 1379 | 1146 | 359 | 18 | 60 | 14753 | 39230 |
| 1997 | 1534 | 1270 | 400 | 22 | 41 | 16121 | 43104 |
| 1998 | 1755 | 1483 | 467 | 21 | 54 | 18105 | 52067 |
| 1999 | 1952 | 1639 | 538 | 27 | 65 | 19788 | 53044 |
| 2000 | 2102 | 1765 | 604 | 24 | 75 | 20937 | 55736 |
| 2001 | 2281 | 1915 | 653 | 22 | 79 | 22320 | 58998 |
| 2002 | 2458 | 2063 | 721 | 28 | 94 | 23660 | 62027 |
| 2003 | 2765 | 2321 | 840 | 31 | 114 | 26191 | 68081 |
| 2004 | 3127 | 2625 | 995 | 35 | 149 | 29145 | 75094 |
| 2005 | 3566 | 2993 | 1325 | 45 | 171 | 32727 | 83555 |
| 2006 | 4086 | 3430 | 1569 | 85 | 225 | 36940 | 93413 |
| 2007 | 4701 | 3946 | 1868 | 118 | 293 | 41872 | 104844 |
| 2008 | 5429 | 4557 | 1983 | 123 | 191 | 47661 | 118129 |
| 2009 | 6189 | 5195 | 2360 | 138* | 215 | 53566 | 131382 |
| 2010* | 6994 | 5871 | 2736 | 123* | 265 | 59693 | 144841 |

*Note:* 1996 refers to 1996/97 etc. Theoretical tax collections are estimated via the income distribution and tax schedule; 2010* tax predictions are based on the new proposed tax code.

## Conclusions

The importance of reforming the direct tax code is illustrated by the following simple statistic. In 1996, personal income tax collections were a paltry Rs. 18,000 crore, and only 9 per cent of total tax revenue. Just 12 years later, personal income tax receipts crossed Rs. 122,000 crore, a near seven fold increase, reflecting an annual growth rate of 16 per cent per annum. In contrast, overall tax revenue has increased at 13.5 per cent rate, and per capita GDP at an annual rate of 11.4 per cent. In the not too distant future, personal income tax, along with corporate income tax, will account for a lion's share of tax revenue; today, direct taxes account for over 40 per cent of total tax revenue, up from 20 per cent in 1996-97. It is imperative that policy be geared towards accelerating this forthcoming reality of direct tax domination. The proposed tax code is a step in the right direction.

This paper has provided estimates of a synthetic tax distribution, a distribution based on NSS data for wage and salary incomes in 1999-2000 and tax schedules for all the years 1989 to 2010. This synthetic "theoretical" tax distribution was compared to actual tax returns. "Matching" the two distributions yielded estimates of tax compliance for the different years. The result: compliance rates have doubled from pre-1997 levels, and are presently in the 55 to 65 per cent range. A strong result of the analysis is that the Laffer curve exists robustly in India. The new proposed direct tax code reduces average tax levels by close to 4 percentage points, a decline that should lead to compliance levels rising by about 18 percentage points (income compliance) and 36 percentage points (return compliance). So far from reducing income tax receipts, *ceteris paribus*, the proposed tax code should lead to increased tax revenue over time and no loss in the year it is enacted. The proposed new direct tax code is very likely to be successful, as all previous tax cuts in India have been.

## References

Acharya, Shankar (1988-1997). "Aspects of the black economy in India", NIPFP, 1986 All India Tax Statistics, various years.

Banerjee, Abhijit and Thomas Piketty (2003). "Top Indian incomes, 1956-2000", Bureau for Research in Economic Analysis of Development, September.

Bhalla, Surjit S. (2010). "Indian economic growth, 1950-2008", in Shankar Acharya and Rakesh Mohan, (eds.), *Indian Economy: Performance and Challenges, Essays in Honour of Montek Singh Ahluwalia*. New Delhi: Oxford University Press.

———. (2004). "Reform of personal income tax in India," *http://www.oxusinvestments.com*, July 2.

———. (2002). "Tax compliance in India", *http://www.oxusresearch.com*, February 12.

———. (1999). "The most kindest cut of all", *Economic Times*, February 4.

Das-Gupta, Arindam (2004a). "The economic theory of tax compliance with special reference to tax compliance costs", March.

———. (2004b). "The compliance cost of the personal income tax in India, 2000-2001: Preliminary estimates", March.

———. (2002). "Central tax and administration reform in the 1990s: An assessment", in Rao, Govinda M. (ed.), *Development, Poverty and Fiscal Policy, Decentralization of Institutions*. Oxford University Press.

Directorate of Income Tax Statistics, Ministry of Finance, Government of India.

Kelkar, Vijay (2002). *Report of the Task Force on Direct Taxes*. Ministry of Finance and Company Affairs, Government of India, December.

National Sample Survey (various dates). *Employment-Unemployment Survey*. Conducted in years 1983, 1993-1994, 1999-2000 and 2004-05.

NCAER (n.d.). *MIMAP Survey, 1994-95*.

———. (n.d.). *National Survey on Household Income and Expenditure, 2004-05*. Unit Level Data Set.

Rao, Govinda M. and Kavita Rao (2009). "Direct taxes code: Need for greater reflection", *Economic and Political Weekly*, September 12.

Shome, Parthasarathi *et al.* (2001). *Tax Policy and Tax Administration for the Tenth Plan*. Planning Commission, Government of India, May.

Virmani, Arvind (1986). "Measuring income tax incentives under evasion: Effective average and marginal rate schedules", Development Research Department (DRD) *Discussion Paper* No. 187, World Bank, September.

———. (1997). "An agenda for tax reform", *Chintan Policy Paper* No. 2, May.

# 8 Inclusive Growth for Creating an Equitable Society

K.C. Chakrabarty

## Introduction

Financial inclusion cannot happen on its own. Therefore, the onus is on the policy makers to ensure the same. Dr. Vijay Kelkar said in his speech at N.P. Sen Memorial Lecture at Hyderabad (13/1/08) that financial inclusion is a quasi-public good:

> Increasingly, in developing countries access to finance is positioned as a public good, which is as important and basic as access to safe water or primary education. The pertinent question to ask here is whether 'Financial Inclusion' can be construed a public good? A good is considered a 'public good' if it meets the conditions of nonrivalness in consumption and non-excludability. The degree of 'publicness' in 'financial inclusion' maybe different from the stand point of a typical public good like say 'defence', but there is little doubt that financial inclusion meets the above two criteria to a large measure and to that extent is a "quasi public good".

There are a number of positive externalities of financial inclusion. One of the important effects is one is able to reap the advantages of network externality of financial inclusion as the value of the entire national financial system increases. Yet another reason why financial inclusion is a quasi-public good is that the consequent fuller participation by all in the financial system makes monetary policy more effective and thus, enhances the prospects of non-inflationary growth.

The 'inclusive growth' as a strategy of economic development received attention owing to a rising concern that the benefits of economic growth have not been equitably shared. Growth is inclusive when it creates economic opportunities along with ensuring equal access to them. Apart from addressing the issue of inequality, the inclusive growth may also make the poverty reduction efforts more effective by explicitly creating productive economic opportunities for the poor and vulnerable sections of the society. The inclusive growth by encompassing the hitherto excluded population can bring in several other benefits as well to the economy. The concept "inclusion" should be seen as a process of including the excluded as agents whose participation is essential in the very design of the development process, and not simply as welfare targets of development programmes (Planning Commission, 2007).

Sighting the extent of financial exclusion in the country, there is urgent requirement of fastening the process of financial inclusion. Some of the figures for financial exclusion are very glaring—45.9 million farmer households out of a total of 89.3 million households do not have access to credit either from the institutional or non-institutional sources (NSSO, 2008); one branch is catering to the banking needs of 16,000 population (June 2007); only 17 credit accounts and 54 saving accounts are there per 100 persons with all the institutions (June 2007); only 13 per cent are availing loans from the banks in the income bracket of less than Rs. 50,000; and 53 per cent people are still taking loans from the institutional and non-institutional sources only for emergency purposes.

'Inclusive growth' remains key objective to be achieved under the Eleventh Five Year Plan (2007-08 to 2011-12). The high growth momentum achieved during 2003-04 to 2007-08, has not been able to bring down unemployment and poverty substantially. In recent decades, economic and social inequalities have increased alongside high growth rates which have exacerbated regional inequalities. Factors like these and many made 'inclusive growth' the focal point of overall growth strategy and major concern for the policy maker in India. Thus, the Eleventh Five Year Plan clearly states that "The development of rural India is an imperative for inclusive and equitable growth, and to unlock huge potential of the population that is presently trapped in poverty with its associated deprivations" (GoI, 2007).

There are supply-side and demand-side factors which drive the inclusive growth; banks are largely to mitigate the supply-side processes that prevent poor and underprivileged from gaining access to the financial system. Also the demand-side factors like low income or asset holding have significant impact on financial inclusion. The Eleventh Five Year Plan specifically mentions 'agriculture' and 'small scale industries' (SSI).

Agriculture not only plays a role of achieving high growth but also inclusive growth for the economy as a whole. It generates about 20 per cent of India's GDP and employs nearly two-third of its population. Targeted Eleventh Plan growth (at 8.5 per cent) warrants a growth of at least 3.9 per cent in the agriculture sector, which would presuppose private sector investment and credit flow to agriculture. The ground level credit (GLC) requirements for the agricultural sector has been worked out at Rs. 16,40,000 crore for the Eleventh Five Year Plan, indicating an annual compounded growth of 17.0 per cent as compared to Rs. 6,39,330 crore of expected GLC during the Tenth Plan period. The role of state governments is of high importance in achieving the target especially in providing suitable infrastructure/extension support for facilitating enhanced credit flow to agriculture.

The Plan also recognises the importance of SSI. It has a share of over 40 per cent of the gross industrial value added in the economy. About 44.0 per cent of the total manufactured exports of the country are directly accounted for by the SSI sector. In terms of employment generation, this sector is next to agriculture sector, employing approximately 295 lakh people. For the small and medium enterprises (SME) sector, the estimated incremental working capital provided by the scheduled commercial banks during the Eleventh Five Year Plan would be at Rs. 1,67,989 crore, which amounts to a growth rate of an average 16.8 per cent per annum. Despite the risk, financing of first time entrepreneurs is a must for financial inclusion and growth.

## Role of Financial Inclusion in Achieving Inclusive Growth

The Committee on Financial Inclusion (Chairman: C. Rangarajan, 2008) defines financial inclusion as the "process of ensuring access to financial services, and timely and adequate credit where needed by vulnerable groups such as weaker sections and low income groups at an affordable cost". To achieve financial inclusion in totality, it is a must to address the constraints like:

- Lack of awareness about the financial products.
- Unaffordable products, high transaction costs, and
- Products which are not convenient, inflexible, not customised and of low quality.

"Financial Inclusion promotes thrift and develops culture of saving and also enables efficient payment mechanism strengthening the resource base of the financial institution which benefits the economy as resources become available for efficient payment mechanism and allocation. The empirical evidence shows that countries with large proportion of population excluded from the formal financial system also show higher poverty ratios and higher inequality" (Thorat, 2008). It has been the endeavour of both the government and the Reserve Bank to expand banking sector across the length and breadth of the country to ensure reasonably priced credit in a timely manner to all the deserving borrowers. Notwithstanding the significant expansion in bank network in unbanked areas after bank nationalisation in India, there are still large segments of the society that remain outside the financial system.

Well-designed poverty alleviation programmes, if effectively implemented, not only supplement the poverty reducing effects of growth but also could promote pro-poor growth. There is need to design financial instruments that would help people to reduce their risk and vulnerability whether it is for smoothening incomes or ensuring higher education for family members or reducing exposure to health shocks.

With the arrival of banking technology and realisation that poor are bankable with good business prospects, financial inclusion initiatives will strengthen financial deepening further and provide resources to the banks to expand credit delivery. Thus, financial inclusion along with the government developmental programmes will lead to an overall financial and economic development in the country.

## Background

The financial sector reforms initiated in the beginning of the 1990s brought a sea change in the profile of the banking sector and enabling them to help in the inclusive growth of the society. Implementation of these reforms had several unique features. Notably, the reforms process was not driven by any banking crisis, nor was it the outcome of any external support package. The design of the reforms was crafted through domestic expertise, taking on board the international experiences in this respect. The reforms were carefully sequenced with respect to the instruments to be used and the objectives to be achieved. Thus, prudential norms and supervisory strengthening were introduced early in the reform cycle, followed by interest rate deregulation and a gradual lowering of statutory pre-emptions. The more complex aspects of legal and accounting measures were ushered in subsequently after establishing basic tenets of the reforms.

The implementation of reforms brought all-round salutary impact on the financial health of the banking system, as evidenced by the significant improvements in a number of prudential parameters, Tables 8.1 and 8.2.

**Table 8.1**

*Non-Performing Loans (NPL) of Scheduled Commercial Banks (Per cent)*

| *End-March* | *Gross NPL/ Gross Advances* | *Gross NPL/ Assets* | *Net NPL/ Net Advances* | *Net NPL/ Assets* |
|---|---|---|---|---|
| *1* | *2* | *3* | *4* | *5* |
| 1996-97 | 15.7 | 7 | 8.1 | 3.3 |
| 1997-98 | 14.4 | 6.4 | 7.3 | 3 |
| 1998-99 | 14.7 | 6.2 | 7.6 | 2.9 |
| 1999-2000 | 12.7 | 5.5 | 6.8 | 2.7 |
| 2000-01 | 11.4 | 4.9 | 6.2 | 2.5 |
| 2001-02 | 10.4 | 4.6 | 5.5 | 2.3 |
| 2002-03 | 8.8 | 4 | 4.4 | 1.9 |
| 2003-04 | 7.2 | 3.3 | 2.8 | 1.2 |
| 2004-05 | 5.2 | 2.5 | 2 | 0.9 |
| 2005-06 | 3.1 | 1.8 | 1.2 | 0.7 |
| 2006-07 | 2.4 | 1.5 | 1 | 0.6 |
| 2007-08 | 2.3 | 1.3 | 1 | 0.6 |

*Source:* Reserve Bank of India (n.d.). *Report of the Trends and Progress of Banking in India.*

Various measures taken under the reform resulted in the improved profitability of banks. The return on assets (RoA) of scheduled commercial banks increased from 0.4 per cent in the year 1991-92 to

0.99 per cent in 2007-08. The banking sector reforms also emphasised the need to improve productivity of the banks through appropriate rationalisation measures so as to reduce the operating cost and improve the profitability. A variety of initiatives were taken by the banks, including adoption of modern technology, which has resulted in improved productivity.

The process of financial inclusion in India can broadly be classified into three phases. During the first phase (1960-1990), the focus was on channelling of credit to the neglected sectors of the economy. Special emphasis was also laid on weaker sections of the society. Second phase (1990-2005) focused mainly on strengthening the financial institutions as part of financial sector reforms. Financial inclusion in this phase was encouraged mainly by the introduction of self-help group (SHG)-bank linkage programme in the early 1990s and Kisan Credit Cards (KCCs) for providing credit to farmers. The SHG-bank linkage programme was launched by National Bank for Agriculture and Rural Development (NABARD) in 1992, with policy support from the Reserve Bank, to facilitate collective decision-making by the poor and provide 'doorstep' banking. During the third phase (2005 onwards), the 'financial inclusion' was explicitly made as a policy objective and thrust was on providing safe facility of savings deposits through 'no-frills' accounts.

The fact that India has not gone through any financial crisis as a result of financial deregulation is not only remarkable, but a testimony to the correctness of the judgment that reforms to global standards need to be adjusted to local conditions (Mohan, 2007). The need of the hour is to have financial sector reforms in a recalibrated manner to address the issues in light of the crisis. India has so far remained relatively insulated from the crisis that global banking system has experienced in the course of the 1990s. Our exposure to troubled subprime assets and related derivatives is negligible in comparison to many other economies.

## Federal Structure and Financial Inclusion

Dr. Kelkar has been a strong advocate of fiscal federalism and decentralisation, to achieve greater financial inclusion. His vision is unanimously shared by policy makers and the institutions promoting

**Table 8.2**

*Cross-Country Select Banking Indicators—A Comparison*

| | *Regulatory Capital to Risk-Weighted Assets (CRAR)* | | | | *Non-Performing Loans to Total Loans* | | | | *Provisions to Non-Performing Loans* | | | | *Return on Assets (RoA)* | | | |
|---|---|---|---|---|---|---|---|---|---|---|---|---|---|---|---|---|
| *Country* | *2002* | *2006* | *2007* | *2008* | *2002* | *2006* | *2007* | *2008* | *2002* | *2006* | *2007* | *2008* | *2002* | *2006* | *2007* | *2008* |
| *1* | *2* | *3* | *4* | *5* | *6* | *7* | *8* | *9* | *10* | *11* | *12* | *13* | *14* | *15* | *16* | *17* |
| **Developing Economies** | | | | | | | | | | | | | | | | |
| Argentina | — | — | 16.9 | 16.8 | 18.1 | 3.4 | 2.7 | 2.5 | 73.8 | 130.2 | 129.6 | 130.9 | -8.9 | 2 | 1.5 | 16 |
| Brazil | 16.6 | 18.9 | 18.7 | 16.6 | 4.5 | 4.1 | 3 | 2.9 | 155.9 | 152.8 | 181.8 | 170.9 | 2.12.5 | 2.9 | 2 | |
| China | — | — | 8.4 | 8.2 | 26 | 7.5 | 6.7 | 2.5 | — | — | 39.2 | 115.3 | — | 0.9 | 1 | — |
| India | 12 | 12.4 | 12.3 | 13 | 10.4 | 3.5 | 2.5 | 2.3 | — | 58.9 | 56.1 | 52.6 | 0.8 | 0.9 | 0.9 | 1 |
| Indonesia | 20.1 | 21.3 | 19.3 | 16.8 | 24 | 13.1 | 4.1 | 3.5 | 130 | 99.7 | 87.7 | 98.5 | 1.4 | 2.6 | 2.8 | 2.6 |
| Korea | 11.2 | 12.8 | 12.3 | 10.9 | 2.4 | 0.8 | 0.7 | 1.1 | 89.6 | 175.2 | 199.1 | 155.4 | 0.6 | 1.1 | 1.1 | — |
| Malaysia | 13.2 | 13.5 | 13.2 | 12.6 | 15.9 | 8.5 | 6.5 | 5.1 | 38.1 | 50.7 | 77.3 | 86.9 | 1.3 | 1.3 | 1.5 | 1.6 |
| Mexico | 15.7 | 16.3 | 15.9 | 15.3 | 3.7 | 2.1 | 2.7 | 2.5 | 138.1 | 207.4 | 169.2 | 184 | 0.7 | 3.1 | 2.7 | 1.8 |
| Philippines | 16.9 | — | 15.7 | 15.5 | 26.5 | 18.6 | 5.8 | 5.2 | 30.1 | 37.4 | 81.5 | 84.1 | 0.8 | 1.3 | 1.3 | 11 |
| Russia | 19.1 | 14.9 | 15.5 | 14.5 | 5.6 | 2.6 | 2.5 | 2.5 | 112.5 | 159.3 | 144 | 140 | 2.6 | 3.2 | 3 | 1.6 |
| South Africa | 12.6 | 12.3 | 12.8 | 12.5 | 2.8 | 1.2 | 1.4 | 2.6 | 46 | — | — | — | 0.4 | 1.4 | 1.4 | 1.8 |
| Thailand | 13 | 13.8 | 14.8 | 15.3 | 15.7 | 7.5 | 7.9 | 6.0 | 62.9 | 79.4 | 86.5 | — | — | 2.3 | 0.1 | — |
| Turkey | 24.4 | 21.1 | 19 | 17.7 | 12.7 | 3.2 | 3.5 | 3.3 | 64.0 | 90.8 | 88.4 | 81.6 | 1.2 | 2.4 | 2.8 | 2.2 |
| **Developed Economies** | | | | | | | | | | | | | | | | |
| Australia | 9.6 | 10.4 | 10.2 | 10.9 | 0.4 | 0.2 | 0.2 | 0.5 | 106.2 | 204.5 | 183.7 | 87.2 | 1.1 | — | 1 | 0.9 |
| Canada | 12.4 | 12.5 | 12.1 | 12.7 | 1.6 | 0.4 | 0.7 | 1.1 | 41.1 | 55.3 | 42.1 | 34.7 | 0.4 | 1 | 0.9 | 1.3 |
| France | 11.5 | — | 10.1 | — | 4.2 | 3.2 | 2.7 | — | 58.4 | 58.7 | 61.4 | — | 0.5 | — | 0.4 | — |
| Germany | 12.7 | — | 12.9 | — | 5 | 4 | 2.7 | — | — | — | 77.3 | — | 0.1 | 0.5 | 0.2 | — |
| Italy | 11.2 | 10.7 | 10.4 | — | 6.5 | 5.3 | 4.6 | — | — | 46 | 49.5 | — | 0.5 | 0.8 | 0.8 | — |
| Japan | 9.4 | 13.1 | 12.9 | 12.3 | 7.4 | 2.5 | 1.5 | 1.5 | — | 30.3 | 26.4 | 24.9 | -0.7 | 0.4 | 0.2 | 0.3 |
| United Kingdom | 13.1 | 12.9 | 12.6 | — | 2.6 | 0.9 | 0.9 | — | 75 | — | — | — | 0.4 | 0.5 | 0.4 | — |
| United States | 13 | 13 | 12.8 | 12.5 | 1.4 | 0.8 | 1.4 | 2.3 | 123.7 | 137.2 | 93.1 | 84.7 | 1.3 | 1.3 | 0.8 | 0.3 |

*Source:* IMF (2009). *Global Finacial Stability Report.*

financial inclusion. State-level Panchayati Raj is the key village level institution. When they involve themselves they bring people to open bank accounts; the need is to identify them. This initiative of identifying rural people has to come from the local government. Banks can only be a catalytic agent but ultimately unless this becomes a people participation, this cannot be done. In Tineri village (in Bihar) project of Punjab National Bank, the financial inclusion has been completed in surrounding 12 villages; everybody is having a bank account and a small overdraft facility, and if they have a genuine credit requirement then the borrower need not go to the moneylender. It is seen that the person can be covered under the life insurance policy and health insurance policy.

## Strategies for Greater Financial Inclusion

The progressive but cautious policies have contributed to efficiency of the financial system while sustaining the growth momentum in an environment of macroeconomic and financial stability. The policy challenge is to continue to ensure financial stability in India during this period of international financial turbulence, while achieving high growth with price stability.

In this respect there are four issues very important for the future regulatory reform, not only in Indian context but also for the many emerging markets. These are as follows:

1. The issue related to 'Know Your Customer (KYC)' in banks.
2. 'Fair Treatment to their Customers (FTC)' from a central banker's perspective.
3. 'Risk Management' and its proper understanding, and
4. Leveraging technology for greater financial inclusion.

To address these and many such challenges, Government of India is working on different strategies with banks and other financial institutions.

### BC and BF Models

Under the guidance of Reserve Bank of India (RBI), two prominent rural banking extension service modes are in place. The first one is called

"Business Facilitator" (BF) and the second one is termed as "Business Correspondent" (BC). BFs and BCs are authorised service providers of banks.

BF is an extension of banking services through the banks to deliver services such as opening of zero balance accounts, no-frill accounts, facilitate loan enablement and recovery and other non-cash services to the unbanked families.

The BC provides an extension of rural banking business services including micro credit, micro insurance and smaller denomination of cash transactions to those who are excluded from the banking stream through individual or institutional business service providers and are authorised by the banks. These services are outsourced to inclusion intermediaries through contract, who are almost like insurance agents. As per the scheme, RBI permitted the engagement of non-profit entities for delivery of these two services. These services were the subjects of discussion by the Committee on Financial Inclusion under the Chairmanship of Dr. C. Rangarajan, constituted by Government of India. The Committee proposed a national mission on financial inclusion.

There are also issues and challenges related to successful working of BC/BF models. One of the major issues to tackle is that of the cash handling; almost all the transactions are cash-based, so larger the volume of cash greater is the risk associated with it; particularly in the isolated regions of the country. Client base is mainly in the rural areas and dealing is mainly with the illiterate mass of the country. Thus, they are susceptible to misguidance and can perceive BCs as banks only. Therefore, financial education is must for all. Viability of BCs is also an issue raised several times; it has been largely related to the operating cost involved.

## Self-Help Groups

Dr. Kelkar emphasised on promoting SHGs-bank linkage programme. He stated that, "One of the most important programmes for promoting financial inclusion through micro-finance is the SHG-Bank linkage programme which aims at improving access of the weaker and other sections of the society from formal financial institutions. The ability of people to pool their micro-savings, provide collective social collateral for banks to lend against and add to the SHGs' funds and the collective allocation of funds to meet emergent credit needs of the SHG members, charge rates which reflect risks and management cost of funds, are the unique feature of this movement which has enabled banks to assist in meeting the credit needs of very poor people without sacrificing their funds and has helped rural women especially to empower themselves both economically and financially".

SHGs represent a unique approach to financial inclusion; the approach combines access to low-cost financial services with a process of self-management and development for the women who are SHG members.

The financial inclusion attained through SHGs is sustainable and scalable on account of its various positive features like:[1]

- They provide a cost-effective credit delivery system, as the transaction costs of lending decrease sharply both to the banks and the borrowers. Banks which have advanced lines of credit report that the repayment rates are high ranging above 95 per cent.
- They provide a forum for collective learning which rural people find more "friendly" and which is consequently more effective than the individual or classroom approach that is commonly adopted.
- They promote a genuine democratic culture where rights and responsibilities are equally valued and internalised; and where sanctions are imposed and accepted.
- They provide the members with opportunities to imbibe norms of behaviour that are based on mutual respect and which can be recognised by the society.
- They foster an "entrepreneurial" culture where members realise that while they need the support of the group to achieve personal

1. Mysore Resettlement and Development Agency (MYRADA). *Rural Management Systems Series*, Paper 28 by Aloysius P. Fernandez.

objectives, their personal interests cannot be promoted at the expense of the group.

- They provide a firm and stable base for dialogue and cooperation in programmes with other institutions like government departments, cooperatives, financial and Panchayati Raj institutions. If the groups are functioning well, they have the credibility and the power to ensure their participation in identifying, planning, budgeting, and implementing Panchayati Raj programmes for the empowerment of the poor.
- They provide the individual member with the support required to exercise control over the pace, timing, size and schedules of loans and programmes, to broaden the pattern of asset provision, to include a package which would help the individual to cover risk rather than to provide a single asset.
- They help to assess the individual member's management capacity which may fall short of what a "viable" investment package requires for optimum returns, as prescribed under regular IRDP norms, but which is manageable by a particular member.

SHGs are not only vehicles of financial inclusion but also they promote participation of women in the rural economy. Gradual awareness which is inculcated by SHGs has helped in reducing child mortality, improved health and the ability of the poor to combat disease through better nutrition, housing and health—especially among women and children.

Success of MYRADA model encouraged for greater linkage between SHGs and banks. This led to the creation of partnership model between the SHGs, banks and NGOs; reviewed in 1995, this led to the evolution of guidelines to banks for opening bank accounts for SHGs. Though there are questions concerning long-term sustainability, cost recovery and loan repayment of SHGs but equally there have been improvement in the lives of rural folks. One reason for its gradual success has been the face that SHGs encourage women participation; women being the axis of a family are able to pass on benefits efficiently to the other members of the family.

There are several success stories in SHGs, like Mission Shakti, a WSHG (women self-help group) development programme initiated by Government of Orissa. Bank of India has opened bank accounts for several SHGs (Kolhapur Zone's Yelavi Branch has a SHG account in the name of "Prabhu Parameshwar Mahila Bachat Gat" and Hinganghat Branch of Nagpur Zone-I has SHG formed by 13 women from the village called Kajalsara, named as Indira Mahila Bachat Group, etc.).

Further success and expansion of SHGs would depend on the strong SHG-bank linkage. Some of the important to do's for this are:

- Opening saving account of all formed SHGs in a specific time frame.
- Consolidation of the groups with respect to regular meetings, savings, participatory decisions, conflict resolution, etc., to complete targeted activities in time.
- Improving literacy and record-keeping skills of SHG leaders and members so that they can maintain SHG records.
- Commencement of inter-loaning among SHG members. (Focus on utilisation of internal loan from consumption to production purposes.)
- Educating SHGs on simple numeracy skills to calculate simple interest rates and instalments of internal loan.
- Grading of SHG for seed capital and CCL with due participation of bankers.

## Bank Branch and ATM Expansion

Reserve Bank has also freed location of ATMs from prior authorisation. In the October 2009 Policy Review, RBI allowed branch opening in towns and villages with population below 50,000. Domestic scheduled commercial banks (other than RRBs) can open branches in towns and villages with less than 50,000 population. This step is also to ensure that one-third of such branches are opened in underbanked districts and states. This has been one exceptional way forward to diminish the digital divide and bring rural masses under the banking network.

## Kisan Credit Cards—Ensuring Timely Credit to Farmers

National Bank for Agricultural and Rural Development (NABARD) formulated a Model Kisan Credit Card Scheme (1998-99) in consultation with major banks in the country. Kisan Credit Card Scheme aims at provision of adequate and timely support from the banking system to the farmers for their cultivation needs including purchase of inputs in a flexible and cost-effective manner.

The features of the KCC are:

- Revolving cash-credit facility with unlimited withdrawals and repayments.
- Meet the production credit need, cultivation expenses and contingency expenses of the farmers.
- Limits based on the basis of operational landholding, cropping pattern and scale of finance. This limit is inclusive of 20 per cent of production credit.
- Each withdrawal to be paid within 12 months.
- Card valid for 3 years subject to annual renewals.
- Credit limits can be enhanced depending on performance and needs.
- Rescheduling is also possible depending upon the situation. If for example the crops fail due to a natural calamity and the farmer is not able to repay his loan, then he could get an extension of upto four years.
- Cash withdrawals through slips accompanied by card and passbook.
- A credit-cum-passbook would be issued.
- All branches engaged in agricultural lending could issue Kisan Credit Cards.

KCC provides access to adequate and timely credit to farmers. It not only simplifies withdrawal of funds from the bank but also it assures availability of credit at any time enabling reduced interest burden for the farmer. It has been equally benefiting for banks; there is noticeable reduction in the transaction cost to the banks, improvement in recycling of funds and better recovery of loans and last but not the least it has resulted better banker–client relationship.

Therefore, all possible efforts should be made for identifying and bringing all the farmers under the KCC scheme; those who are so far not covered by the KCC scheme including tenant farmers, oral lessees, share croppers and defaulters. The banks should ensure that all the crop loans are routed through KCC only with at least 2 per cent of their crop financing directed towards tenant farmers/oral lessees.

### Unique Identification Number—Including Digitally

Once implemented, unique identification number (UID), it will ensure all essential services, amenities and benefits to each and every individual in the country. A single universal identity number is going to remove duplication of identity.

The Unique Identification Authority of India (UIDAI) was established in February 2009 under the chairmanship of Shri Nandan Nilekani. The purpose of the UIDAI is to issue a unique identification number (UID) to all Indian residents that is: (a) robust enough to eliminate duplicate and fake identities, and (b) can be verified and authenticated in an easy, cost-effective way. UID will solve much of banks' logistical and know-your-customer (KYC) issues, and bring rural masses under the cover of banking. Reaching out to the unbanked areas, it will reduce overall transaction cost for all the intermediaries.

Enrolling agencies are to make the UID number a primary field of their database. This will have a cleansing effect on all existing databases, eventually enabling enrolling agencies to clean their databases and further streamline operations.

Uniformity in data assimilation will ensure that the data of a person enrolled by NREGS can be reliably used by a Grameen Bank. Therefore, this will gradually eliminate the problem of re-verification of the same details about the same individual again and again by each agency.

## Mobile Commerce: The Emerging Paradigm

Mobile commerce or M-commerce is an area which is rapidly changing the way people conduct their financial transactions. Besides, this is an area which offers abundant scope for inclusive growth. This is also an area which promises business opportunities to service providers and other players in the field of mobile communications. M-commerce has its own set of challenges which require greater attention from the regulators across the globe.

E-commerce is a process of providing the buyers of goods and services, the option to carry out such transactions, and pay for the same, without being physically present. E-commerce platforms can bring in efficiency and cost benefits to buyers. But the key to such arrangements is the delivery. The Internet is only one of the mediums to reach to the buyer; the confidence of the buyer depends on the reliability, safety and security of the delivery system and the trustworthiness of the merchants. Same would be applicable to M-commerce. Mobiles by the same logic can only be a facilitator and the mobile service providers (MSPs), the service provider for this channel.

In E-commerce or M-commerce, 'delivery' becomes the critical core competence on which businesses will be evaluated and preferred. Its speed, quality and responsiveness are the decisive competitive factor determining the success and sustainability of the company.

The three aspects related to the payment delivery and banking technology in India which needs to be considered are:

1. Banking technology is of recent origin in the country. Scaling up may require more time.
2. Payment is only one aspect of banking. Financial inclusion goes beyond remittances. Other products and services are also required which banks are equipped to provide.
3. Given the above aspects and that the enabling provisions like appointment of BCs have been permitted only recently, it would be early to conclude that banks have not been successful so far.

Keeping pace with the developments, Reserve Bank of India introduced the Electronic Clearing Service (ECS), followed by the Electronic Fund Transfer System, later extended as the National Electronic Fund Transfer (NEFT) and the Real Time Gross Settlement (RTGS). All these systems offered a secure and efficient platform for transfer of funds between bank accounts without the need for paper-based payment instruments.

a) ECS: The volume of ECS (credit) transaction increased from 69,019 thousand in 2006-07 to 88,394 thousand in 2008-09. The volume of ECS (debit) transactions increased from 75,202 thousand to 1,60,055 thousand during the given period.

b) NEFT: The number of CBS-enabled bank branches offering NEFT service has increased from 42,900 to 54,200 in 2008-09 and to 60,839 as on September 30, 2009.

   The volume of transactions in EFT/NEFT increased from 4,776 thousand in 2006-07 to 32,161 thousand in 2008-09. The aggregate value of transactions increased from Rs. 77,446 crore to Rs. 2,51,956 crore during this period.

c) RTGS: The number of bank branches offering RTGS service has increased from 43,512 to 5,000 in 2008-09 and to 60,144 as on September 30, 2009.

   The daily average volume of transactions is 90,000 for about Rs. 1,200 billion of which 82,000 transactions for about Rs. 980 billion pertained to customer transactions as at end of August 2009.

## Financial Inclusion Using Technology (M-Commerce): Issues and Challenges

While E-commerce has skipped the majority of the population due to the cost of setting-up such channels, M-commerce has the capability to be inclusive due to the widespread use of the mobile phones.

Mobile phone services are growing rapidly and the number of mobile phone connections is estimated to be about 440 million, reaching roughly 38 per cent of the country's population. The benefits of M-commerce should reach the common man at the remotest locations in the country. However, the extent and the manner in which M-commerce should be facilitated needs a cautious and well-considered approach, keeping in view the concerns on money laundering and financial terrorism and the stability of the payment and settlement systems.

The most complicated challenge is to ensure security of financial transaction, being executed from some remote location and transmission of financial information over the air. This is to be addressed jointly by mobile application developers, wireless network service providers and the banks' IT departments.

At the first level of dispensing banking services, SMS alert for credit or debit, status of transactions and other information providing services—is operational. The challenge lies in extending it to the next level, such as transaction of payments, transfer and stop payments is yet to take off in the big way.

To meet the long-term objective of a nation-wide mobile payment framework, there is a need for a robust clearing and settlement infrastructure operating on a 24×7 basis. Banks are yet to enter in to suitable multilateral arrangements to create mobile switches or inter-bank payment gateways as allowed by the Reserve Bank of India.

Also, there are some challenges which banks face with mobile service providers. These are:

- Facilitation of mobile banking requires tie-ups with individual service providers for enabling such services. Banks face difficulties in entering into such partnerships.
- MSPs do not open up channels for facilitating mobile banking services by banks opening up USSD (unstructured supplementary services data) channel for mobile banking and enabling the accessing of mobile banking facilities through all GPRS connections.

Recognising the importance of mobile banking, the Reserve Bank of India issued the guidelines for mobile banking transactions in October 2008. The guidelines permit banks to provide mobile banking transactions and mandates that all transactions have to originate from one bank account and terminate in another bank account. These guidelines have been discussed in different fora and the perception in certain quarters has been that the guidelines are restrictive as they do not permit non-bank entities, especially the mobile service providers to provide such services. The protagonists of this view often refer to the reported success of the M-PESA model adopted by Kenya and feel that the same could be adopted or adapted in our country. The general argument is that a non-bank-led model with appropriate regulatory mechanism in place would not only be as safe as a bank-led model but also enable greater penetration into underbanked and non-banked areas and thereby contribute to the financial inclusion process.

M-PESA is in effect a virtual prepaid payment product, allowing the mobile service provider to retain the prepaid amount and permitting, *inter alia*, person to person remittance. A paper "Poor People Using Mobile Financial Services: Observations on Customer Usage and Impact from M-PESA" published by CGAP (Consultative Group to Assist the Poor) states that person-to-person transfer for maintenance of family dominates the use of M-PESA in Kenya. In comparison, mobile banking offers the facility of accessing banking products, which includes payments/remittances from bank account to bank account—either inter-bank or intra-bank.

Before embarking on the question of extending M-commerce facility, it is necessary to understand the risks. In this connection, a paper submitted by the World Bank on the "Integrity in Mobile Financial Services" identified four risk factors *viz.*, anonymity, elusiveness, rapidity and poor oversight. Anonymity is the risk of not knowing a customer's actual identity.

- Elusiveness is the ability to disguise mobile transaction totals, origins and destinations;
- Rapidity is the speed with which illicit transactions can occur;
- Poor oversight identity refers to the level of regulation of service providers;

Any model of mobile financial services needs to address these issues.

Despite a wide network of bank branches spread across the length and breadth of the country, banking has still not reached a large section of the population. They are deprived of basic banking services like a savings account or minimal credit facilities. Banking penetration was not there because earlier technology was not available. But now, technology is available. Reserve Bank has taken measures to achieve increased financial inclusion through the "Banking Correspondent (BC)" model. The RBI also formulated a biometric access/smart card-based scheme of Electronic Benefit Transfer (EBT) by banks to facilitate routing of social security benefits; National Rural Employment Guarantee Act payments and other government payments could be routed. The scheme, which involves subsidising the cost of issue of the biometric access/smart cards by banks, was initially implemented in Andhra Pradesh in 2008 and has been extended across the country till June 30, 2010. According to the annual report of India Post for the year 2008-09, there are over 1.55 lakh post offices in India, of which 89 per cent are in the rural areas. And post offices offer money transfer services through their money order and instant money order schemes. One of the important concerns in any money transfer transaction is the bonafide of the underlying. This concern is not restricted to India but felt across the globe.

The Know Your Customer (KYC) guidelines/Anti-Money Laundering (AML) guidelines have been well established in banks and appropriate mechanism is in place for reporting high value transactions to the financial intelligence unit of the Government of India. The MSP-led model would have concerns from the point of view of money laundering, and the safety and security of the transactions. The customer identification processes followed in case of prepaid customers are lax as the MSPs consider this as low risk from their financial standpoint. Given the large number of such cards being issued and the number of outlets through which they are issued, as a regulator of the payment and settlement systems in the country, it is difficult to contain the risk of anonymity in a MSP-led model. M-PESA model has the comfort of a national ID scheme which is in existence in Kenya. Interestingly, as per the indications available on the UID Project, the team is veering round to the bank-led model to further financial inclusion in India. Also, apart from KYC norms, MSPs would also have to enhance transparency in pricing and improve their infrastructure.

The advocates of a MSP-led mobile commerce list two advantages of the system, namely: (i) leveraging the spread agent network and (ii) transaction cost. The widespread agent network is an attractive proposition for extending financial services. But does this require that the service is provided by the MSP only? Knowing the availability of a large network of banks in the country, cannot this agent network be utilised by banks in partnership with MSPs, for extending financial services? Keeping in view the concerns about money laundering and financial terrorism, it is preferred to have a partnership where the MSPs gain from the over the air (OTA) transaction volume and banks leveraging the channels for wider reach. There needs to be clear distinction of roles. Reserve Bank is exploring a better model across the world.

In this context, two successful models of partnership between banks and MSPs observed are—Wizzit in South Africa and GCash in the Philippines. Wizzit Bank is a virtual bank which is a subsidiary of Bank of Athens in South Africa. It provides the unbanked population in SA with bank accounts on mobile phones which can be used to make person-to-person payments, transfers and prepaid purchases. Besides, account holders are also provided a maestro card for cash withdrawal. The MSPs support this facility as carriers of such transaction instructions.

Philippines have been the pioneer in enabling financial services through use of mobile phones. The first product introduced in the country was SMART money—a partnership between SMART Telecom and Banco de Oro. Subsequently, GCash a telecom-led model was subsequently introduced by Globe Telecom. The country has seen the development of partnership between the mobile payment platforms provided and rural banks there.

## Demographic Dynamics in India—Financial Inclusion

India is in the midst of a demographic transition. The demographic transition that India is going through will result in addition of millions of youth, who are potentially a bankable population and present a unique opportunity for banking system to expand their customer base. It has been estimated that the population in the 15-24 age group grew from around 175 million in 1995 to 190 million in 2000 and 210 million in 2005, increasing by an average of 3.1 million a year between 1995 and 2000 and 5 million between 2000 and 2005. In 2020, the average Indian will be only 29 years old, compared with 37 in China and the US, 45 in West Europe and 48 in Japan.

Besides technology, India's demographic advantage is a key factor that has immensely added to India's economic potential—it is popularly called as 'demographic dividend'. Share of the working age group (15-64) in the population has been increasing from 63 per cent in 2006 and projected at 68 per cent in 2026. However, for these demographic changes to provide upward push to economic growth, it needs to be accompanied by a process of skill formation and employment opportunities. This would require larger investment in human capital formation and encouragement to entrepreneurial activities by creating conducing environment. Current performance of the education sector particularly in terms of quality leaves much scope for improvement.

Going forward, it is required to have flexible systems, modular approach and small units of competency-based courses. More aggressive approaches are required to strengthen the education system in rural areas. Some of the schemes have been executed successfully in this regard and while we continue with these schemes, the need is also to modify them keeping in view the future of rural India, eventually India.

Some of the important initiatives, so far, have been the Operation Blackboard (1987), Non-Formal Education Scheme (1987), the Shiksha Karmi Project (1987), Mahila Samakhya (1988), Mid-Day Meal Scheme (1995) and the Sarva Shiksha Abhiyan (2001) which aimed at completion of eight years of schooling by all children between 6-14 years, by 2010. Elementary education being made fundamental right by the 83rd Constitutional Amendment, Supreme Court's insistence on states to provide hot cooked meals in schools, are improving enrolments, especially among girls.

## Educating to Enhance Inclusion

The establishment of financial literacy and credit counselling centres (FLCC) is an important milestone in furthering financial inclusion. Financial inclusion is a much broader term which can be construed as the process of ensuring fair, timely and adequate access to financial services, namely, saving, credit, payment and remittance facilities and insurance services at an affordable cost in a fair and transparent manner by the mainstream institutional players. Educating people and making them financially literate thus becomes integral to achieving financial inclusion, which is why centres such as these are needed.

## Financial Education

Financial education can broadly be defined as the capacity to have familiarity with and understanding of the financial market products, especially rewards and risks in order to make informed choices. It primarily relates to personal financial education to enable individuals to take effective actions to improve overall well-being and avoid distress in financial matters. The focus of any discussion on financial education is thus primarily on the individual, who usually has limited resources and skills to appreciate the complexities of financial dealings with financial intermediaries on matters relating to personal finances on a day-to-day basis.

Lack of literacy in general and financial literacy in particular, is the main hurdle in expanding the coverage of financial services to the poorer segments of society. Notwithstanding the initiatives taken so far, given the large magnitude of the problem, concerted efforts need to be made in this direction. Banks should, therefore, come forward to set up literacy centres and guide their clients about the features, benefits and risks of various financial products. With no well-established banking relationships, the un-banked poor are pushed towards expensive alternatives. These centres can educate the people about proper financial management tools, inculcate saving habits and generate demand for financial products and services which in turn will boost financial inclusion. This process of education could benefit the banks as the centres while interacting with customers would be in a much better position to understand their specific requirements, which could then be a critical input in appropriate product design.

Financial education is also an integral component of customer protection. Despite concerted efforts, the current level of transparency coupled with the difficulty of consumers in identifying and understanding the fine print from the large volume of information, leads to an information asymmetry between the financial intermediary and the customer.

## Credit Counselling

Credit counselling can be defined as 'counselling that explores the possibility of repaying debts outside bankruptcy and educates the debtor about credit, budgeting, and financial management'. It serves three purposes:

1. It examines the ways to solve current financial problems.
2. It educates about the costs of misusing a credit; it improves financial management.
3. It encourages the distressed people to access the formal financial system.

As per the All India Debt and Investment Survey, 2003, nearly a fourth of the households were indebted in 2002. The per cent of indebtedness households in rural areas increased sharply from 23 in 1991 to 27 in 2003; the corresponding figures for urban areas during the same period were 19 and 18, respectively. As per the NSSO survey (2003), out of 89.35 million farmer households, 43.42 million (48.6 per cent) were reported to be indebted. Farmer's indebtedness was highest in Andhra Pradesh, followed by Tamil Nadu and Punjab. The average outstanding loan per farmer household was highest in Punjab, followed by Kerala, Haryana, Andhra Pradesh and Tamil Nadu.

Through the provision of timely and professional advice, common people can be helped to manage their debt, improve money management skills and gain access to the structured financial system. Counselling can help solve current financial problems, create awareness about the costs of misusing a credit, can improve financial management and help develop realistic spending plans. Debt counselling/credit counselling can be both preventive and curative. In case of preventive counselling, the centres could provide awareness regarding cost of credit, availability of backward and forward linkages, where warranted, etc. The clients could be encouraged to avail of credit on the basis of their repaying capacity. Preventive counselling can be through the media, workshops and seminars. In the case of curative counselling, the clients may approach the counselling centres to work out individual debt management plans for resolving their unmanageable debt portfolio. Here, the centres can work out effective debt restructuring plans that could include repayment of debt to informal sources, if necessary, in consultation with the bank branch.

## Specific Objectives of FLCCs

FLCCs are to provide free financial literacy/education and credit counselling. The specific objectives of the FLCCs would be:

i. To provide financial counselling services through face-to-face interaction as well as through other available media like e-mail, fax, mobile, etc., as per convenience of the interested persons, including education on responsible borrowing, proactive and early savings, and offering debt counselling to individuals who are indebted to formal and/or informal financial sectors.

ii. To educate the people in rural and urban areas with regard to various financial products and services available from the formal financial sector.

iii. To make the people aware of the advantages of being connected with the formal financial sector.

iv. To formulate debt restructuring plans for borrowers in distress and recommend the same to formal financial institutions, including cooperatives, for consideration, and

v. To take up any such activity that promotes financial literacy, awareness of the banking services, financial planning and amelioration of debt-related distress of an individual.

FLCCs are not to act as investment advice centres/marketing centres for products of any particular bank/banks. All the stakeholders are being encouraged to push aggressively for greater financial inclusion. The Banking Codes and Standards Board of India (BCSBI) has recently brought out an updated code to ensure that the banks formulate and adhere to their own comprehensive code of conduct for minimum standards of banking services, which individual customers can legitimately expect. And finally, the Banking Ombudsman Scheme has been instituted for redressal of grievances against deficient banking services, covering all the states and union territories.

## Conclusion: Towards Greater Financial Inclusion

"Indian BPL—214 million earning on an average Rs. 10 per day, out of which 16 million people are living in rural areas.

Of the world's 6.4 billion poor, about 2.6 billion live on less than US $2 per day. The poor have largely untapped potential for consumption, production, innovation and entrepreneurial activity. The need is to do business with them so as to bring them out in the market place. This is a sure way of freeing them from the poverty. The more business models integrate and include the poor, the higher are the chances for the companies to increase their revenues while fulfilling the millennium development goals (MDGs)."[2]

In this regard, India faces some great challenges ahead on the path of financial inclusion:

1. By 2012, out of next 250 million Indian wireless users, 100 million (40 per cent) are likely to be from rural areas:
    a. Mobile phones to act as local banks, playing a major role to solve power and connectivity problem,
2. Accessibility: Remoteness of villages,
3. Connectivity,
4. Errors in account opening and verification process,
5. Relaxation of KYC norms for migrant population,
6. Finding suitable BCs,
7. Pilot projects to go beyond experimental stage,
8. Standardisation of card specifications, and
9. Interoperability among the different technological systems as the solutions being offered today are proprietary in nature.

Greater the financial inclusion, greater the impact would be on India's economy. Financial inclusion is a quasi-public good because of its positive spillover on economy and community. Enhanced financial inclusion will bring rural as well as underserved areas of the country

2. *Creating Value for All: Strategies for Doing Business with the Poor.* Report by UN Development Programme.

into the mainstream. This will have greater impact on the lives of the farmers because availability of easy finance has been the one big reason for misery of rural India. Also, it will lead to more rapid modernisation of agriculture. The new agriculture, by nature, would need more working capital and it is capital-intensive as it depends upon modern inputs and equipments. There would be increased growth, equitable distribution and growth in both rural and urban areas because financial inclusion will mobilise the bottom of the pyramid (Kelkar, 2008).

The most important positive impact of promoting financial inclusion would be in the form of grassroot innovations and entrepreneurship.

"The involvement of Panchayati Raj Institutions is critical for ensuring the success of schemes (for inclusive growth). The Eleventh Five Year Plan firmly weaves all these initiatives together and focuses on marginalised sections and regions without sacrificing enterprise and growth."[3]

With the arrival of banking technology and the realisation that the poor are bankable with good business prospects, financial inclusion initiatives will strengthen financial deepening further. The banking technology initiatives meant for financial inclusion should be collaborative and innovative with an objective to reduce the transaction costs. Thus, financial inclusion along with the government developmental programmes will lead to an overall financial and economic development in the country and as in the case for most developing countries, extending the banking services to everyone in the country will be the key driver towards inclusive growth.

3. Excerpt from Prime Minister's opening remarks at the 54th meeting of the National Development Council, December 19, 2007.

## References

Government of India (2007). *Eleventh Five Year Plan (2007-2012).* New Delhi: Planning Commission.

Kelkar, Vijay (2008). "Financial Inclusion for 'Inclusive Growth'", in Raj Kapila and Uma Kapila (eds.), *Economic Developments in India* 121. New Delhi: Academic Foundation.

Mohan, Rakesh (2007). *India's Financial Sector Reforms: Fostering Growth While Containing Risk.* Address at Yale University on December 3.

NSSO (2008). *NSSO 60th Round Report.* Government of India.

Planning Commission (2007). *Towards Inclusive Growth: The Gender Dimension.* November 15.

Thorat, Usha (2008). *Independence Commemoration Lecture, 2008.* Delivered at Central Bank of Sri Lanka, Colombo on February 28.

# 9 Financial Inclusion via Universal Access to Electronic Payments

Laveesh Bhandari and Sumita Kale*

> By financial inclusion, we mean delivery of financial services, including banking services and credit at an affordable cost to the vast sections of disadvantaged and low-income groups. The various financial services would include access to savings, loans, insurance, payments and remittance facilities by the formal financial system to those who tend to be excluded (Kelkar, 2008).

## Introduction

The Rangarajan Committee defined financial inclusion as "the process of ensuring access to financial services and timely and adequate credit where needed by vulnerable groups such as weaker sections and low income groups at an affordable cost." As far as definitions go, the committee headed by the former RBI governor and also reflected in Dr. Kelkar's views made a very significant departure from the past and that accepted internationally.[1] The Indian definitions are more inclusive, deeper, and less constraining for policy makers.

India has made an important contribution to the concept of financial inclusion—it now incorporates not just banking, but also

---

* This paper draws from our past work on financial inclusion, electronic payments, mobile value-added services. We are grateful to Harshvardhan Singh, Ashok Desai, Bibek Debroy, Payal Malik and Navin Surya of Intrex and Subho Ray of IAMAI for their support, comments on this paper and those that it draws from. This paper however contains the views of the authors and does not reflect those of either Indicus Analytics or any of the entities that have supported us. All comments welcome. *laveesh@indicus.net, sumita@indicus.net*

1. The international definition tends to be similar to this, "[It] is the delivery of banking services at affordable costs to vast sections of disadvantaged and low income groups" (*http://en.wikipedia.org/wiki/Financial_inclusion*)

elements of insurance and very significantly payments and remittances. Second, it is being increasingly accepted that financial inclusion is not about who provides the services—banks or non-banks, large or small or for that matter formal or informal—but the type, quality and terms at which such services are being provided.

This paper argues that universal access to electronic transactions is critical for ensuring financial inclusion. The RBI has through its recent actions created a highly progressive regulatory regime that would enable both innovation and entry of new providers of financial and e-transaction services. Moreover, the ideal mode or 'pipe' through which such services can be provided—the mobile phone—is already widely accessible for the underprivileged. However, constraints in the mobile VAS (value-added services) sector are preventing further movement in this space. An enabling environment requires the mobile service providers (MSPs) to be more accepting of entry by non-MSP entities, competition and transparency, barring which regulatory action in the MVAS will become critical to ensure greater financial inclusion. Just as the RBI has created an enabling environment in the financial regulation space, the TRAI and/or mobile industry needs to create an enabling environment in the electronic communication space. Only when this is achieved can we hope for further cost efficient innovations that will finally ensure financial services for all.

It is well recognised that a large number of households and especially those in rural areas do not have bank accounts. It is also well known that the formal financial sector has not been expanding rapidly enough where services to the masses are concerned. In fact, there is a relative stagnancy (as a later section reveals). Data from the National Sample Survey Organisation show that other formal sector modes of various financial services (e.g. via post offices) are also not growing rapidly enough. Though the informal sector (such as the moneylender) has been taking up some of this unmet demand, even that has been quite inadequate in reaching out to the large masses that require financial services, and later sections show this quite effectively.

The problem is well known—the formal financial sector has been unable to meet the requirements of the poor and the under-privileged, the non-formal sector has been meeting some of their needs albeit at high cost, and despite many experiments and pilots, no cost-effective model has yet been found. Increasingly technology is being seen as the way out. That is, ICT technologies, it is thought, would be able to reduce the costs of delivery of financial services and thereby enable widespread access to those at the bottom of the pyramid.

**Box 9.1**

*Continued Failure of Conventional Financial System in Reaching to the Poor*

In March 2005, commercial banks had 338 million savings and current accounts as against 290 million in 2000. Rural accounts went up from 172 million to 200 million—representing an increase of 28 million, while urban accounts increased by 20 million from 118 million to 138 million. The rate of growth annually was around 3 per cent just a little over the population growth. State wise data would show certain areas where there is hardly any increase. The number of loan accounts increased from 54 million in 2000 to 77 million in March 2005 (7.3 per cent CAGR). However the higher growth rate was on account of urban areas. In rural areas, the number of loan accounts went up from 40 million to 47 million (3.3 per cent) whereas the urban areas showed a stronger growth from 14 million to 30 million loan account or growth rate of 16.5 per cent. The growth in the number of small borrower accounts in rural areas was even lower at 2.5 per cent whereas the growth in the number for urban areas was 13.8 per cent between 2000 and 2005. There has been hardly any increase in outreach or scale in the last five years except for some growth in branches and loan accounts in urban areas. ....On the other hand, there are 93 million mobile users today—the CAGR since 1999 is 85 per cent.

*The number of mobile phones currently is more than the number of borrowers from the banking system. There is a clear need to increase the outreach and scale up operations at existing outlets*. (emphasis ours)

*Source:* Thorat, 2006.

This paper makes the case that financial inclusion, in terms of access to a range of financial services, will be an outcome of widespread use of electronic payments. That is, increased use of technology that will enable low cost delivery is a necessary precondition, but another precondition is that the uncovered have easy access to electronic payment mechanisms for their transactions. In the process, the electronic payments regime needs to ensure that no single group has sole control over these services—whether they are mobile service providers (MSPs) or banks.

The rest of this paper proceeds as follows. Section 2 delves into the scope and scale of financial exclusion, as well as the characteristics of the 'uncovered' households and their requirements. It makes the point that the low and irregular incomes and expenditures of under-privileged households, with significant proportion of credit requirements being for unproductive purposes, lack of collateral and lack of recorded assets or transactions make these households unviable for the formal sector to service.

Section 3 makes the point that electronic transactions have the great advantage of low cost and complete records of transactions as well as the economic network that the potential borrower is a part of. These records can then be used by lenders such as micro-credit institutions to leverage for credit purposes. The important part is that whatever be the type or the mode through which the transaction occurs—whether through a prepaid card or through an Internet account, or through the mobile or some as yet undiscovered means—as long as it is electronic, the records would be accessible for future use.

Section 4 takes a detour into the experience with financial inclusion and underscores the point that current mechanisms such as micro-finance institutions (MFIs) and bank correspondents cannot be expected to fully address the problem of financial exclusion. In fact wide use of electronic payments would strengthen such mechanisms as well, and may give rise to many others as yet unthought of. It then makes the point that the RBI has come up with a highly enabling set of orders governing electronic transactions.

Section 5 highlights the importance of the mobile phone as the most likely means of carrying information in the electronic form on a 24×7 basis between the household and the financial service provider. However, our experience with competitive forces within the mobile services industry has not been entirely positive where introduction of innovative services is concerned. Unlike the voice segment, the mobile value-added services (or MVAS) segment has seen little competition and little innovation. This we argue is due to the nature of the service, where voice and data are bundled commodities and the regulatory action and competitive response has been limited to the voice segment. Either through industry coordination or through regulatory and policy action, higher revenue sharing and easy entry for diverse financial service/ content providers will need to be ensured. The section also proposes a set of coordinated or policy/regulatory measures that need to be undertaken in the MVAS space for ensuring that critical innovations are not stifled.

Finally, the concluding section, Section 6 underlines the fact, that we really do not know which kind of services and which type of models will be able to profitably meet the micro-credit requirements of the masses. But by loosening competitive forces at all points in the chain, we would have created a highly enabling environment for innovations to occur.

## The Problem of Financial Inclusion

The National Sample Survey Organisation conducts a decennial survey on financial activities of Indian households—the All-India Debt and Investment Survey (AIDIS). This survey was last conducted in 2003 where more than 110,000 households were surveyed in rural and urban India. The survey, though dated, provides important insights into the problem of financial inclusion. Some data from the survey report are replayed here.

About 26.5 per cent of rural and 17.8 per cent of urban households have taken some form of debt. Of these, the better-off are far more likely to have their requirements met from institutional sources (formal financial system) and the worse-off rely mostly on the non-institutional (unorganised or informal mechanisms) sources. However, it is evident that indebtedness is lower among the poor and this is likely because of lack of availability of even non-formal sources for those not so well-off.

The non-formal sector typically provides lower amounts than the formal sector in both rural and urban areas. However, it is able to provide credit at significantly higher debt to asset (DAR) ratios than the formal sector. Significantly, the poorest segments tend to have significantly higher DARs in both rural and urban areas.

There is some evidence that the share of the formal financial sector has fallen in both rural and urban areas, this may since have changed—but the point remains that the formal sector has not been able to increase its activities to the extent required. And the poor are the most likely to have been 'left out'. Among the non-formal means, the moneylender and family and friends are the most important. The critical characteristic of these two entities is that they capitalise on the repeated nature of their interaction with the debtor. In other words, where adequate collateral is not available, it is the repeated nature of other interactions that are able to ensure some guarantee to the lender—this is the same principle that many MFIs work upon.

There is another reason why many institutional sources are unable to meet the requirements of the under-privileged. A very high proportion of debt of the under-privileged is for consumption purposes, and this holds for both urban and rural areas. What is typically classified as consumption is, in fact, a critical element of survival and progress of a community—expenditures for health, marriages and social functions are important components under the overall consumption head.

In rural areas, of the 27 per cent indebted households, 13 per cent are in debt for household consumption and this accounts for 35 per cent of the debt. Investment in farm and related business accounts for 41 per cent of the total debt and is taken by barely 10 per cent of all the households. In urban areas, of the 18 per cent households that are indebted 12 per cent have taken household consumption related debt accounting for 58 per cent of the total household debt.

By far, the easiest to ensure financial inclusion would be for those households that have some assets—land, cattle etc. However, the bulk of the uncovered require credit for what is typically classified as non-productive expenditure. It is highly unlikely that any financial institution would be able to provide access to such credit, whatever be the cost of provision. In fact, consumption credit for those without adequate collateral is best if it is provided by the community, whether through an informal sector moneylender or through 'friends and family'. At the same time, such credit is not unimportant. Consumption expenditure—whether for consumption smoothing, or for health care, or even for some social functions, is an important aspect of a poor household's survival and prosperity.

The lack of adequate security is an important issue—of the 27 per cent of the rural households that were indebted in 2003 as many as 18 per cent availed of credit only on the basis of personal security and this accounted for 48 per cent of the total debt of such households. In the case of urban households, such reliance is even more—12 out of 18 per cent indebted households relied upon personal security and this accounted for 40 per cent of the total debt.

But the aggregates hide an important aspect of household debt in India—the majority of the indebted households reported an average value of less than 10,000 in rural areas and 30,000 in urban areas. These figures, admittedly, would have increased since 2002, and there would be some under-reporting here as well. But even after accounting for these, the fact remains that most households' debt lies in a range that will be costly for the formal institutions to service. Moreover, the lack of adequate collateral will make it even more difficult for such institutions. Last, the cost of appraisal has many elements in it, but the human resource element will be among the most important components. This points to the need to create a system where the time taken in the appraisal of such loan applications is minimised.

All in all, the problem of credit for under-privileged households is not just an issue of using technology to reduce transaction costs. It is a problem that originates in the occupational and asset structure of households and is further worsened by the large spread of the unorganised sector with consequent lack of records; a problem that is made even more difficult for the higher cost formal FIs because of the low ticket value and 'non-productive' requirements of poor households. Current mechanisms aimed at addressing the problem of financial inclusion are bound to be unsuccessful in meeting the goal of 100 per cent coverage of poor households. Therefore, what is needed is a solution that takes into account the peculiar needs of these households.

## A Transaction-based Approach to Financial Inclusion

This section makes the case that for the requirements at hand, and given the characteristics of the debt and the households taking it, the first step is to ensure that households make greater use of electronic payments. In other words, the point being made is that a history of transactions facilitates provision of credit. And given the large component of unorganised sector and unrecorded transactions, the best way of creating a history of transactions is through the use of electronic transactions, through the use of electronic money. Later sections will argue that the fears expressed related to e-money, namely, safety, security, money laundering, financial stability, etc., though not unfounded, are all addressable at low cost.

First what is electronic money, and why is it so different from cash.[2] E-money can be defined as "...monetary value as represented by a claim on the issuer which is:

(i) stored on an electronic device; and

(ii) accepted as a means of payment by persons other than the issuer."

E-money may be carried on a number of electronic devices and may be downloaded from an ATM, a shop-based terminal or the Internet or be stored on a mobile phone instrument.

Electronic money performs the same functions as physical cash: it can be used to buy different goods and services; may or may not be redeemed for physical cash; and may be exchanged person to person. It may be used in the physical world by inserting a card into a terminal or by using contactless wireless technology; and in the virtual world, over the Internet from a PC or a mobile phone.

Depending upon the regulatory framework, e-money can be provided by banks and also non-banking entities. Here a distinction will typically need to be made in that the non-banking entities (such as those providing prepaid cash cards) are not allowed to undertake any activities that are not closely related to e-money issuance. For instance,

2. This and the following two paragraphs borrow liberally from "The Regulation of Electronic Money Issuers," *Consultation Paper* 117, The Financial Services Authority, UK, 2001.

the granting of credit by e-money issuers would of course need to be specifically prohibited.

Despite many different models in operation, it is not clear which systems would be best suited for Indian conditions. This is the foremost policy and regulatory issue—ensuring that a flexible regime is developed that encourages innovation and experimentation, entry of many types of new players and at the same time ensuring security and stability of the financial system.

Having said that, one can argue that the mobile phone may very well be a component of ensuring universal access. This is purely for one reason—the mobile phone enables electronic delivery and electronic log-keeping on a 24×7 basis and eliminates travel costs of the consumers. But this advantage of the mobile phone also suggests that the mobile phone should merely be treated as a direct pipe to the consumer, nothing more and nothing less. The regulatory/policy regime therefore needs to ensure that different types of entities are able to provide financial and transactional services on this electronic pipe—not just banks or MSPs. But more on this later.

## What the Under-privileged Require

At the cost of repetition, the poor have certain characteristics that will make it difficult for the conventional models to provide credit services.

- First, most have irregular incomes. And their transactions are also irregular. This is because casual wage labour is typically on a daily basis, and also because self-employment, whether in agriculture or otherwise has many uncertainties associated with it, not to mention a high degree of seasonality.
- Second, and this is natural given low incomes, each transaction is also of low value.
- Third, as discussed in previous sections, their credit requirements and deposits also tend to be of low value.
- Fourth, the poor have few assets.
- Fifth, they have poor records of the assets that they do possess.

- Sixth, the under-privileged are highly time constrained and cannot easily take time out during peak hours.
- Seventh, the bulk of credit requirements are for what are typically considered to be non-productive consumption purposes.

While financial inclusion is largely seen as a problem affecting rural areas, the crux of the problem actually lies in the income characteristics of the household. According to RBI statistics, 72 per cent of those earning less than Rs. 50,000 lack a bank account—when it comes to access to banks, the distinction between rural and urban matters less than the income differential. Without appreciating the particular needs of the poor, it would not be possible to create appropriate policy responses.

Undoubtedly the government has formulated policies, put in many rules and regulations, tried to mandate rural branches, lending to the under-privileged, controlled moneylenders, and each of these had some success in reaching out to under-privileged, but never has it been enough. As of today, as per the government's own admission, barely 27 per cent of rural households are able to access a financial institution (see *Economic Survey 2007-08*). Recent initiatives, though promising, will need to be made even more cost-effective and accessible for the poor.

Take, for instance, micro-finance. Despite more than three decades of micro-finance institutions operating in South Asia, their household penetration has not increased beyond 3 per cent (Gonzalez and Rosenberg, 2006).

Or consider bank correspondents who reduce cost of delivery and increase access as they do not require the setting up of a bank branch and are also located close to the user. India has taken important steps towards the creation of such 'correspondents', an initiative borrowed from Latin America where retail vendors, lottery outlets and post offices double as bank branches for customers. However, it is also well known that even in Brazil where they are considered to be the most successful, users tend to be those who receive welfare payments, or use it for utility bill payments etc. Only a minority of the users use services such as savings deposits etc.

So what is the problem? Formal credit giving organisations would require some appraisal of creditworthiness. Lack of assets, missing records, irregular incomes and transactional history, loans for consumption, all conspire against formal sector credit—whether it is given directly by banks or through entities such as bank correspondents. That leaves network-based credit mechanisms such as those followed by self-help groups (SHGs). The problem here is that of stability of community-based networks. Migration and rapid economic growth create conditions that weaken traditional communities very rapidly. Multiple credit from multiple networks, high cost of credit, interest rate arbitrage, dependence on subsidy or benefits from government are some elements affecting their ability to provide credit universally. This is not of course to say that SHGs and MFIs have no long-term role, merely, that they have certain weaknesses that will prevent them to serve the needs of the under-privileged universally.

Credit, whether in larger or smaller amounts, for the rich or poor, requires that the borrowers have the ability to repay. In the absence of adequate collateral or organised sector regular employment, a history of transaction becomes critical. Given that the poor are typically employed in the unorganised sector, transactional history is missing as well.

E-money and electronic transactions have the great advantage of being recorded and logged and easily accessible. The only additional requirement is that adequate confidentiality and identification sharing precautions be taken. With the advent of the UID or spread of PAN cards or the ID to be assigned by the Home Ministry post-Census 2011, a common and unique ID could be used for credit purposes and for transactional history. Moreover, modern analytic methods further enable the identification of economic relationships that the prospective borrower typically has. The applicant can potentially share such records with prospective lenders.

On the side of the vendor of the good or service, providers must determine which of the transactions have high transaction cost for the poor such as remittances to the village, or visit to the bank branch to access cash. Focusing on transactions where cash is inconvenient is the best way to bring people into the fold of the modern financial system and raise efficiencies through savings in cost and time—cash on delivery payments, payments related to business requirements of the masses (about half of all Indians are self-employed, a percentage that is much higher among the poor), insurance payments, salary payments for schemes such as NREGA, small wage payments by private entities such as construction contractors, etc.

But it is not merely small day-to-day transactions. The self-employed account for a large proportion of the poor. Only a very small percentage of these firms have access to formal sector bank credit. The third census of small scale industries conducted in 2001-02 showed that while 14 per cent of the registered units enjoyed bank credit, just 3 per cent of the unregistered units had bank loans. Credit to the small sector has not kept pace with other sectors and the Report on Financing the Unorganised Sector by NCEUS 2008 has this to say, "Had the SSI sector received the same percentage of gross bank credit as it got between 1994-1995 and 1999-2000 i.e. 15 per cent of the net bank credit, the actual credit to this sector would have been Rs. 203,190 crores instead of Rs. 101,385 crores in 2006. The addition of about Rs. 1,02,000 crores would have doubled the employment, output and export. On the basis of current statistics of production, employment and exports, we find that the nation lost about 30 million of man days employment, about Rs. 5,00,000 crores of production and about Rs. 1,50,000 crores of exports. *A sector which has the potential to grow at a much higher rate than 9 to 10 per cent and create large employment was denied this opportunity*...(emphasis ours)." It is quite apparent that alternatives to the bank-based model must be sought urgently to bring the bottom of the pyramid into the growth trajectory of the rest of the economy.

A look at the comparative costs of provision of services through various channels shows that removing the physical presence of the bank is by far the cheapest method of transacting (See Figure 9.1). So even banking business in general will profit through technological advances and convergence with digital systems of payment.

In other words, the goal of financial inclusion is best met through the convergence of digital and payment systems in a manner that will

**Figure 9.1**

*Costs of Transaction*

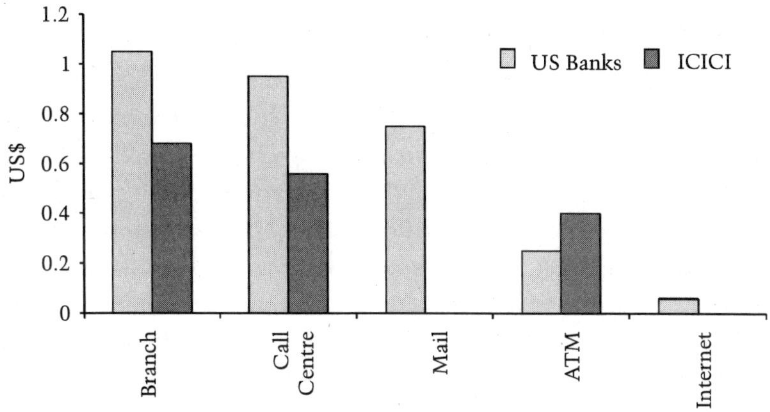


*Source:* CGAP Focus Note 32, 2006.

bring in the small low income cash-dependent customer. This is because true financial inclusion is one that will allow each citizen to enjoy the fruits of the modern payment and settlement system.

**Box 9.2**

*Network Externalities in the Financial Space*

With new technology there are significant positive externalities from being connected to others on the same network. Whether this is through the Internet on computers, television cables or mobile phones, as the number of devices increase and connectivity increases, there will be an exponential rise in the benefits to new users on the digital payment landscape.

"As more people become connected to the network, the value to each individual of acquiring a mobile phone increases, as there are more people who can be called. A similar effect is to be expected in terms of m-transactions and if so, it is at the point where network effects are triggered that we will see truly transformational impacts. Before any such point is reached, the role of financial and telecoms regulators will be key." Nick Hughes, Head of International Mobile Payment Services, Vodafone in "The Transformational Potential of M-transactions", *Policy Paper Series*, No. 6. July 2007.

The above discussion underscores an important component of our argument—that day-to-day or irregular e-transactions will enable greater access to financial services. The second component of our argument is that e-transactions do not necessarily require a bank account.

Experiments on financial inclusion through digital payments have been successful in many parts of the world and the great impact such models could have on financial inclusion objectives is well understood. There are various models e.g. PayPal, Paymate, M-PESA, GCash, ITZ Cash etc., that work through the Internet, through mobile phones, through agents or POS terminals and allow consumers to make retail transactions in a secure and convenient environment. Another trend for the future is the use of digital interactive television to make transactions. This has taken off in developed countries of the West and can be seen as a potential access point for financial services in developing countries too.

While mobile density is rising at an unprecedented pace in India, with more than 10 million subscribers added every month, broadband connectivity is also going up, the wireless subscriber base has crossed 525 million.[3] Meanwhile, under the government's national e-governance plan to set up one common service centre amongst every six villages in the country, more than 50,000 centres have been set up in 27 states by December 2009.[4] Payment systems that use this growing network will be in a position to reach the masses that have so far been excluded from the formal banking system. For this to become an actuality, it is important to create an environment that will enable greater numbers of such service providers and greater range of services for digital payments.

It is important for retailers to connect with these payment systems in a way that allows the spread of the service amongst low income unbanked consumers. For instance, the Indian Railways allows purchase of the tickets through kiosks or through the Internet using a variety of methods. In 2008-09, more than 40 million tickets were booked online, a 130 per cent rise over the previous year.[5] While credit cards accounted

3. TRAI data as on 31st December 2009.
4. *http://www.mit.gov.in/download/csc130110.pdf*
5. *http://www.medianama.com/2009/10/223-130-rise-in-online-ticket-sales-for-irctc-in-2008-2009/*

for 41 per cent of successful transactions, net banking 31 per cent and cash cards 26 per cent of the online business of more than Rs. 450 crore in August 2008. [6] What is more interesting is that net banking was the least successful transaction method with a 65 per cent success rate while cash-card transactions had the highest success rate of more than 80 per cent. The average amount transacted was less than Rs. 1000 (Rs. 878 for cash cards). The typical customers for cash cards are those who do not have credit, debit cards or net banking facilities, in other words are not seen as attractive customers for banks. They can, however, use point of sales terminals to purchase cards and make retail transactions in amounts as small as Rs. 100. It is for users like these that e-payments can prove to be a boon.

In other words, even if regulations limit provision of credit to banks, they need not limit provision of electronic transaction services to the banking sector alone. Till very recently this was a critical issue, however, recent announcements by the RBI following the Payments and Systems Bill of 2007, have opened the sector for non-bank entities, loosened their coverage to include semi-open systems, and increased the amounts that can be transacted. In the space of electronic payments, Indian financial regulation is perhaps the most advanced among all countries of the world. Broadly, the directions by the RBI are following the framework below.

On the financial regulation space, we do not believe any more loosening is desirable or possible. The RBI has taken a highly proactive stance as reflected in its order entitled "Issuance and Operation of Pre-paid Payment Instruments in India (Reserve Bank) Directions, 2009". But despite this highly liberal take at the regime governing electronic transactions, the MSPs have not followed up by loosening of their highly constraining practices. Indeed, the last bottleneck in enabling widespread access to such electronic transactional services is in the domain of telecom industry.

6. *Medianama*, September 8, 2008.

**Table 9.1**

*E-money: Concepts and Issues*

| *Topic* | *Specifics* | *Notes* |
|---|---|---|
| Definition | E-money: monetary value stored on an electronic device and accepted as a means of payments by third parties. | Allows for all types of systems, based on cards or other means and removes single purpose cards from the ambit of such regulation. |
| Inclusion | E-money includes a range of modes and media, specifically including but not limited to value being carried in various types of electronic devices including smart cards, magnetic strip based media, etc.; can be used to purchase products and services, redeemed for cash and whose value can be updated. | Various new forms are going to emerge that are currently difficult to predict; the definition should be inclusive.<br>The regulatory framework needs to be technology neutral. |
| Issuer | Both banks and non-banks are allowed to issue; certain norms, reporting and information criteria etc. Also small issuers should be encouraged to enter. | A level playing field between banks and non-banks needs to be established and this needs to be explicitly recognised. |
| Risk mitigation (tech.) | Payment system to build in the following risks and associated costs: unauthorised creation, transfer or redemption; incorrect attribution of funds, etc. | Build in monitoring processes of the same in the regulatory framework.<br>Concerns of risks many times get translated into limiting activity. Better reporting and associated monitoring mechanism can eliminate many of these concerns. |
| Use of deposits | The payment from the consumer to the issuer will need to be protected. There are many ways of doing so including adequacy norms, restrictions on usage of deposits received, etc. | This is the key concern for allowing non-banks. By ensuring better protection of the users, non-bank entry will be made easier in this field. |
| Granting of credit | Credit providing entities governed by stricter norms. | Currently MFIs are allowed to provide micro-credit facilities by RBI. Lower norms for systems not based on credit. |
| Authorisation (entry) | Only granted to those who meet the following criteria related to explicit:<br>Legal status and identity, pre-specified threshold conditions. | This procedure needs to be as smooth and as open as is possible. It should explicitly be recognised that small issuers' entry should be facilitated and not barred in the interest of financial stability concerns. |

*Contd...*

*...contd...*

| *Topic* | *Specifics* | *Notes* |
|---|---|---|
| Supervision | The laws should allow for supervision including ability of the regulator to examine all transactions of the issuer; all transactions also need to be maintained in clearly laid out, uniformly implemented database and data warehousing systems. | The regulator should be able to crosscheck various informational claims made by the issuers in case it so desires. |
| Enforcement | Enforcement powers should rest with regulator, which would include cancellation of permissions, fines and censures, prohibition of activities and individuals, initiation of court proceedings etc.<br>In case of non-compliance of the regulator's orders or in case of some disagreement between the regulator and the issuers, some arbitration/resolution mechanism would be built in. | A balance would need to be ensured between two forces—the need to provide adequate powers to the regulator. And the need to maintain some third party oversight over the regulator as well. |
| Prudential requirements | Corporate structure: a formal structure of the entity undertaking this activity should be essential. | With cleanly laid out systems of commands and associated responsibilities. |
| Capital | A minimum initial capital requirement is one such option. Scales dependent upon the amount of initial capital could be another possibility that would enable both small and large players to enter. | The minimum initial capital amount should not be too high; this would ensure that scales are not necessarily high and at the same time, unprepared entities are prevented from entering. |
| Asset-liability management | Non-bank issuers must have investments of an amount not less than outstanding e-money liabilities. | To ensure both stability and confidence in the system. |
| Liquidity | Issuers must have sufficiently liquid assets; such norms can be easily specified. | To ensure both stability and confidence in the system. |
| Safety and security | Recognise that low value cards are not viable money laundering options, as other methods are much easier and less costly. | By ensuring that databases can be shared with the regulator, real time monitoring of criminal activities as well as money laundering is possible. |
| User identification | None for low value cards, as this will increase costs of delivery and therefore reduce spread. | Recognise that e-money is a substitute for cash. Moreover, user identification one of the primary factors why the poor are kept out of the banking sector. Large seasonal migrant labour, poor urban migrants are only some examples. |

*Source:* Bhandari, 2007.

## The Importance of the Mobile

Of all the electronic transaction delivery mechanisms, the mobile phone is by far the most likely candidate for providing a cost-efficient pipe to masses. And it is here that policy attention now needs to be focused. It should be noted that whatever be the system of e-money—whether prepaid card, e-wallet, Internet transaction, etc., the mobile can provide the last mile access to the masses. That is, the last component of our argument is that the mobile phone is an unparalleled tool to provide electronic transactions. And that it is too important to be left solely in the hands of the mobile service providers.

At the core, the MSPs provide the consumer with a service that transfers data packets from one instrument to another. Whether it is voice or data, the conversion from the input to data packets and back to the output mode is done at the level of the instrument. We therefore argue that the MSP is in effect providing a pipe to the consumer, and charges for its services of transferring data packets from one instrument to another. This is an important characteristic of the MSP. All other services that it provides such as access to the Internet, MVAS (mobile value-added services), etc., are add-on services that are in many (though not all) cases tied to the main service of enabling the transfer of data packets.

The MVAS market, of which financial transactions form a part, has grown suboptimally in India. The share of VAS revenues is barely 10 per cent after a decade of introduction of such services—the bulk of it being person-to-person SMS. Whereas VAS revenues account for about 30 per cent of the total revenues in China and Japan, in Europe they contribute around 20 per cent.

To begin with, despite the increase in the range of VAS on offer in India in the last decade, the usage on a per user basis has not increased, and may in fact have fallen. Second, the problem is systemic and not limited to a few operators. Third, remove entertainment and there is little that the masses can do with VAS in India currently. There are few social networking, education, health, employment, etc., services that are currently available. Industry sources also reveal that the entertainment services are mostly consumed by urban youth and that there is limited usage of VAS among the higher age groups as well as in rural areas.

**Table 9.2**

*Share of Non-Voice Revenue to Total Mobile Revenue*

| *Country* | *Share of Non-voice Revenue in Total* | *Details* |
|---|---|---|
| Germany | 20.2 | (Vodafone 2005) |
| Italy | 16.7 | (Vodafone 2005) |
| United Kingdom | 20.3 | (Vodafone 2005) |
| United States | 8.9 | (Vodafone 2005) |
| Germany | 18.0 | (Tmobile 2006 H1) |
| Japan | 27.0 | (KDDI 2005) |
| Korea | 26.0 | (SK Telecom, Wireless Internet 2005) |
| China | 27.3 | (Estimated 2008) |

*Source:* OECD, 2007; Holtkamp, 2006.

MSPs in India tend to keep a high share of the revenues, 60-70 per cent, while content aggregators receive 15-20 per cent and content providers 10-15 per cent. Where intellectual property rights are involved, the share to content or financial service providers is larger (around 35-40 per cent), but since this includes compensation for IPR, the actual share to content providers remains low. The entire revenue from P2P SMS goes to the operators and revenue sharing is only relevant for the remaining 60 per cent of business, though each operator has a different revenue sharing model. Moreover, content that is sold more gets the same share as content that interests a limited market. The prices to the consumer are also rarely determined by the content provider. This practice is typical to India—in Europe, Japan, Korea etc., the share of the MVAS content provider is far higher at around 70 per cent. They also have greater freedom in choice of content, software or services that can be loaded on the mobile.

Moreover, there are (admittedly unproven) claims of billing and revenue leakages between the operators and the content providers, lack of transparency in statistics of content transactions, efficiency in settlements, of credible systems to address disagreements and in grievance redressal mechanisms. Further, when information systems connecting the end user, operator and content provider are not in place, it is difficult to keep track of the revenues accrued, and actual and the optimal potential of earnings is not achieved. Content providers (that could include financial service providers) are at the end of the stream and unless they have a system of validating usage, they must be content with the billing accounts given to them by the operator. Delays in payments compound the problems, especially for small VAS providers. This problem would also affect SHGs, community-based financial services and small NGOs in providing innovative solutions.

Flexibility in billing models are also crucial—whether the consumer subscribes to a service or whether content can be provided on pay-as-you do principles—currently such models are offered to only a limited set of larger content providers. Typically the MSPs are not built to address the requirements of a small entity providing such services or piloting innovations.

Further, and this is significant given the nature of electronic transactions, the MSPs do not share information on the type of mobile instruments being used by different types of consumers. This affects the development of software that is in line with technical specifications of the instruments being used.

The point being made is that there is a market failure in the MVAS segment, that is a result of bundled services. Competitive pressures have not been generated adequately wherein the MSPs compete for better content and services that can be loaded on the 'mobile pipe'. This failure is also affecting the progress of the financial transactions on the mobile space.

To reiterate, whether as an access point to the Internet, or as a holder of value through a cash card, or as a means of identification, or a direct enabler of electronic transactions—the mobile is critical for the success of electronic transactions.

Greater entry of transaction service providers needs to be enabled by a range of changes. These changes can be made by coordination within the cellular industry, or forced through regulatory and policy measures. Transactions need to be enabled by enabling transparencies; content and service providers need to be incentivised by providing them with adequate flexibility in pricing and earning from their content; all of this requires that there be adequate infrastructure and coordination between different players in the market; access to a common short codes that works across all providers, etc.

These recommendations are given in brief below.

### Short Codes: Unique for each Content Provider and Universally Accepted by all MSPs

A short-code assignment system needs to be put in place that is integrated across all operators. That is, a single number should be assigned to every content provider, and this code should work across all MSPs whether they are GSM or CDMA, or for that matter whether the service is 2G or 3G. This would be an important shift from the current system—the short code needs to be content/service provider-specific.

For a country such as India with a highly heterogeneous population with highly varying tastes and preferences, a large range of content and content providers would need to be accommodated. This necessarily requires a large set of numbers available for content providers. Therefore, adequate numbers of short codes need to be made available freely and fairly. This would entail certain one-time costs for MSPs to shift to the new system.

### Building Transparency on Users and Usage

In the interest of a level playing field, all information that is available to the MSP on users and usage will need to be made available to the content providers as well (subject, of course, to privacy considerations). Information on user, handset, transactions that is available with the MSP needs to be transferred to the content provider. Typically, larger content providers and aggregators are able to negotiate better deals with the MSPs. Information on such prices needs to be openly available in the industry.

The sharing of information in a free and fair manner is one of the most important aspects of a vibrant industry. Such information will enable greater investment, better and more appropriate design, and better targeting of content. Since the credibility of information is a key issue, auditing of this information-sharing process by external entities can create such an environment.

## Infrastructure Improvements and Better Integration

- It is expected that infrastructure issues such as bandwidth congestion will be addressed in the near future with the sorting out of the spectrum allocation problem.
- Currently, location-based services are constrained by a lack of a digitised map of the country. A coordinated approach will help accelerate the development of an exhaustive all-India digitised map.
- A high level of integration between the MSP systems and the handset can ensure the smooth delivery of a range of MVAS options. This requires that handsets be well integrated with the MSP. A standardised system would help.
- It is currently claimed by some MSPs and content aggregators that they do not have the built-in software that enables them to generate or share information on content-specific usage. Such information systems that are integrated across different players need to be a precondition for entry into this market.
- Currently, mobile phones sold in India are not necessarily Indian language-friendly. Hence, many instruments—whether manufactured in India or imported—are sold without the ability to support text in Indian languages.

## Greater, Flexible and Simpler Revenue Sharing

- The broad principle here should be that the MSP is merely a facilitator of financial service/content provider-consumer interaction. The provider needs to have the flexibility over pricing of his content and the manner in which it is implemented.
- The MSP needs to separately price the various services rendered. For instance, the MSP needs to separately report charges for packet delivery, platform, marketing costs and various other items.
- The MSP also needs to provide the flexibility to the service/ content provider to choose only those items which he desires.

- The MSPs need to provide the service/content provider with the flexibility to adequately price its product.
- The MSP needs to provide the content provider an option to chose between: (a) payment on a rupee amount per unit/packet, and (b) percentage of revenue sharing basis, or (c) a one-time single user charge.

## Other

- Authentication standards for downloads of content do not exist currently; these need to be set up and implemented across the board.
- Security of transactions need to be encouraged through proper identification and transactional cross-checks.
- The universal acceptance of IPR and an industry backed monitoring system also needs to be put in place.
- By providing customers with the option of not receiving promotional SMS, operators can help create a more favourable environment for VAS adoption.
- MSPs need to work with handset manufacturers to create certain industry standards that incorporate local language options.

As Dr. Kelkar (2008) noted, "as policy instruments, markets are better in promoting inclusive pattern of outcomes as they do not differentiate among citizens. Ironically, it is a State action which is more differentiating in nature and, therefore, can be non-inclusive. I am mindful that while markets may be caste, colour, religion, gender-blind, they are not income or wealth neutral and there is a need for regulation to ensure that markets are transparent and competitive. Therefore, Government's role as an umpire is of vital importance towards ensuring the desired outcomes while deploying market instruments."

The solution to the financial transactions on the mobile pipe lies in the realm of ensuring broad principles of transparency, flexibility, coordination and fairness to all concerned. If industry cannot through collective action create such an environment, then regulatory and policy oversight becomes necessary to achieve these ends. This has to be done in both the financial as well as in the telecom space.

## Conclusion

Despite decades of progress in the financial systems and markets in India, the masses continue to depend on cash for their transactions and remain outside the scope of the formal financial sector. There is a vast and diverse group of people whose financial needs are going unmet—marginal farmers, agricultural labourers, migrants, employees and entrepreneurs in the unorganised sector, socially excluded groups etc. Their cash flows of income, savings and consumption are of low levels and often of uncertain, irregular nature, making them unattractive clients for the formal financial sector. Yet, bringing the poor and poorest into the system has large savings in the present transaction costs of dealing with cash and has the potential of boosting economic growth. Thus, financial inclusion is recognised as a goal by all policy makers as the economic growth and development story will remain incomplete without participation by the poorest of the poor.

Presently policy makers in the government and at the RBI continue to emphasise the role of the banks, even though it is clear that market failure has arisen in meeting the goal of financial inclusion precisely because of a mismatch of the needs of the formal financial sector and the low income consumer. In the last two years, though, there has been a welcome shift in their approach with the RBI repeatedly making it clear that if banks fail to deliver on the financial inclusion front, a non-bank-led model will be put in place. For a non-bank model to work, however, the problems in the MVAS market space have to be dealt with.

Looking ahead, there is significant activity expected in the m-payments sphere. An Inter-Ministerial Group for Financial Services on Mobiles set up in November 2009 is on track with formulating guidelines for further progress. The Group has also zeroed onto the need to facilitate management of large number of small-value accounts and micro-transactions involved in the delivery of basic financial services. Of all the possibilities of electronic transactions, the mobile is the most suitable candidate for ensuring rapid growth of inclusive services. Consequently, it is critical to address the issues that have constrained the growth of

MVAS, as these will be the key to enabling financial inclusion in the real sense. Clearly, the intent to cater to the needs of the poor is there and if all agencies and regulators work in tandem, the next few years could well see a dramatic transformation in the way majority of Indians make their financial transactions.

To sum up, the RBI in its order of April 2009[7] has already created an environment that facilitates an enabling regime and a level playing field for all players, banks as well as non-banks. The mobile industry and TRAI now need to take up the baton that will finally bring in true financial inclusion.

## References

Bhandari, Laveesh (2007). "Inclusion, e-payments and the payments and settlement systems bill", *White Paper*. Indicus Analytics.

CGAP (2006). "Using technology to build inclusive financial systems", *Focus Note* No. 32. Consultative Group to Assist the Poor.

Gonzalez, Adrian and Richard Rosenberg (2006). "The state of microfinance—Outreach, profitability, and poverty: Findings from a database of 2600 microfinance institutions" (*mimeo*). CGAP, World Bank. (*http://info.worldbank.org/etools/docs/library/232702/Rosenberg_OutreachEfficiencyProfitability.doc*)

Holtkamp, Bernhard (2006). *Mobile Value-added Services in China*. VAS China Project, Funded by the European Union. January.

OECD (2007). *OECD Communications Outlook*. Paris.

Kelkar, Vijay (2008). "Financial inclusion for 'inclusive growth'", *N.P. Sen Memorial Lecture*. Hyderabad: Administrative Staff College of India. 13 January.

Thorat, Usha (2006). "Financial inclusion for sustainable development: Role of IT and intermediaries", *Annual Bankers' Conference*, RBI. Hyderabad.

7. Amended in August 2009 to allow non-banks to issue prepaid financial instruments.

## Appendix[8]

### Table A-9.1

*Incidence of Indebtedness (IOI) of Households as on 30.6.02 to Institutional and Non-institutional Credit Agencies by Household Assets Holding Class (AHC)*

| AHC | Rural | | | Urban | | |
|---|---|---|---|---|---|---|
| (Rs. '000) | Institutional | Non-Inst. | All | Institutional | Non-Inst. | All |
| (1) | (2) | (3) | (4) | (5) | (6) | (7) |
| Less than 15 | 3.6 | 12.0 | 15.0 | 1.4 | 9.5 | 10.7 |
| 15–30 | 6.2 | 13.9 | 19.0 | 2.4 | 12.8 | 14.8 |
| 30–60 | 8.7 | 17.7 | 25.2 | 4.5 | 11.0 | 14.8 |
| 60–100 | 10.9 | 17.7 | 26.5 | 7.2 | 11.9 | 18.3 |
| 100–150 | 13.6 | 17.9 | 28.9 | 8.3 | 12.2 | 19.7 |
| 150–200 | 14.6 | 17.1 | 28.7 | 8.9 | 12.0 | 20.0 |
| 200–300 | 16.2 | 15.7 | 28.7 | 11.1 | 10.1 | 19.9 |
| 300–450 | 18.7 | 13.2 | 28.7 | 12.1 | 8.2 | 18.7 |
| 450–800 | 22.0 | 13.0 | 31.0 | 16.9 | 7.2 | 22.5 |
| 800 & above | 26.7 | 10.3 | 32.9 | 18.5 | 4.2 | 21.4 |
| All | 13.4 | 15.5 | 26.5 | 9.3 | 9.4 | 17.8 |

8. The following tables are taken from NSSO AIDIS Survey of 2003.

## Table A-9.2

*Average Amount of Debt (AOD) and Debt-Asset Ratio (DAR) by Household Assets Holding Class (AHC) as on 30.6.02*

| Assets Holding Class (Rs. '000) | AVA (Rs.) | AOD (Rs.) Institutional | AOD (Rs.) Non-Inst. | AOD (Rs.) All | Debt-Asset Ratio (%) Institutional | Debt-Asset Ratio (%) Non-Inst. | Debt-Asset Ratio (%) All |
|---|---|---|---|---|---|---|---|
| **Rural** | | | | | | | |
| Less than 15 | 7,071 | 299 | 1,124 | 1,423 | 4.23 | 15.90 | 20.12 |
| 15-30 | 22,523 | 643 | 1,600 | 2,243 | 2.85 | 7.10 | 9.96 |
| 30-60 | 44,609 | 990 | 2,163 | 3,153 | 2.22 | 4.85 | 7.07 |
| 60-100 | 78,431 | 1,313 | 2,988 | 4,301 | 1.67 | 3.81 | 5.48 |
| 100-150 | 123,412 | 2,075 | 3,224 | 5,299 | 1.68 | 2.61 | 4.29 |
| 150-200 | 173,382 | 2,404 | 3,292 | 5,696 | 1.39 | 1.90 | 3.29 |
| 200-300 | 244,339 | 3,411 | 3,648 | 7,059 | 1.40 | 1.49 | 2.89 |
| 300-450 | 366,134 | 5,770 | 4,087 | 9,857 | 1.58 | 1.12 | 2.69 |
| 450-800 | 591,676 | 10,166 | 4,919 | 15,085 | 1.72 | 0.83 | 2.55 |
| 800 & above | 1,668,644 | 26,577 | 6,837 | 33,414 | 1.59 | 0.41 | 2.00 |
| All | 265,606 | 4,302 | 3,237 | 7,539 | 1.62 | 1.22 | 2.84 |
| **Urban** | | | | | | | |
| Less than 15 | 5,400 | 201 | 1,267 | 1,468 | 3.72 | 23.46 | 27.19 |
| 15-30 | 21,759 | 558 | 2,882 | 3,440 | 2.56 | 13.25 | 15.81 |
| 30-60 | 44,532 | 1,240 | 2,437 | 3,677 | 2.78 | 5.47 | 8.26 |
| 60-100 | 78,981 | 2,294 | 2,117 | 4,411 | 2.90 | 2.68 | 5.58 |
| 100-150 | 123,601 | 2,472 | 2,733 | 5,205 | 2.00 | 2.21 | 4.21 |
| 150-200 | 173,451 | 3,011 | 2,839 | 5,850 | 1.74 | 1.64 | 3.37 |
| 200-300 | 244,921 | 4,840 | 3,844 | 8,684 | 1.98 | 1.57 | 3.55 |
| 300-450 | 369,455 | 7,596 | 3,485 | 11,081 | 2.06 | 0.94 | 3.00 |
| 450-800 | 593,813 | 16,065 | 3,896 | 19,961 | 2.71 | 0.66 | 3.36 |
| 800 & above | 1,858,475 | 36,663 | 4,217 | 40,880 | 1.97 | 0.23 | 2.20 |
| All | 417,158 | 8,843 | 2,926 | 11,771 | 2.12 | 0.70 | 2.82 |

*Note:* AVA: Average Value of Assets.

## Table A-9.3

*Percentage Share of Institutional Agencies in Outstanding Cash Debt for Each of Occupational Categories*

| Category | 1981 (37th) | 1991 (48th) | 2002 (59th) |
|---|---|---|---|
| **Rural** | | | |
| Cultivator | 63 | 66 | 61 |
| Non-cultivator | 37 | 55 | 46 |
| All | 61 | 64 | 57 |
| **Urban** | | | |
| Self-employed | 58 | 69 | 67 |
| Others | 62 | 74 | 80 |
| All | 60 | 72 | 75 |

## Table A-9.4

*Percentage Share of Institutional Agencies to the Total Cash Dues of the Households as on 30.6.02 by Household Assets Holding Class*

| Household Assets Holding Class (AHC) (Rs. '000) | Rural | | | Urban | | |
|---|---|---|---|---|---|---|
| | Institutional Agency | Non-Inst. Agency | All | Institutional Agency | Non-Inst. Agency | All |
| Less than 15 | 21 | 79 | 100 | 14 | 86 | 100 |
| 15–30 | 29 | 71 | 100 | 16 | 84 | 100 |
| 30–60 | 31 | 69 | 100 | 34 | 66 | 100 |
| 60–100 | 31 | 70 | 100 | 52 | 48 | 100 |
| 100–150 | 39 | 61 | 100 | 48 | 53 | 100 |
| 150–200 | 42 | 58 | 100 | 52 | 49 | 100 |
| 200–300 | 48 | 52 | 100 | 56 | 44 | 100 |
| 300–450 | 59 | 42 | 100 | 69 | 31 | 100 |
| 450–800 | 67 | 33 | 100 | 81 | 20 | 100 |
| 800 & above | 80 | 21 | 100 | 90 | 10 | 100 |
| All | 57 | 43 | 100 | 75 | 25 | 100 |

## Table A-9.5

*Percentage Share of Different Credit Agencies to the Total Cash Dues of the Households as on 30.6.02*

| Credit Agency | Rural | Urban |
|---|---|---|
| Government etc. | 2.3 | 7.6 |
| Cooperative societies/bank | 27.3 | 20.5 |
| Commercial banks etc. | 24.5 | 29.7 |
| Insurance | 0.3 | 3.5 |
| Provident fund | 0.3 | 2.0 |
| Financial corporation/institution | 1.1 | 7.0 |
| Financial company | 0.6 | 2.0 |
| Other institutional agencies | 0.7 | 2.9 |
| All institutional agencies | 57.1 | 75.1 |
| Landlord | 1.0 | 0.2 |
| Agricultural moneylender | 10.0 | 0.9 |
| Professional moneylender | 19.6 | 13.2 |
| Traders | 2.6 | 1.0 |
| Relatives & friends | 7.1 | 7.6 |
| Doctors, lawyers, etc. | 0.3 | 0.1 |
| Others | 2.3 | 1.8 |
| All non-institutional agencies | 42.9 | 24.9 |
| Unspecified | 0.0 | 0.0 |
| All agencies | 100.0 | 100.0 |

**Table A-9.6**

*Percentage of Indebted Households (P) and Percentage Share (S) of Dues Outstanding as on 30.6.02 by Purpose of Loan*

| Purpose of Loan | All-India | | | |
|---|---|---|---|---|
| | Rural | | Urban | |
| | P | S | P | S |
| Capital expenditure in farm business | 6 | 27 | 1 | 3 |
| Current expenditure in farm business | 5 | 14 | 0 | 2 |
| All expenditure in farm business | 10 | 41 | 1 | 5 |
| Capital expenditure in non-farm business | 2 | 9 | 2 | 17 |
| Current expenditure in non-farm business | 1 | 3 | 1 | 3 |
| All expenditure in non-farm business | 3 | 12 | 3 | 20 |
| Household expenditure | 13 | 35 | 12 | 58 |
| Expenditure on litigation | 0 | 0 | 0 | 0 |
| Repayment of debt | 0 | 1 | 0 | 2 |
| Financial investment expenditure | 0 | 1 | 0 | 2 |
| Others | 2 | 10 | 2 | 14 |
| All (non-business) expenditure in household | 16 | 47 | 15 | 75 |
| All (incl. n.r.) | 27 | 100 | 18 | 100 |

*Note:* n.r.: Not Reported.

**Table A-9.7**

*Percentage of Indebted Households (P) and Percentage Share (S) of Cash Dues Outstanding as on 30.6.02 by Type of Security*

| Type of Security | Rural | | Urban | |
|---|---|---|---|---|
| | P | S | P | S |
| Personal security | 18 | 48 | 12 | 40 |
| Surety security etc. | 2 | 8 | 2 | 9 |
| Crop | 1 | 4 | 0 | 0 |
| First charge on immovable property | 3 | 16 | 2 | 22 |
| Mortgage of immov. prop. | 4 | 20 | 2 | 22 |
| Bullion/ornaments | 1 | 2 | 1 | 1 |
| Share of companies etc. | 0 | 0 | 0 | 1 |
| Agricultural commodities | 0 | 1 | 0 | 0 |
| Other movable property | 0 | 1 | 0 | 1 |
| Other type of security | 1 | 2 | 1 | 3 |
| All (incl. n.r.) | 27 | 100 | 18 | 100 |

*Note:* n.r.: Not Reported.

### Table A-9.8

*Percentage of Households Reporting (P) Outstanding Debt as on 30.6.02 and Percentage Share (S) of such Debt over Size Group of Outstanding Debt*

| *Size Group of Outstanding Debt (Rs. '000)* | *Rural* | | *Urban* | |
|---|---|---|---|---|
| | *P* | *S* | *P* | *S* |
| Less than 2 | 2.7 | 0.5 | 1.1 | 0.1 |
| 2–4 | 4.4 | 1.8 | 1.8 | 0.5 |
| 4–6 | 4.5 | 3.2 | 2.3 | 1.1 |
| 6–10 | 4.2 | 4.6 | 1.7 | 1.2 |
| 10–15 | 5.1 | 8.6 | 2.8 | 2.9 |
| 15–20 | 2.7 | 6.3 | 1.7 | 2.5 |
| 20–30 | 3.8 | 12.9 | 2.7 | 5.9 |
| 30–50 | 2.5 | 13.4 | 2.6 | 8.8 |
| 50–100 | 1.8 | 16.7 | 2.4 | 14.6 |
| 100 & more | 1.2 | 32.1 | 2.7 | 62.4 |
| All | 26.5 | 100 | 17.8 | 100 |

# 10 India's Elementary Education Challenge

Bibek Debroy[1]

## Introduction and the "Right"

Elementary education is defined as that between classes I and VIII and this is again sub-divided into primary (Classes I-V) and upper primary (Classes VI-VIII). The Indian Constitution was amended in 2002 through the 86th Amendment. While this changed Articles 45 and 51A too, the substantive change was the insertion of a new Article 21A on right to education.[2]

This stated, "The State shall provide free and compulsory education to all children of the age of six to fourteen years in such manner as the State may, by law, determine." This followed a Supreme Court judgment in 1993, when the court ruled that the right to education was a fundamental right and flowed from Article 21 on the right to life. Therefore, every citizen should have the right to free education till the age of 14 years. A draft Right to Education Bill was circulated in 2005. While this varies in some details from the legislation of 2009 and is only of historical interest now, the Preamble to the 2005 Bill sets out the background rather well. "Whereas the Preamble to the Constitution resolves to secure to all citizens of India Justice, social, economic and political; Liberty of thought, expression, belief, faith and worship; Equality of status and of opportunity; and to promote among them all fraternity, assuring the dignity of the individual and the unity and integrity of the Nation; and whereas, despite the original Article 45

1. An earlier version of this paper was published as an Institute for South Asian Studies (ISAS) *Working Paper*.
2. Article 45 was for children under 6 years (pre-school) and Article 51A concerned responsibilities of parents and guardians.

of Directive Principles of the Constitution having made it the duty of the State to provide free and compulsory education to all children up to age fourteen in ten years (1960), the number of out of school children particularly from the disadvantaged groups and those engaged in labour, and those receiving poor quality education has remained very large; And whereas, the 86th Constitutional Amendment Act 2002 has provided for free and compulsory education of all children in the age group of six to fourteen years as a Fundamental Right under Article 21A of the Constitution, in such manner as the State may, by law, determine; And whereas the above Act also provides under Article 45 that the State shall endeavour to provide early childhood care and education for all children until they complete the age of six years; And whereas the above Act further provides under Article 51-A (k) that it shall be a fundamental duty of every citizen of India who is a parent or guardian to provide opportunities for education to his child/ward between the age of six and fourteen years; And whereas it is considered important and essential to create a humane and equitable society that incorporates the secular values and the ethnic, religious and cultural diversities of India; And whereas it is recognised that the objectives of democracy, social justice and equality can be achieved only through the provision of elementary education of equitable quality to all; And whereas it is also imperative to improve the present delivery system of elementary education by, inter alia, greater decentralisation of its management, and making it sensitive to the needs of children, especially of those belonging to disadvantaged groups..."

However, the first UPA government between 2004 and 2009 decided not to push this Bill, apparently because of the high financial costs.[3] During UPA-I, policies were largely determined by the National Common Minimum Programme (NCMP). There is no such equivalent for UPA-II, elected in May 2009. The Congress party's electoral manifesto is the closest approximation. While this did not mention the right to free education anywhere, the manifesto's focus on social sectors and education was obvious. This meant all varieties of education, not

3. "The Right of Children to Free and Compulsory Education Bill, 2008", PRS Legislative Research, *http://www.prsindia.org/index.php?name=Sections&id=12&parent_category=&category=59&action=bill_details&bill_id=734*

just elementary education. On elementary education, the manifesto stated, "It (UPA-I) has imparted a new momentum to the Sarva Shiksha Abhiyaan for primary education. It has also introduced a cooked mid-day meal scheme in all primary schools that feeds 15 crore children every day.... In order to ensure quality school education for all children, we have already made a beginning by approving the setting up of one model school in every block of the country. Every year, over the next five years, we will add one more model school in every block....The Indian National Congress will introduce special incentives for the girl child to correct the adverse sex ratio and to ensure education of girl children. Girl children in districts that have an adverse sex ratio and/or low enrollment of girls, monetary incentives will be given to the girl child to be credited to the girl child's account on her completing primary school, middle school, secondary school and higher secondary school."

But the Bill had been placed before the Rajya Sabha in December 2008, which had been unaffected by the declaration of general elections. The Bill had also been referred to a Standing Committee on Human Resource Development. When UPA-II was elected, this legislation figured prominently in the 100-day agenda floated by the Ministry of Human Resource Development. The Bill was finally passed by the Rajya Sabha on 20th June 2009 and by the Lok Sabha on 4th August 2009.

The important strands of this legislation are the following.[4] First, all children between the ages of 6 and 14 have the right to free and compulsory education in a "neighbourhood" school.[5] A child who is above 6 and is not enrolled in a school, will be enrolled in a class that is appropriate for age.[6] Second, no child can be held back, expelled or required to pass a board examination before the completion of elementary education. Third, schools cannot screen applicants at the admissions stage. Fourth, schools cannot charge capitation fees. Fifth, Kendriya Vidyalayas, Navodaya Vidyalayas, Sainik Schools and unaided

4. There is a Constitutional issue about the tenability of reservations, including that for minority schools, which we are downplaying. But such Constitutional challenges are possible.

5. There is the qualification that even if the child is older than 14, elementary education will be free until it is completed.

6. Such children have the right to special training.

schools will have to ensure that 25 per cent of their students are from disadvantaged and economically weaker groups. New schools will not be established unless they meet these norms and existing schools have been given three years to comply. Sixth, other than Kendriya Vidyalayas, Navodaya Vidyalayas and Sainik Schools, government schools are exempted from penalties if they do not comply with the provisions. Therefore, barring these three types of schools, there is an effective abdication from the responsibility of delivering elementary education by the government. Seventh, the responsibility of delivering elementary education through neighbourhood schools is on state and local governments, with no clear division of responsibility between the two. There is a lack of accountability and no penalties are proposed on authorities if delivery does not occur. The idea is that specific academic authorities, like national and state advisory councils will be established. Each school will also have a school management committee, with representatives from local authorities, parents and teachers. Eighth, all schools must comply with pupil/teacher norms and in addition, private schools also have to comply with physical infrastructure norms. However, the pupil/teacher norms are based on the total number of students, so that they allow for multi-grade teaching. Ninth, to the extent of that extra 25 per cent, the government will reimburse private schools the actual cost of providing this education, or the equivalent cost in a government school, whichever is lower.

## The State of India's Elementary Education

For what it is worth, this new piece of legislation gives children a right to schooling. It does not give children a right to education. While this paper is on elementary education, education itself is a continuum and cuts across elementary education, secondary education, vocational education and higher education. The overall context is the demographic dividend, flagged among others, by Vijay Kelkar. For instance, in the 2004 K.R. Narayanan Lecture at the Australian National University (Kelkar, 2006), he talked about incremental growth that comes from increased quality and quantity of the labour force. The theme is explored in greater detail in a paper written for the Strategic Studies Institute, with educational reforms flagged under the head of meso-economic reforms. To quote, "In addition to its intrinsic value, education is also valued for what it can do in terms of human resource capabilities. It is this sector that could make or break India. Compared to 1951, when more than four-fifths of its adults were illiterate, India reached a remarkable level of achievement by 1997, when almost two-thirds of its adult population had attained literacy. Compared to China, however, the gap is huge: with an equally large population and similar size of illiterate population in the 1950s, the PRC has now virtually eliminated illiteracy among its younger population and raised adult literacy to 80 per cent. To reduce such a gap requires an enormous effort with resources on a matching scale. It is estimated that an additional amount equal to 1.9 per cent of GDP would be required annually to provide schooling to those who are not currently in school" (Kelkar, 2002). The simple point is that there is no automaticity about the demographic dividend leading to incremental growth. There are problems with education, skills, morbidity and mortality, often with significant inter-state differences. Having said this, this paper focuses on elementary education alone. There are two reasons for this. First, one cannot cover everything in a single paper. Second, elementary education reform has been on the visible agenda and there is evidence that demand, and not just supply, has shifted. Demand-driven reforms tend to work better than supply-driven ones.

In 2005, the World Bank published a report on India and the knowledge economy (Dahlman and Utz, 2005). The expression "knowledge economy" can be precisely defined, but that is irrelevant for present purposes. The thrust of the World Bank report is on education's role as a fundamental enabler of the knowledge economy and the knowledge economy's requirement of a new set of skills and competencies. While the figures quoted in this report are now dated, this report said, "India has made substantial progress in increasing literacy and increasing primary and secondary enrollments and overall education attainment. But the country still accounts for one-quarter of the world's 104 million children out of school. The participation of girls in the 6-14-year-old age group in elementary education is low. And considerable gaps exist in access to secondary education, particularly for girls. But, the Indian leadership is very committed to increasing educational attainment. The national program for universal elementary education, Sarva Shiksha Abhiyan or Education for All, was initiated in 2001 and the constitution was amended in 2002 to make elementary education a fundamental right of every child." On issues, with a focus on elementary education, the report said the following: "Improving efficiency in the use of public resources in the education system, and making the education system as a whole more responsive to market needs, as well as ensuring expanded access to education that fosters critical thinking and learning skills for all, not just the elites; Enhancing the quality of primary and secondary education, including tackling issues related to quality and relevance, with special emphasis on ameliorating teacher vacancies and absenteeism, reversing high dropout rates, and correcting inadequate teaching and learning materials and uneven levels of learning achievement. This is especially important for India to meet the goal of providing eight years of schooling for all children by 2010; Ensuring consistency between the skills taught in primary and secondary education and the needs of the knowledge economy; introducing materials and methods to teach students "how to learn," rather than stressing occupation-specific knowledge." It is necessary to mention that public expenditure on education was 3.7 per cent of GDP in 1991 and has been 3.8 per cent between 2002 and 2005.[7]

In December 2006, the Planning Commission produced the Approach Paper to the 11th Five Year Plan (2007-2012). The introductory chapter of this document stated, "A key element of 11th Plan strategy should be to provide essential education and health services to those large parts of our population who are still excluded from these. Education is the critical factor that empowers participation in the growth process, but our performance has been less than satisfactory, both overall and in bridging gender and other divides. Overall literacy is still less than 70 per cent and rural female literacy less than 50 per cent with corresponding rates even lower among the marginalised groups and minorities. While the *Sarva Shiksha Abhiyan* has expanded primary school enrolment, it is far from providing quality education. Looking ahead, we cannot be satisfied with only universal primary education; we must move towards universal secondary education too as quickly as

7. *Human Development Report 2007/2008*, UNDP and Oxford University Press, 2007.

possible." Further down, the chapter said, "While both education and curative health services are available for those who can afford to pay, quality service is beyond the reach of the common people. Other privately provided services are of highly variable quality. In this situation, access to essential services can only be through public financing. In most cases this means public provision or partnership with non-profit and civil society organisations. A major institutional challenge is that even where service providers exist, the quality of delivery is poor and those responsible for delivering the services cannot be held accountable. Unless such accountability is established and cutting edge service providers trained, it will be difficult to ensure significant improvement in delivery even if large resources are made available." Although this statement is about education at a very general level, some additional points have now been flagged. First, there is a question of access to the relatively poor. Second, flowing from the first argument, a case has been made for public financing, which is then equated with public provisioning, without making the jump from one to the other at all clear. Third, an implicit argument has been made about regulation. Fourth, another implicit argument has been made about lack of accountability in public expenditure.

While quality is an issue, indeed an important one, the major emphasis of the Tenth Five Year Plan (2002-2007) was on universalisation of elementary education (UEE). This was supposed to be driven by five objectives: (a) universal access; (b) universal enrolment; (c) universal retention; (d) universal achievement; and (e) equity. And the main schemes to drive these were the Sarva Shiksha Abhiyan (SSA), the DPEP (District Primary Education Programme),[8] the National Programme of Nutritional Support to Primary Education (NPNSPE),[9] the Teacher Education Scheme, the Kasturba Gandhi Balika Vidyalaya Scheme (KGBVS),[10] Operation Blackboard for physical infrastructure, the

8. The precursor to the SSA and a centrally sponsored scheme. This was an externally funded project for primary education. It was decentralised and had a community focus. There was another externally funded project known as Mahila Samakhya.

9. Also known as the Mid-Day Meal Scheme.

10. This is for residential schools for girls, for SCs/STs/OBCs and schools that have to be set up in difficult terrain. This was launched in 2004. Seventy-five per cent of the enrolment is reserved for the target categories. The remaining 25 per cent is open, provided it is from BPL (below the poverty line) households.

Shiksha Karmi Project on teacher absenteeism and the Lok Jumbish Project on girls' education. Other than mid-day meals, SSA now subsumes the others. As an explanation of what SSA is expected to do, a quote from the Ministry of Human Resource Development is appropriate.[11] "Sarva Shiksha Abhiyan (SSA) is Government of India's flagship programme for achievement of Universalisation of Elementary Education (UEE) in a time bound manner....SSA is being implemented in partnership with State Governments to cover the entire country and address the needs of 192 million children in 1.1 million habitations. The programme seeks to open new schools in those habitations which do not have schooling facilities and strengthen existing school infrastructure through provision of additional class rooms, toilets, drinking water, maintenance grant and school improvement grants. Existing schools with inadequate teacher strength are provided with additional teachers, while the capacity of existing teachers is being strengthened by extensive training, grants for developing teaching-learning materials and strengthening of the academic support structure at a cluster, block and district level." SSA was launched in 2001-02, with a Centre/state funding ratio of 85/15 during the Ninth Plan and 75/25 during the Tenth Plan. During the Eleventh Plan, the ratio was 65/35 for the first two years, 60/40 for the third year, 55/45 for the fourth year and 50/50 thereafter. However, for the north-eastern states, the ratio continued to be 90/10.

The precursor to these attempts during the Ninth Plan was a National Policy of Education. This was formulated in 1986 and then was revised in 1992. This suggested three thrust areas in elementary education: (i) universal access and enrolment; (ii) universal retention of children up to 14 years of age; and (iii) a substantial improvement in the quality of education to enable all children to achieve essential levels of learning.

To the extent one can pin it down quantitatively, SSA should therefore be judged by its successes on access, enrolment, retention, achievement and equity. The Tenth Plan indeed had some specific timelines, timelines also of the SSA (Planning Commission, 2008).

11. *http://education.nic.in/Elementary/elementary.asp*

First, by 2005, all children should be in regular schools, back to school camps and so on. Second, by 2007, all gender and social category gaps should be bridged in primary education. By 2010, these should be bridged for the entire category of elementary education. Third, there should be universal retention by 2010.

The "success" is most evident for universal access. 177,677 new schools were opened since 1991 and 94 per cent of the rural population now has a school within a distance of 1 km.[12] Roughly once every five years, the Ministry of Human Resources Development conducts All India School Education Surveys (AISES) through National Council of Educational Research and Training (NCERT). This provides data on how far a school is. To give a perspective to the discussion, there were 642,000 primary schools in 1999-2000 and 198,000 upper primary schools. By 2004-05, there were 767,520 primary schools and 274,731 upper primary schools. There were 1.9 million primary school teachers and 1.3 million upper primary school teachers in 1999-2000. By 2004-05, there were 2.3 million primary school teachers and 1.4 million upper primary school teachers. Enrolment in primary school increased from 113.61 million in 1999-2000 to 131.69 million in 2004-05 and enrolment in upper primary school increased from 42.00 million in 1999-2000 to 51.67 million in 2004-05.

One should not form the impression that SSA is only about new schools. It also allows expenditure for improving physical infrastructure. Having said this, it is clear that lack of physical access is much less of a problem now. National University of Educational Planning and Administration (NUEPA) brings out a District Information System for Education (DISE). While DISE is a survey rather than a census, the detail of quality and disaggregation in the DISE database is remarkable and the coverage of DISE has also been increasing. Based on DISE, NUEPA (2008) concludes the following: "It is also important to note that activities under SSA got momentum from the year 2002 onwards and a large number of Primary and Upper Primary schools/sections have been opened across the country which is also reflected in the ratio of Primary to Upper Primary schools/sections."

12. *Annual Report 2005-06*, Ministry of Human Resource Development.

Though the number of upper primary schools has increased, 65.14 per cent of schools are still independent primary schools.[13] Only 17.55 per cent of primary schools are integrated with upper primary schools. Only 5.65 per cent of upper primary schools are attached to secondary and higher secondary schools. As an indicative target, there should be one upper primary school or section for every two primary schools or sections. The national average now is 2.45. However, what this masks is that the ratio is as high as 5.4 in West Bengal and 4.5 in Arunachal Pradesh. Many schools are also a fair distance away from the cluster resource centre (CRC) and are rarely visited by the CRC coordinator.[14] 70.12 per cent of primary schools have *pucca* (permanent) buildings, 9.08 per cent have partially *pucca* buildings and 3.38 per cent only possess *kuchcha* (temporary) buildings. These numbers do not look that bad at an all-India level. However, few schools in the north-east have *pucca* buildings. 7.02 per cent of primary schools in Mizoram have *pucca* buildings. At an all-India level, a school has 4.1 classrooms, though the figure varies between 3.7 in rural India and 7.3 in urban India. However, Assam only has 1.5 classrooms per school, while Jharkhand has 1.3. 9.7 per cent of schools still have single classrooms and most of these are primary schools. 65.26 per cent of primary schools in Assam have only a single classroom. On an average, there are 36 students per classroom. However, for primary schools, the ratio is 92 in Bihar, 79 in Jharkhand and 53 in UP. 11.76 per cent of schools in rural areas are still single-teacher schools, with very high numbers in Assam, Jharkhand, MP, Rajasthan and UP. While 85 per cent of schools have drinking water facilities, the number is as low as 69.5 per cent in Jharkhand, 43.3 per cent in Meghalaya, 61.8 per cent in Assam and 68.4 per cent in Nagaland. Only 42.58 per cent of schools have separate toilets for girls. 16.2 per cent of schools in Bihar have separate toilets for girls and the figures are 15.5 per cent in Jharkhand, 13.3 per cent in Chhattisgarh, 8.8 per cent in Meghalaya, 10.0 per cent in Assam, 12.2 per cent in Arunachal Pradesh and 17.9 per cent in Manipur.[15] For

13. Unless otherwise specified, the school and facility indicators in this paragraph are from DISE (NUEPA, 2008).

14. 35.36 per cent of schools are within 1 km from the CRC. During the previous academic year, 63.46 per cent of schools were visited by the CRC coordinator and 53.99 per cent of schools were inspected by school inspectors.

15. There are other indicators too, which we will skip, such as computers, ramps, kitchen sheds, boundary walls, playgrounds, electricity connections, book banks, medical check-ups and residential facilities.

government schools, the average number of teachers per school is as low as 2.2 in Uttarakhand, 2.6 in Madhya Pradesh, 2.9 in Chhattisgarh, 3.0 in Orissa and 2.8 in Meghalaya. The number of female teachers is as low as 27.9 per cent in Bihar, with figures of 28.4 per cent for Jharkhand, 29.8 per cent for West Bengal, 25.6 per cent for Tripura and 28.4 per cent for Rajasthan.[16] Pupil/teacher ratios are as high as 55 in UP and 65 in Bihar. 55.77 per cent of regular primary school teachers do not even possess higher secondary level qualifications. Few teachers have in-service training and several states employ para-teachers as opposed to regular teachers, with a figure as high as 41.3 per cent in Jharkhand.[17]

While the number of schools has increased, four points emerge. First, there are still problems with physical access. Second, notwithstanding SSA expenditure, physical infrastructure in many schools is deficient. Third, there are problems with teachers. Fourth, there are significant inter-state variations in these. Table 10.1 illustrates this. This table requires an explanation. The second column, on the number of elementary schools per 100,000 population, is from the 11th Five Year Plan document. There are national norms on distance and population size, before a school is opened. But these are indicative and different states have their own norms. But to the extent that is an indicator, among large states, we clearly still have a shortage of schools in states like Bihar. However, a better indicator of access is obtained from the access index in the third and fourth columns of Table 10.1. The access index has been constructed by NUEPA.[18] A mixed picture emerges for primary and upper primary. For primary education, there are

16. SSA requires that 50 per cent of newly-appointed teachers must be women.

17. Other than Jharkhand, there are large numbers of para-teachers in Andhra Pradesh, Bihar, Chhattisgarh, Madhya Pradesh, Rajasthan, Uttar Pradesh and West Bengal. The 1986 National Policy on Education provided for non-formal education (NFE) centres "for school drop-outs, for children from habitations without schools, working children and girls who cannot attend whole-day schools". There are many such NFE centres in Uttar Pradesh, Bihar, Andhra Pradesh, Madhya Pradesh, Orissa and Rajasthan, employing what are called para-teachers. NFEs cost less than regular schools and there is no evidence to suggest that such students perform worse than those in regular schools.

18. *Ibid.* It is based on the percentage of habitations not served, the number of schools per 1000 child population and the ratio of primary to upper primary schools, the last included only for the upper primary index. The indices are constructed separately for primary and upper primary and to obtain the index, the variables are weighted and aggregated using principal components. The higher the value of the index, the better.

serious access problems in Kerala[19] and the Andaman & Nicobar islands and Meghalaya and Mizoram do extremely well. For upper primary education, there are serious access problems in Arunachal, Jharkhand and West Bengal and Gujarat, Mizoram, Chandigarh and Daman & Diu perform extremely well. Moving on to the infrastructure[20] indices in the fifth and sixth columns of Table 10.1, for primary schools, there are serious problems in Assam, Bihar, Jharkhand and Meghalaya, with Haryana, Kerala, Delhi and Puducherry performing extremely well. The upper primary infrastructure is dismal in Bihar, but extremely good in Goa, Haryana, Kerala, Punjab, Sikkim, Tamil Nadu, Uttar Pradesh, Uttarakhand, Andaman & Nicobar Islands, Chandigarh, Delhi, Lakshadweep and Puducherry. For primary, the teacher index is low in Bihar, Jharkhand, Madhya Pradesh and Uttar Pradesh, but good in Kerala, Andaman & Nicobar Islands, Chandigarh, Delhi, Lakshadweep and Puducherry. For upper primary, the teacher index is low in Orissa and remarkably low in Uttar Pradesh, but high in Andhra Pradesh, Goa, Kerala, Tamil Nadu, Andaman & Nicobar Islands, Chandigarh, Delhi and Puducherry. Beyond the variation between states, there is a great deal of variation between primary and upper primary school too.

From access, let us now move on to enrolment. That there has been an improvement in enrolment is undeniable. In primary classes, the gross enrolment ratio was 96.3 in 2001-02 and by 2004-05, it increased to 107.8.[21] In primary classes, gross enrolment ratios of less than 80.00 characterise Assam, Gujarat, Jammu & Kashmir, Orissa and Chandigarh.[22] While enrolment in primary school has increased, gender disparity has also declined. For instance, while the gross enrolment ratio has increased for boys from 105.3 in 2001-02 to 110.7 in 2004-05, for girls it has increased from 86.9 in 2001-02 to 104.7 in 2004-05. Though gender disparity still remains, especially in some states, the gains for girls have been commensurately more in primary classes. The gains have

19. This is a bit of a surprise and contrary to *a priori* expectations.

20. *Ibid.* This is based on drinking water, common toilets, girls' toilets and average student/classroom ratios.

21. *Eleventh Five Year Plan, ibid.* Unless otherwise specified, the subsequent figures in this paragraph are also from the same source.

22. These are figures from September 2003 and from *Annual Report, ibid.*

**Table 10.1**

*Elementary Education Indicators*

| State | Elementary Schools per 100,000 Population | Primary Access Index | Upper Primary Access Index | Primary Infrastructure Index | Upper Primary Infrastructure Index | Primary Teacher Index | Upper Primary Teacher Index |
|---|---|---|---|---|---|---|---|
| Andhra Pradesh | 99 | 0.610 | 0.567 | 0.604 | 0.773 | 0.681 | 0.823 |
| Arunachal Pradesh | 163 | 0.468 | 0.184 | 0.463 | 0.644 | 0.464 | 0.691 |
| Assam | 137 | 0.593 | 0.521 | 0.302 | 0.425 | 0.402 | 0.614 |
| Bihar | 57 | 0.437 | 0.495 | 0.260 | 0.237 | 0.241 | 0.400 |
| Chhattisgarh | 203 | 0.624 | 0.607 | 0.483 | 0.570 | 0.491 | 0.481 |
| Goa | 76 | 0.506 | 0.516 | 0.686 | 0.861 | 0.736 | 0.854 |
| Gujarat | 73 | 0.530 | 0.770 | 0.711 | 0.742 | 0.701 | 0.723 |
| Haryana | 63 | 0.483 | 0.648 | 0.801 | 0.871 | 0.587 | 0.640 |
| Himachal Pradesh | 212 | 0.595 | 0.681 | 0.679 | 0.791 | 0.698 | 0.783 |
| J&K | 153 | 0.580 | 0.664 | 0.526 | 0.671 | 0.697 | 0.781 |
| Jharkhand | 76 | 0.453 | 0.347 | 0.306 | 0.429 | 0.303 | 0.503 |
| Karnataka | 97 | 0.537 | 0.690 | 0.677 | 0.757 | 0.670 | 0.731 |
| Kerala | 30 | 0.326 | 0.609 | 0.866 | 0.909 | 0.898 | 0.902 |
| Madhya Pradesh | 205 | 0.593 | 0.590 | 0.540 | 0.581 | 0.355 | 0.380 |
| Maharashtra | 67 | 0.503 | 0.660 | 0.660 | 0.767 | 0.700 | 0.739 |
| Manipur | 150 | 0.530 | 0.500 | 0.553 | 0.702 | 0.603 | 0.716 |
| Meghalaya | 317 | 0.850 | 0.491 | 0.350 | 0.490 | 0.617 | 0.729 |
| Mizoram | 263 | 0.716 | 0.758 | 0.653 | 0.710 | 0.756 | 0.747 |
| Nagaland | 97 | 0.588 | 0.485 | 0.604 | 0.656 | 0.662 | 0.682 |
| Orissa | 162 | 0.511 | 0.537 | 0.575 | 0.574 | 0.539 | 0.338 |
| Punjab | 62 | 0.526 | 0.639 | 0.887 | 0.907 | 0.615 | 0.738 |
| Rajasthan | 137 | 0.487 | 0.616 | 0.643 | 0.765 | 0.463 | 0.674 |
| Sikkim | 155 | 0.601 | 0.521 | 0.764 | 0.833 | 0.780 | 0.771 |
| Tamil Nadu | 63 | 0.501 | 0.538 | 0.771 | 0.829 | 0.763 | 0.863 |
| Tripura | 84 | 0.402 | 0.615 | 0.548 | 0.539 | 0.625 | 0.658 |
| Uttar Pradesh | 95 | 0.450 | 0.499 | 0.741 | 0.830 | 0.378 | 0.229 |
| Uttarakhand | 207 | 0.572 | 0.623 | 0.759 | 0.808 | 0.568 | 0.453 |
| West Bengal | 63 | 0.513 | 0.290 | 0.497 | 0.511 | 0.476 | 0.536 |
| Andaman & Nicobar | 69 | 0.237 | 0.442 | 0.723 | 0.810 | 0.849 | 0.904 |
| Chandigarh | 3 | 0.365 | 0.739 | 0.792 | 0.829 | 0.933 | 0.970 |
| Dadra and Nagar Haveli | 91 | 0.507 | 0.670 | 0.524 | 0.582 | 0.430 | 0.629 |
| Daman & Diu | 40 | 0.389 | 0.713 | 0.679 | 0.745 | 0.736 | 0.744 |
| Delhi | 20 | 0.520 | 0.689 | 0.909 | 0.916 | 0.888 | 0.932 |
| Lakshadweep | 38 | 0.533 | 0.605 | 0.704 | 0.842 | 0.834 | 0.780 |
| Puducherry | 45 | 0.480 | 0.684 | 0.863 | 0.875 | 0.855 | 0.891 |

been relatively less for upper primary. In upper primary, the gross enrolment ratio has increased from 60.2 in 2001-02 to 69.9 in 2004-05. While the improvement has been from 67.8 in 2001-02 to 74.3 in 2004-2005 for boys, it has been from 52.1 in 2001-02 to 65.1 in 2004-05 for girls. While the increase has been relatively more for girls, the differential has not dropped by as much as it has for primary classes. For girls in upper primary, the gross enrolment ratio is still as low as 19.21 in Bihar, 32.19 in Jharkhand and 42.97 in Uttar Pradesh.[23] The number of out of school children was estimated to be 32 million in 2001-02 and by July 2006, it had dropped to 7 million. There were 9.5 million out of school children in 2005-06 and a break-up shows that these were concentrated in Bihar (3.2 million), UP (3.0 million), West Bengal (1.2 million), Madhya Pradesh (1.1 million), Rajasthan (80,000) and Jharkhand (62,000).[24] "Social and gender disparity, existing at both primary and upper primary education levels, continues to be an issue to be tackled with more concentrated and sustained efforts, especially in Bihar, Rajasthan, Jharkhand, Madhya Pradesh, Gujarat and Uttar Pradesh..... The social composition of out-of-school children indicates that 9.97 per cent of Muslim children, 9.54 per cent of Scheduled Tribes (STs), 8.17 per cent of Scheduled Castes (SCs), and 6.97 per cent of Other Backward Class (OBC) children were out of school and an overwhelming majority (68.7 per cent) was concentrated in five States, *viz.*, Bihar (23.6 per cent), UP (22.2 per cent), West Bengal (9 per cent), MP (8 per cent) and Rajasthan (5.9 per cent)."[25]

"During 2004-05 there were 76 districts with more than 50,000 out of school children. During 2005-06 the number of such districts dropped to 48. Of these 19 were in Bihar, 15 in UP, 5 in West Bengal, 2 each in Assam & Chhattisgarh, 1 each in AP, Haryana, Maharashtra, MP & Tripura. The States and UTs reported only 29 districts with more than 50,000 out of school children at the beginning of 2006-07.... It is true that many States have conducted school enrolment drives and teachers have entered the names of all eligible children in the school registers.

23. These are figures from September 2003 and from *Annual Report, ibid.*

24. *Annual Report, ibid.* There were also significant numbers in Andhra Pradesh, Assam, Maharashtra and Gujarat.

25. *Eleventh Five Year Plan, ibid.*

Some of these children may not be attending schools and therefore can only be called 'nominally enrolled'. Thus the actual number of children actually attending school may be lower than the number projected by the States and UTs."[26]

One should not play down the point about considerable variation within states. "There are large variations between states, between districts within a state and between blocks within a district with respect to availability of schools, especially upper primary schools, physical infrastructure of schools and the availability of teachers (Dhir and Sankar, 2009).[27]

Table 10.2 shows some elementary education outcome indicators. The second column in Table 10.2 is from the 11th Five Year Plan document and shows the gross enrolment ratio, combined for primary and upper primary school. Therefore, it does not capture the transition from primary to upper primary, a point that we will return to later. However, at this aggregated level, it highlights the point made earlier, about low enrolment in states like Bihar, Jammu & Kashmir, Jharkhand, Nagaland, Punjab, Chandigarh and Lakshadweep. The aforementioned DISE database reinforces the same points. For primary schooling, though the gender parity index is low in states like Bihar, Chandigarh, Jammu & Kashmir, Gujarat, Punjab and Rajasthan, it is not that bad. However, for upper primary schooling, the gender parity index is extremely low in states like Rajasthan, Bihar, Dadra & Nagar Haveli, Gujarat, Jammu & Kashmir, Jharkhand and Madhya Pradesh. But it is one thing to get children enrolled in school. It is a completely different thing to retain them there, ensure that they do not drop out and ensure that they transit to higher grades.

"It is increasingly realised that retaining the disadvantaged children enrolled in schools is a far more challenging task than enrolling them into educational system. Around 22 per cent of children dropped out in classes I and II. Several factors, apart from their adverse socio-economic conditions are responsible for this. The opportunity cost of girl-child

26. Chapter on *Elementary Education for the Eleventh Plan Working Group Report*, Ministry of Human Resource Development, undated.

27. This paper constructs an educational index for districts and argues that public fund flows should be linked to these district-level deprivations.

education is quite high in the rural set up and she is often a 'nowhere child', neither in the school nor in the labour force but doing domestic work, mostly sibling care. It is well documented that the presence of female teachers often serves as a role model for girls and positively influences their enrolment and attendance. But, then, in the educationally backward States, there are few women teachers to particularly attract girls to school and retain them.... The fact that children drop out of school early or fail to acquire basic literacy and numeracy skills partially reflects poor quality of education. The average school attendance was around 70 per cent of the enrolment in 2004-05. In States like UP and Bihar, the average attendance was as low as 57 per cent and 42 per cent, respectively. One-third of the teachers in MP, 25 per cent in Bihar, and 20 per cent in UP do not attend schools. Besides, the repetition rates in such States are also very high, resulting in wastage of human and material resources. Teacher attendance, ability, and motivation appear to be the weakest links of elementary education programmes. Lack of universal pre-schooling (Early Childhood Care and Education, ECCE) and consequent poor vocabulary and poor conceptual development of mind makes even enrolled children less participative in the class, even for learning by rote."[28]

The drop-out rate for elementary school is 50.8 per cent, 50.5 per cent for boys and 51.3 per cent for girls.[29] At 29.0 per cent, it is slightly better for primary school, 31.8 per cent for boys and 25.4 per cent for girls. However, drop-out rates are much higher for SCs and STs. For SCs, it is 34.2 per cent in primary school, 32.7 per cent for boys and 36.1 per cent for girls. And for all of elementary education, it is 57.3 per cent for SCs, 55.2 per cent for boys and 60.0 per cent for girls. For STs, it is 42.3 per cent in primary school, 42.6 per cent for boys and 42.0 per cent for girls. And for all of elementary education, it is 65.9 per cent for STs, 65.0 per cent for boys and 67.1 per cent for girls. However, there are inter-state variations too. The third column in Table 10.2 has data for 2003-04.[30] Primary school drop-out rates are especially high in Assam,

28. *Eleventh Five Year Plan, ibid.*

29. Unless otherwise specified, figures in this paragraph are from *Eleventh Five Year Plan, ibid.*

30. These are from *Annual Report, ibid.* The overall data are for 2004-05. Separate data are not available for the newly-formed states of Chhattisgarh, Jharkhand and Uttarakhand.

Bihar, Meghalaya, Mizoram, Rajasthan and Sikkim. The gender difference is not pronounced for drop-out rates in primary school. Indeed, as mentioned earlier, drop-out rates are, on an average, lower for girls. The fourth column in Table 10.2 has drop-out rates for all of elementary schools taken together. While data are not separately available for upper primary, primary figures read in conjunction with elementary figures show that there is a serious upper primary drop-out problem in all states, barring Himachal Pradesh, Goa, Kerala, Lakshadweep, Puducherry and Chandigarh. The problem is particularly serious in States like Assam, Bihar, Meghalaya, Rajasthan and Sikkim. The DISE database uses not only the drop-out rate, but also other measures like the survival rate, the retention rate and the average promotion rate to gauge the internal efficiency of the education system.[31] Based on these, a coefficient of efficiency is worked out and this is shown in the fifth column of Table 10.2. Measured by this indicator, Orissa is the worst-performer, by a long shot. Finally, the last two columns of Table 10.2 shows the outcome index, generated through the DISE database. This is based on enrolment ratios (with separate numbers on SCs, STs and gender parity), repetition rates, drop-out rates, ratio of exit grade over Grade I enrolment and the percentage of appeared children who have passed. The outcome index shows a slightly different picture from that obtained through input measures. For example, the less than satisfactory performances based on outcomes are in Arunachal Pradesh, Bihar, Goa, Haryana, Jharkhand, Madhya Pradesh, Meghalaya, Orissa, Punjab, Sikkim, Tripura, West Bengal and Dadra and Nagar Haveli (for upper primary).

To add to the warts and blemishes, learning achievements are poor.[32] These are thrown up in several surveys. For instance, a NCERT study is often quoted.[33] To take Grade VII as an example, the average

31. *Ibid.* The apparent survival rate is the share of enrolment in Grade II and subsequent primary grades in relation to the enrolment in Grade I. It is a stock statistic, based on the enrolment data for a single year. The retention rate is the enrolment in Grade V (minus repeaters) linked to enrolment in Grade I four years ago. The inverse of this (subtracted from 100) is the drop-out rate. This too is a stock measure, whereas promotion rates, repetition rates and transition rates (from primary to upper primary) are flow measures.

32. The aforementioned outcome index captures one element of this.

33. *Eleventh Five Year Plan, ibid.* and PRS, *ibid.*

marks scored by students in mathematics was 29.87 per cent and that in social science was 32.96 per cent. More specifically, in the Grade III tests, Manipur, Karnataka and Nagaland performed the best and Madhya Pradesh, Chhattisgarh and Uttarakhand students performed the worst. In the Grade V tests, Manipur, Bihar, Tamil Nadu and West Bengal performed the best and Goa, Himachal Pradesh and Jammu & Kashmir performed the worst. In the Grade VII tests, Assam, Andhra Pradesh and Mizoram performed the best and Orissa and Karnataka performed the worst. In the Grade VIII tests, West Bengal, Manipur and Nagaland performed the best and Punjab and Chhattisgarh performed the worst. "Clearly, the achievement levels of students are low. The survey carried out by *Pratham* called ASER 2005 has also brought out the inadequate abilities of students in the primary grades to read and carry out simple mathematical operations."[34]

## The Way Forward

The Eleventh Five Year Plan document concludes the following. "Unless there is a strong effort to address the systemic issues of regular functioning of schools, teacher attendance and competence, accountability of educational administrators, pragmatic teacher transfer and promotion policies, effective decentralisation of school management and transfer of powers to Panchayati Raj Institutions (PRIs), it would be difficult to build upon the gains of SSA. It is important to focus on good quality education of common standards, pedagogy, and syllabi to ensure minimum learning levels. In the liberalised global economy where there is a pursuit for achieving excellence, the legitimate role of private providers of quality education not only needs to be recognised, but also encouraged. Public-Private Partnership (PPP) need not necessarily mean only seeking private investments to supplement governmental efforts, but also encouraging innovation in education that the government schools may lack. Schools under private management (unaided) have been expanding at a faster rate. However, a vast majority of the poor, particularly in rural areas, is solely dependent on government schools."[35]

---

34. Chapter on *Elementary Education*, Ministry of Human Resource Development, *ibid*.
35. *Eleventh Five Year Plan, ibid*.

**Table 10.2**

*Elementary Education Outcome Indicators*

| *State* | *Gross Enrolment Ratio, Primary +* | *Primary School Drop-out Rates* | *Elementary School Drop-out Rates* | *Coefficient of Efficiency* | *Outcome Index, Primary* | *Outcome Index, Upper Primary* |
|---|---|---|---|---|---|---|
| Andhra Pradesh | 86.99 | 42.61 | 59.79 | 88.6 | 0.646 | 0.609 |
| Arunachal Pradesh | 106.70 | 46.34 | 63.52 | 66.6 | 0.332 | 0.354 |
| Assam | 91.92 | 53.15 | 70.81 | 76.1 | 0.557 | 0.533 |
| Bihar | 65.16 | 59.03 | 78.03 | 83.9 | 0.388 | 0.228 |
| Chhattisgarh | 112.63 | | | 77.8 | 0.539 | 0.448 |
| Goa | 106.04 | 1.90 | 9.43 | 97.1 | 0.515 | 0.330 |
| Gujarat | 101.70 | 26.02 | 46.94 | 80.1 | 0.593 | 0.560 |
| Haryana | 80.01 | 13.31 | 21.26 | 75.6 | 0.385 | 0.335 |
| Himachal Pradesh | 108.74 | 16.98 | 14.28 | 95.0 | 0.683 | 0.684 |
| J&K | 74.45 | 36.65 | 47.49 | 91.1 | 0.577 | 0.547 |
| Jharkhand | 75.82 | | | 83.6 | 0.460 | 0.316 |
| Karnataka | 98.76 | 9.75 | 50.59 | 87.2 | 0.662 | 0.638 |
| Kerala | 95.35 | 0.00 | 9.54 | 93.1 | 0.665 | 0.693 |
| Madhya Pradesh | 114.09 | 23.78 | 46.81 | 83.5 | 0.492 | 0.384 |
| Maharashtra | 105.70 | 13.07 | 33.25 | 82.0 | 0.629 | 0.659 |
| Manipur | 129.65 | 26.41 | 30.61 | 72.8 | 0.475 | 0.653 |
| Meghalaya | 121.93 | 53.42 | 71.13 | 65.5 | 0.402 | 0.371 |
| Mizoram | 109.51 | 55.61 | 64.19 | 71.7 | 0.525 | 0.415 |
| Nagaland | 75.76 | 32.81 | 44.83 | 81.5 | 0.482 | 0.440 |
| Orissa | 108.47 | 38.19 | 61.72 | 53.9 | 0.467 | 0.326 |
| Punjab | 72.57 | 22.03 | 35.19 | 90.0 | 0.453 | 0.308 |
| Rajasthan | 102.67 | 57.94 | 68.50 | 73.5 | 0.502 | 0.448 |
| Sikkim | 111.49 | 53.85 | 73.29 | 63.5 | 0.511 | 0.375 |
| Tamil Nadu | 113.96 | 3.23 | 25.15 | 97.5 | 0.735 | 0.763 |
| Tripura | 109.59 | 44.80 | 64.29 | 79.5 | 0.504 | 0.376 |
| Uttar Pradesh | 87.04 | 13.51 | 42.84 | 83.3 | 0.528 | 0.464 |
| Uttarakhand | 106.39 | | | 78.2 | 0.513 | 0.673 |
| West Bengal | 94.67 | 33.46 | 63.77 | 71.9 | 0.527 | 0.295 |
| Andaman & Nicobar | 107.97 | 0.35 | 18.86 | 98.4 | 0.605 | 0.520 |
| Chandigarh | 71.87 | 3.62 | 2.03 | | 0.503 | 0.446 |
| Dadra & Nagar Haveli | 113.70 | 28.40 | 45.24 | 95.8 | 0.563 | 0.393 |
| Daman & Diu | 128.25 | 0.00 | 17.36 | 71.7 | 0.441 | 0.425 |
| Delhi | 91.84 | 22.03 | 27.71 | 99.8 | 0.564 | 0.409 |
| Lakshadweep | 58.75 | 3.03 | 4.90 | | 0.498 | 0.592 |
| Puducherry | 121.34 | 0.00 | 4.60 | | 0.663 | 0.640 |

The Ministry of Human Resource Development makes the following points.[36] There is evidence to show that the country is moving towards the goal of universal elementary education. Access to schooling has improved. There is a trend towards greater decentralisation and community participation. Household surveys have become a feature of planning and village education committees (VECs) are slowly being formed. They are taking charge through the construction of schools and the managing of teacher and school grants. This decentralisation is an important component and hence a longer quote is justified. "The SSA framework for implementation emphasizes decentralisation and delegation to the grass-root level in order to ensure community-based implementation and ownership of schools. Through this community-based approach, planning at habitation level, monitoring of school activities and a number of interventions are to be carried out by the VECs or its equivalent. A number of steps have already been taken in all States to decentralise powers to Village Education Committees (VECs)/ Panchayats/Urban local bodies through legislation or through Government orders. States have set up local community-based bodies to implement elementary education programmes over the last decade in the light of the 72/73rd Constitutional Amendments for decentralisation and the requirements of the DPEP programme, where project funds necessitated setting-up of decentralised local community based bodies. Some states already had vibrant local structures like PTAs in Kerala and ZP[37] institutions in Maharashtra and Gujarat. Under SSA, this process has been further reinforced, as funds for the programme flow through local community-based bodies for all school related expenditures, which in fact constitute more than 50 per cent funds of SSA. However, the nomenclature of the community level structure varies fom state to state. They are known as VECs, School Development Management Committees (SDMCs), Mother Teacher Councils (MTC) or Parent Teacher Associations (PTAs) in different states. The pattern of VECs also differs from state to state. Some VECs are statutory under Education Acts/State PRI Acts or through State Government executive orders. States like Maharashtra, Madhya Pradesh, Uttar Pradesh,

36. *Annual Report, ibid.*

37. *Zilla Parishad.*

Andhra Pradesh, Gujarat, Himachal Pradesh, Kerala and Bihar have decentralised powers to VECs/Panchayat/Urban local bodies through Act. Andaman & Nicobar, Chandigarh, West Bengal, Karnataka, Tamil Nadu, Punjab, Delhi, Haryana and Jharkhand have decentralised powers to VECs/Panchayat/Urban local bodies through State orders.....One of the major examples of Community Empowerment is of Nagaland which under "Communitisation of Nagaland Public Institutions & Services Act, 2002", empowers the Village Education Committee with administrative and financial powers for the management of elementary schools under its jurisdiction including the power to disburse salary to teachers after exercising the powers of "No work no pay". The Nagaland Communitisation Programme has been circulated by the Department as a good model and States have been advised to look at it."

The government's recently published *Economic Survey*[38] had the following quotes, though they are often about public goods in general, or about education in general. "The Government in recent years has increased its outlays in the social sector. However, the reach of public and quasi-public goods and services supplied by the state to people still leave a lot of scope for improvement. There are still leakages in the schemes and the benefits in full do not reach the intended target groups of people." In addition, "Education in India comes under the concurrent list and thus both the Central and State Governments are involved leading to multiple controls and regulations by the governments and statutory bodies. There is an urgent need for replacement of bureaucratic controls in education by professional regulators along with private-public partnership to ensure universal primary education. ...Rating the quality of educational institutions and all education service providers (private and public) may be helpful. Entry of registered societies (non-profit) and publicly listed (education) companies in all fields of education, subject to the regulatory framework which ensures quality and reasonable pricing may be encouraged." Elsewhere, "Targeted and outcome oriented review and reform of elementary education, public health institutions and curative health infrastructure; Empower the poor and weaker sections through government funded smart card based

38. *Economic Survey, 2008-09*, Department of Economic Affairs, Ministry of Finance, Government of India.

payments to public sector providers of education and health. Set up rating system for providers of social services (education, health, social welfare), covering public sector, non-profits and NGOs and private sector."

In essence, the issues are exceedingly simple. First, to the extent elementary education will still have to be driven by public sector provisioning, how does one improve efficiency and make the system more accountable? Second, can subsidies be routed directly to students instead of to education providers, breaking the link between public sector provisioning and public sector financing? Smart cards or other IT-based mechanisms are only one option. The point is that subsidies are not incompatible with choice, competition and efficiency, provided that alternative providers exist, to whom education vouchers can be taken. This cannot work if there are market failures and no alternatives to the government school system. Third, are there regulatory barriers that impede the entry of private sector school providers? Fourth, what kind of regulation should be imposed on providers?

A key question remains the choice between government and private schools (Panagariya, 2008). But before that, some figures from the DISE database, on the nature of school management, are useful.[39] In 2006-07, 81 per cent of schools were government schools and this percentage has been declining. Government schools included 68.64 per cent schools run by the Department of Education, 25.02 per cent run by local bodies and 5.34 per cent run by the Tribal Welfare Department. 18.86 per cent of schools have private management and this figure has been increasing down the years. Within privately managed schools, 30.79 per cent are private aided schools and 69.21 per cent are unaided. The share of private schools, both aided and unaided, is high in states like Kerala (58.27 per cent), Delhi (37.05 per cent), Meghalaya (59.40 per cent), Jammu & Kashmir (20.47 per cent), Karnataka (19.01 per cent), Maharashtra (28.39 per cent), Puducherry (35.03 per cent), Rajasthan (21.26 per cent) and Uttar Pradesh (23.68 per cent). But in a state like Bihar, the share is as low as 1.55 per cent.

39. *Elementary Education in India, ibid.*

Do private schools perform better than government schools? Reviewing the limited literature available, Arvind Panagariya concludes, "Children in private schools exhibit higher attendance rates and test scores than those in government schools, even after controlling for family and school characteristics... A key distinguishing feature of private schools is the lower teacher absence rate. ...Private-school teachers receive salaries that are typically one-fifth and sometimes as low as one-tenth, of those received by government-school teachers. Private schools also hire more teachers and have lower pupil-to-teacher ratios than government schools. The authors[40] find that one important reason why absenteeism in private schools is lower is the ability of the head teacher to discipline the teachers under him.... A final important finding of Muralidharan and Kremer is that private schools are more likely to be established in villages where teacher absenteeism is higher in government schools, rather than in richer areas. In richer areas, where government schools perform satisfactorily, private schools have not emerged. Therefore, it stands to reason that it is the dysfunctional nature of government schools rather than increased incomes that are providing impetus to progressive privatisation of elementary education in India."[41]

Echoing the argument advanced in *Economic Survey*, the policy conclusion follows. "The official view in India is that funding is the key problem ailing elementary education in India. Officials acknowledge the existence of teacher absenteeism, but see increased expenditures as the most important key to solving the problem. This is entirely misguided. Under the current system, the state government pays salaries to the teachers, but the administrations at the village, block, district and city levels where they serve have no supervisory authority over them. Under such a system, throwing good money after bad cannot solve absenteeism. The solution—transfer of power to hire, supervise, and fire

40. This is an unpublished study by Karthik Muralidharan and Michael Kremer. Panagariya also quotes from a study done by James Tooley and Pauline Dixon for the Centre for Civil Society, Delhi. In addition, the 1999 PROBE (*Public Report on Basic Education in India*), Oxford University Press, has similar findings on superiority of private schools. It is incorrect to presume that private schools only exist in urban areas. Muralidharan and Kremer found that 28 per cent of rural children in India have access to fee-charging private primary schools.

41. *Ibid.*

the teachers to the jurisdictions in which they serve—has been known for some time, but the government lacks the political courage to implement it. The most efficient practical solution to the problem is to open the door wider to the private sector and subject the public sector to competition. This solution not only promises better-quality education, it also requires minimal resources. Specifically, the government should give education vouchers worth 2000 rupees per child, on average, to children aged 5 to 14 years whose parents are in the bottom 30 per cent of the income distribution... Currently, the poor have no choice but to send their children to a government school, irrespective of the quality of education the school offers. With vouchers, they would have the means to send children to a decent public school... The vouchers would place private and government schools on an equal footing. Currently, the poor are captive to the government schools since they provide free education, while private schools do so only on a limited scale. Once government schools have to compete for students, they are bound to feel the heat of competition, forcing reluctant teachers to begin delivering the services expected of them.... An alternative to the voucher is a cash transfer based on the number of school-going children in a family designated as below the poverty line."[42]

This pre-supposes the existence of private schools as an alternative and there are supply-side issues there. But before that, a demand-side problem needs to be flagged, though demand for elementary education has indeed increased.[43] For instance, for Muslims, "Social mobilisation to promote the demand for education, especially for older girls—This will require a special effort from teachers, educational administrators and programme functionaries to work with parents, religious leaders, panchayat representatives etc. to overcome barriers due to social and cultural traditions." To add to this, "Gender and social group disparities exist across large parts of the country, but there are important regional and State-wise differences. There is some overlap between areas/pockets which are generally educationally backward and those that have high gender and social group disparities, e.g. parts of Bihar, Jharkhand, Chhattisgarh, South Orissa, Rajasthan and Madhya Pradesh. The

42. *Ibid.*

43. Chapter on *Elementary Education, ibid.*

disadvantage faced by girls and children belonging to Scheduled Castes and Scheduled Tribes has its basis in cultural and traditional factors as well as social discrimination and discrimination at the school. Socio-cultural factors and a history of neglect (in some parts of the country) have also adversely affected the educational outcomes of children belonging to the Muslim community. Some children belonging to ethnic and linguistic minorities also face disadvantages in coping with the regular school system." And there is an issue that is both a demand-side and a supply-side problem. "Certain specific groups of children face a severe disadvantage in their participation in elementary education owing to the specific difficult circumstances in which they and their families are placed. These include street children in large cities; children working in shops, dhabas, hotels, garages, manufacturing units, at home for piece-rate work, agricultural child workers, domestic servants in urban and rural areas; children who migrate seasonally with their parents including children of construction workers and nomadic tribes etc....Urban poor live in under served/un-served settlements without basic amenities such as livelihood, access to water, sanitation etc. Their settlements are often not recognised by local authorities for service provision under the impression that these would qualify them for land rights in the city. Land tenure policy of local governments and the nature of stay of poor in cities and their access to basic services, greatly influences education processes among the disadvantaged groups."

On the supply-side, as has been mentioned before, non-availability of the private school route is not a rural/urban problem, since private schools also exist in rural areas. However, a great deal of variation exists across states in availability of private schools and this relates to a problem that is rarely discussed or highlighted. This concerns the licensing requirements for opening a private school. A case study is available for Delhi to illustrate the nature of the problem (Wadhwa, 2001). First, to open a school, an association or a group of individuals has to be registered under the Societies Registration Act as a "non-profit" institution. Since there is no reason why education should be for altruistic motives alone, this also means that accounts of schools are never transparent and money is siphoned off under other heads, not to speak of capitation fees charged at the time of admission. Nor should one forget the high costs of urban land. Second, the society has to obtain an "Essentiality Certificate" from the Department of Education (DOE). This certifies that a school is required in a particular zone, without which, the society cannot be allotted land. *De facto*, this works like a licence, limiting the supply of schools. Third, land needs to be allotted to the school and a sponsorship letter from the Department of Education is forwarded to land-owning agencies like DDA (Delhi Development Authority) or Municipal Corporation of Delhi (MCD). Fourth, once the school has been established, it needs to apply for recognition. Recognition up to Grade V is granted by MCD and recognition up to Grade VIII is granted by DOE. The application to DOE requires 17 documents, including "a duly approved Scheme of Management, Completion Certificate, Sanctioned Building Plan, Water Testing Report, Health Certificate. All this is governed as per the rules mentioned in Delhi Education Act, 1973" (Wadhwa, 2001). Finally, the school needs to apply for affiliation with CBSE (Central Board for Secondary Education). Without this, the terminal examination cannot be taken through the school. Needless to say, few of these clearances are available without bribes. "By the end of the 1990s, the poor had begun to do what the middle class had done three decades ago—search for alternatives to government schools—and cheap private schools surged across the country to cater to the new demand. Across states such as Punjab, Haryana, Kerala and Maharashtra, enrolment in state schools has fallen steeply, as students shift to private schools....These schools remained illegal due to the long, tedious tap-dance with bureaucracy that is necessary to get a license. Recognition of schools can consequently take years, and involves in Delhi, for example, fourteen licenses from several different authorities" (Nilekani, 2008). While this is for Delhi, other states have licensing requirements that are not dissimilar. These entry barriers should also be eased to facilitate private sector entry. Surveys, including by NUEPA, have shown that children from poor households often enrol in two schools—a government one, to obtain free textbooks, uniforms and mid-day meals, and a private one, for education. In addition, the private school is often unrecognised, because of the procedural requirements and the terminal examination has to be taken through the government system. One instance of unreasonable procedural requirements is physical infrastructural requirements, given the premium on scarce urban land.

The present government/private ratio is thus a distorted one and should increase even more in favour of the private sector, especially if the licensing requirements are eased. Nevertheless, the government sector will remain important and an improvement in its functioning is not an issue that can be ducked. "While a sizeable number of children from urban, socially and economically better off background and boys moved to private sectors, almost all of the children who started attending schools from rural, social and economically marginalised groups and girls started increasingly attend the school went to government schools. Overall, it government accounted for 3/4ths of all children attending schools" (Sankar, 2008). There is no quarrel about the fundamental problem. "Unless there is a strong effort to address the systemic issues of regular functioning of schools, teacher attendance, school supervision, accountability of educational administrators, delegation of powers to VEC/PRIs, teacher transfer & promotion policies and effective decentralisation of school management, the gains of SSA will be difficult to sustain."[44] It is more than a question of sustaining the gains of SSA. It is because these issues have not been satisfactorily addressed that the gains of SSA and its precursors have been far short of expectations.

Perhaps one should mention that India does not perform that well in cross-country comparisons on teacher-absenteeism in government schools (Rogers and Vagas, 2009). In a six-country study, 25 per cent of Indian teachers were absent from school, compared to 16 per cent in Bangladesh. Only Uganda performed worse at 27 per cent. These are absence rates from the school, rather than from the classroom. "Teacher absence ranged from a low of 15 per cent in Maharashtra, one of the most developed Indian states, to a high of 38 per cent in Bihar and 42 per cent in Jharkhand." In addition, "For example, in the state of Maharashtra, the absence rate was 15 per cent, about 60 per cent of teachers were not engaged in teaching when the survey teams arrived. By contrast, in Bihar and Jharkhand, where absence rates were about 40 per

44. Chapter on *Elementary Education*, Sankar (2008).

cent, only 25 to 26 per cent of teachers were actively teaching." This is fundamentally a problem of lack of accountability. One should not form the impression that there has been no improvement in accountability in government schools. But these tend to be sporadic and vary from state to state, district to district within a state and block to block within a district. Therefore, notwithstanding improvements here and there, there is no general template for reform. On 21st February 2005, at the first meeting of the Governing Council of the National Mission for SSA, the Prime Minister said, "One of the key ways of making government systems effective is to strengthen the Panchayats and Urban Local Bodies. For this, we need to build up the capacity of these decentralised bodies and empower their elected representatives. This is best done through effective devolution of funds. I note with satisfaction that this is the route taken by 'Sarva Shiksha Abhiyan', where more than 70 per cent of the funds are being spent through Panchayats and other school-based peoples' committees."[45] Decentralisation, devolution, accountability, transparency and third party scrutiny have not worked everywhere.

To return to the introductory section, one way to interpret the legislated right to elementary education is that the buck has been passed to the private sector, with the government abdicating its provisioning responsibility, though not its financial responsibility. This may be an uncharitable and extreme view, but there is a grain of truth in it. However, if *de facto* privatisation is the route, one should make it *de jure*, by removing entry barriers on the private sector, including those that prevent profit-making, and replacing licensing controls with appropriate regulation that is based on outcomes and not on inputs. This does not negate the possibility or necessity of subsidies through education vouchers and other means. In conclusion, let us remember that Vijay Kelkar's work is not about direct and indirect tax reform alone, or fiscal policy and finance commissions, or energy policy and infrastructure. In at least one interview[46], he has advocated education vouchers to increase efficiency of public expenditure in education.

45. *http://pmindia.nic.in/speech/content.asp?id=77*

46. *India Today*, 16 January 2006.

## References

Dahlman, Carl and Anuja Utz (2005). *India and the Knowledge Economy: Leveraging Strengths and Opportunities*. Washington DC: World Bank.

Dhir, Jhingran and Deepa Sankar (2009). "Addressing educational disparity, using district level education development indices for equitable resource allocations in India", *Policy Research Working Paper* No. 4955. June. World Bank.

Kelkar, Vijay (2002). "South Asia in 2020: Economic outlook", in Michael R. Chambers (ed.), *South Asia in 2020: Future Strategic Balances and Alliances*. Strategic Studies Institute.

———. (2006). "India: On the growth turnpike", in Raghbendra Jha (ed.), *The First Ten K.R. Narayanan Orations: Essays by Eminent Persons on the Rapidly Transforming Indian Economy*. Australian National University Press.

National University of Educational Planning and Administration (NUEPA) (2008). *Elementary Education in India, Progress towards UEE, Analytical Report 2006-07*.

Nilekani, Nandan (2008). *Imagining India: Ideas for the New Century*. Penguin and Allen Lane.

Panagariya, Arvind (2008). *India: The Emerging Giant*. Oxford University Press.

Planning Commission (2006). *Towards Faster and More Inclusive Growth, An Approach to the $11^{th}$ Five Year Plan*. New Delhi: Government of India. December. *http://planningcommission.nic.in/plans/planrel/app11_16jan.pdf*

———. (2008). *Eleventh Five Year Plan, 2007-2012*. Vol.II: *Social Sector*. New Delhi: Government of India and Oxford University Press.

Rogers, F. Halsey and Emiliana Vagas (2009). "No more cutting class? Reducing teacher absence and providing incentives for performance", *Policy Research Working Paper* No. 4847, February. World Bank.

Sankar, Deepa (2008). "What is the progress in elementary education participation in India during the last two decades? An Analysis using NSS education rounds", *Working Paper* No. 42112, South Asia Sector for Human Development. October. World Bank.

Wadhwa, Mayank (2001). *Licenses to Open a School: It's all About Money*. New Delhi: Centre for Civil Society.

# 11 Developing the Market for Land

Shubhashis Gangopadhyay

Land is becoming the most important factor in India's struggle to achieve a set of development goals—increased urbanisation, improved infrastructure, establishment of new industrial and commercial facilities and the setting up of special economic zones (SEZs). There are three (among others) legal institutions that affect land markets in India: (a) zoning, or land-use, laws, (b) terms and conditions under which land was "given" for setting up factories in the past and, of course, (c) government acquisition of privately owned land. In this paper, I will focus on the last aspect though all three could be important in particular cases. Land acquisition by government has become a major political issue after the experiences with the proposed, and finally aborted, Nano plant in Singur, West Bengal. It is important to take a look at this entire episode and the thought processes that went behind the actions of the various groups that got involved in the happenings in Singur.

However, I have a limited purpose in this paper. First, I want to describe an event that happened in another country and how that was tackled. Second, I want to compare it with what happened in Singur. Finally, I want to raise some issues that become important to resolve before land transactions can become more meaningfully smooth in a development context.

## Poletown and Singur

In 1981, General Motors decided to move its Cadillac plant away from the Detroit region and relocate it to a place in the south of the country. It made clear to the local government that the only way the Cadillac plant would be kept open was if the (elected) authorities of the city of Detroit made extensive infrastructure improvements. This prompted the cities of Detroit and Hamtramck to collaborate in a grand plan to bring industry back to what was perceived as a "dying" city.[1] This would keep the US automobile establishment in Detroit, arrest the drop in employment and generate tax revenues for the city allowing it to mobilise resources for other developmental and public projects.

General Motors and Detroit Mayor Coleman Young together formulated a plan under which the city would give land to General Motors who would then build a state-of-the-art plant, crossing the border with Hamtramck, which would include the neighbourhood of Poletown. This would generate direct jobs for 6000 workers and unspecified indirect jobs through the setting-up of ancillary production units that will be supplying inputs and parts to the automobile major.

The earmarked land was home to a number of different communities—Poles as well as Albanians, Yugoslavs, African-Americans, Yemenis and Filipinos. Some of the Poles have been there for generations, since the influx of Polish workers to the auto plants in the 1920s and 1930s, and even before. A total of 1300 homes and 600 businesses had to relocate for the plan to go through.

Since it was a "depressed" neighbourhood, many homeowners readily agreed. Of course, such a decision was also helped by the offer prices made by the government—starting at USD 6,000 and averaging about USD 13,000. In addition, there were two other sops offered by the government—an additional amount up to a maximum of USD 15,000 could be given if the new house bought by the household was more than the buyout price and a bonus of USD 3,500 to be given to households if they moved within a stipulated time. The government's cost of acquiring the property and developing it was estimated at USD 200 million but the price charged by the government to General Motors was USD 8 million.

However, importantly, not everyone was willing to move. The Poletown neighbourhood association and some other individuals filed suit in Wayne Circuit Court.

1. Recall Prime Minister Rajiv Gandhi describing Kolkata in the late eighties as a dying city!

Back in India, on May 18, 2006, the Tata group of companies announced that they were going to set up a car factory in West Bengal. Unlike the luxury car Cadillac proposed by General Motors in Detroit, Tata wanted to produce the globally cheapest "people's" car which was later christened as Nano.

According to a public statement by the state Industry Minister, five different sites were offered by the government to Tata, who chose Singur. Formal announcement of the land to be acquired was announced on July 27, 2006, by the Chief Minister and a 6-month deadline for the acquisition was set. The government also announced that it will avoid, as much as possible, land on which two crops were grown and will definitely not acquire triple-cropping land. The Singur block is not only situated on a major highway leading into Kolkata (the state capital), it was also a very fertile agricultural block.

The Tata automobile plant was to be the first major step in the re-industrialisation of the state. Over the years, industry has been leaving West Bengal citing labour union activities and lack of infrastructure as major concerns. The government which had just won a popular mandate was determined to woo industry back to the state as a means of generating employment and income.

According to the State Bureau of Applied Economics and Statistics, there were 10,437 hectares of farmland in Singur block, out of which on 9,099 hectares more than one crop was produced. Like in most parts of India, landholding was skewed towards small farmers. In Singur, 9020 farmers owned a total of 635 acres of the land that was to be acquired. Paddy was the major crop produced by the farmers.

According to government calculations, paddy fetched revenues of INR 9,940 per *bigha* of land. Given a cost of cultivation equal to INR 5,500, farmers earned an annual income of INR 4,400 from paddy cultivation. The government offered a compensation of INR 100,000 per *bigha* (roughly one-third of an acre). This price was apparently 30 per cent more than the market price prevailing in the region. If the buyout price was invested in safe assets (like bank fixed deposits), then the farmers would have obtained an annual return of INR 7,000 (interest of 7 per cent per annum). An additional 10 per cent of the price was to be given to those who surrendered their land within the stipulated period and without any dispute. Much of the land was cultivated by tenant farmers and the government offered a lumpsum payment of INR 250,000 to them. The company stated that the automobile factory would generate 2,000 jobs within the plant and 10,000 outside the plant through its ancillary industries. The company started fencing the land on December 1, 2006.

The first visit of the site by the company had taken place on May 25, 2006 when about a thousand villagers protested against land acquisition. At the time of the fencing, 347 affidavits opposing the transfer of land had been submitted and there was written consent for 586 acres only. Given that the target amount of land to be acquired was about a thousand acres, less than 60 per cent of it was voluntarily surrendered.

Three groups supported the transfer of land—absentee landowners, registered share-croppers and those losing a part of their land. This was largely because of the policies that the ruling party (in power since 1977) had earlier initiated in which, tenant cultivators, once registered, could not be evicted as long as they shared a government-determined proportion (50 per cent) of the value of their produce with the landowner. The government offer to buy out the land benefitted the landowners who got full value of their land as against 50 per cent of the revenue from the land in perpetuity. Tenants, similarly got value for an asset that they really did not own!

Three groups opposed the land transfer—unregistered share-croppers, daily wage earners associated with agriculture and those losing all their land. For these groups, it was a loss of livelihood with the first two not being compensated at all. The government was quick to respond to the grievances of the non-registered share-croppers and offered to give them the same compensation as the registered ones. However, being unregistered, and hence without records, there was a strong feeling that only activists and sympathisers of the ruling party would benefit as unregistered tenants.

By the beginning of February 2007, 700 locals had been inducted as factory guards by WBIDC (West Bengal Industrial Development Corporation), 2,792 as daily wage labourers had been hired for civil work in and around the factory site and a couple of rudimentary workshops were set up to train women in sewing (to stitch uniforms) and the men in elementary machine work. Once again, the people who got left out of these jobs were the erstwhile agricultural labourers who had not owned land or been tenants (registered or otherwise).

While there were similarities between what happened in Singur (a state ruled by a party with strong communist affiliations) and in Poletown (where the ruling party strongly believed in capitalism and free enterprise), the major point of departure was in the way those opposed to the land transfer behaved. Recall that in Poletown the residents' association filed a suit in the local court; in Singur, the people took to violent street protests. It is important to know why.

## Laws Governing Government Acquisition

The original Indian Constitution guaranteed the right to property as a fundamental right. As early as 1951, immediately after the adoption of the Constitution, the Parliament clashed with the judiciary on this matter. The first order of business in the newly formed nation was the promulgation of a number of laws and statutes aimed at land reforms and the rights of tenants. Obviously, the landowners went to court. The courts opposed the land reform laws declaring them unconstitutional on the basis that owning property was a fundamental right guaranteed in the Constitution.

The Parliament responded by putting all land related matters into the Ninth Schedule of the Constitution. The Ninth Schedule, introduced as the First Amendment as early as 1951, listed the matters on which Parliament could pass laws without any judicial review. Once land related laws became a part of this Schedule, it was not possible for any one to challenge them in court on the grounds that they were against the guarantee of the fundamental rights of a citizen.

The next milestone in land laws came during the two years of 1971 and 1972. Parliament gave itself the absolute right to amend all parts of the Constitution including the part that guaranteed the fundamental rights of the citizens. Hence, disputes regarding land reforms and land acquisitions by the government could no longer come under judicial review.

Almost all countries allow the concept of "eminent domain". This gives the government the right to seize private property for public use in exchange for fair market value. Thus, the acquisition of land by the state for public purposes is a general phenomenon. This allows the building of roads, for example, which are used by the general public. It also allows the building of dams for power generation that usually leads to moving people out of their current possession of land. The issue then is what can and cannot be considered as public use. For roads, or the provision of public goods, public use is easy to understand. However, what happened in both Singur and Poletown was the take-over by the state of private property to transfer it to another private party—General Motors in Poletown and Tata in Singur.

A case came up in the Indian Supreme Court in 1971 where a property owner challenged the acquisition of his land by a state government to build a factory. In the first instance, the land was earmarked for the setting up of a public sector unit. However, for various reasons, the public sector unit could not be set up and the land was given to the private sector to develop it. The challenge in court was that this is not for public use but for private gain. The court's position was that public purpose was to be decided by the legislature. This was enshrined in law by the amended Land Acquisition Act of 1984 whereby government could transfer private land from one to another party once the new activity, or project, could be justified as serving a public purpose. The year is 1984, soon after the Poletown judgement which was a very similar precedent but being set by the law courts instead of the legislature.

## Poletown Revisited

In Poletown, the challenge was to the use of the power of eminent domain to acquire one's property to transfer it to another private entity to bolster the economy. The contention of the plaintiffs was that General Motors was the primary beneficiary of this transfer. In any economic activity, new value is generated and extracted by all those participating in the activity. This includes the government which earns additional revenue. This is what markets do, for commodities, services and assets and hence, the contention was that one does not need the government to affect such transfers of assets. The defendants' contention was that the acquisition was to create an industrial site which will generate employment, economic activity and add to the state coffers. The benefit to General Motors was purely incidental.

Even though the court found for the defendant, there was a dissenting judgement by one of the judges. The dissent is worth recounting. His point was that this finding for the defendant was a case of the end justifying the means.

In Michigan (state where Detroit is situated), there have been enough instances of acquisition of private land for public use. They have been justified as attempts to improve the "instruments of commerce" and through this process various highways, railroads and canals have been built. The dissenting judge maintained that there were three characteristics of such acquisitions: "(a) public necessity of the extreme sort, (b) continuing accountability to the public, and (c) selection of land according to facts of independent public significance." He felt that these conditions were not satisfied for the General Motors automobile plant.

Private property is an essential concept in market driven, rule of law economies. Thus, any suspension of such property rights must have a solid argument. One must be able to argue that the objectives of a market economy will be better served in a specific instance if private property rights are suspended. The dissenting judge maintained that while there is a sound theoretical argument in certain cases for the involuntary transfer of private ownership to public ownership, there are no sound arguments for the government forcing a private party to give up land to another private. In other words, why should the government act as a non-market intermediary in what is an essentially private transaction and can be left to the land market to accomplish?

Moreover, for the sake of argument, suppose that the creation of new employment is a desired public purpose goal. Who is going to implement this? If at some time in the future, General Motors in its bid to maximise profit, decides to shed labour, will the government hold it liable because it had promised 6000 new jobs? If not, who satisfies the stated public purpose of increased employment? If, on the other hand, the government holds General Motors accountable, it will interfere in its market activity and this is against the basic tenet of a market economy based on free enterprise. In other words, the position is either one of zero accountability or, one where the government becomes an interventionist entity.

Of course, the dissenting judge made a much stronger judgement: "with this case the Court has subordinated a constitutional right to private corporate interests."

The dissenting judge's observations were important in a number of ways. The 1982 judgement opened the floodgates. It gave a huge incentive to local governments to use eminent domain to take over land from private parties in the name of development. It encouraged companies and developers to make wild claims of what would happen after the take-over. Indeed, the Poletown project itself did not live up to expectations. Many claim that, in the ultimate analysis, it destroyed more jobs than it created.

In a quite unprecedented move, on July 30, 2004, the Michigan Supreme Court reversed its Poletown decision. It said that for forceful acquisition by government, it is not enough to argue that an entity's profit maximisation contributed to the health of the general economy, an argument that was essentially made in the Poletown case.

At the same time, the Michigan Supreme Court also decided another important eminent domain case. In this case, the Detroit Wayne County Stadium Authority forcefully acquired the property of a certain Ms. Frida Alibri promising her that it would not be given to a private party. However, the property was transferred to a private corporation. Alibri filed to get her property back and the court upheld her complaint. Recall that this is essentially similar to the 1971 case in the Indian Supreme Court where the plaintiff objected to land being taken for a public sector unit and then given to a private corporation. It is uncanny that there should be two near identical cases in the two largest democracies concerning the government's ability to forcefully acquire land. In India, everything went in favour of the government and against the private citizen. In the US, while initially the state was given precedence, the position was finally reversed and eminent domain was not allowed to be used to transfer land from one private entity to another using the argument of "public purpose".

## Is a Third Party Necessary?

The question that still remains is whether we need a third party—like the government—to effect land transfer between private parties when such transfers will lead to overall development but where the new activities are not owned and operated by the state. Note that this involves not only land for new industry, but also the acquisition of land by municipal bodies to be handed over to private owners for residential and/or commercial use in the drive towards increased urbanisation. In short, is it possible to find a pure market solution to the problem wherein, suppliers voluntarily surrender their property to the buyer in exchange for monetary compensations?

The important aspect of such land transactions is that there is usually a large number of small sellers (farmers in Singur and homeowners in Poletown) and one big buyer (General Motors in Poletown and Tata in Singur). Another major characteristic of such transfers of property is that little additional value is generated if all current owners do not voluntarily sell their land. In other words, there is a certain degree of lumpiness—half the land has a value that is much less than half of what all the land could generate. So, to extract the full value, all the potential suppliers of the land must voluntarily surrender their land to the bidder.

There are at least three reasons why market-driven voluntary transactions may not work. First, since the transactions have to be voluntary and this is a one-off sale (in the sense that parcels of these lands are not routinely bought and sold), the buyer has to negotiate with each landowner the price for the land he, or she, owns. The time and effort spent by the buyer to carry out these negotiations, referred to in the literature as transaction costs, can become prohibitively high. Second, the negotiations are between small owners with limited resources and a big company with vast amount of resources. These resources are not simply financial but include real estate lawyers, accountants and networks of people. This gives rise to great disparities in what the literature terms as bargaining strength between the suppliers and the buyer. This may result in sellers getting a much lower price than what they could get if the buyer was similar (in their ownership of resources) to the sellers. In other words, one may require an agency which negotiates on behalf of all the farmers together so that the disparity in bargaining strength can be mitigated. Thus, instead of multilateral transactions that would happen in the market place, one may require bilateral negotiations where an agency or association of sellers interacts with the buyer.

The third problem is a bit more complicated and is referred to in the literature as the "hold-up" problem. Suppose that there are three identical and adjacent plots of land owned by A, B and C respectively. Each of the current owners, given their use of the land, values the plot at 100. Some public authority wants to build a road from one extreme end of these plots to the other extreme end. Once the road is built, it will generate a value of 350. Thus, if all the three plots of land were bought by the authority, the value generated would be greater than the current value being generated (300=100+100+100) from these assets. For argument's sake, suppose that the buyer has already bought the land from A and B, C is the last person with whom the buyer needs to negotiate. Suppose the price paid to A and B for the land was 110. A and B voluntarily transferred their land because 110 is greater than 100.

So, when the buyer goes to C, the buyer has already spent 220. If the negotiations with C break down, the buyer would lose 220 because an unfinished road, regardless of what proportion of it is unfinished, gives zero value. If C is aware of this then C is in an excellent bargaining position. For suppose C makes a take it or leave it offer of 200; i.e., if the buyer pays at least 200, C will sell, otherwise not. The buyer has two options—to accept and pay 200 for C's land or, reject C's offer and not build the road. If the buyer accepts, the buyer gets the value of 350 from the finished road at a price 420 (110+110+200). This means the buyer makes a loss of 70 (420–350). If the buyer reject's C's offer, the buyer gets zero value from the unfinished road but has already paid 220 to A and B, the buyer's loss is then 220. In both cases the buyer is making a loss and it makes sense for the buyer to choose that option which minimises the loss. And so, the buyer should accept C's offer. A simple generalisation of the argument immediately leads us to the following conclusion: an aware C should charge something as close to 350 as possible for his/her land. For example, an offer price of 349 if accepted means a loss of 219 (350 – (110 + 110 + 349)) to the buyer; if rejected, it means a loss of 220, which is a greater loss than that of 219.

This is sufficient to understand the "hold-up" problem. The last seller always has a great advantage in all voluntary transactions. Since there is no reason to believe that A, or B, or C is any less smart than the other, each will want to be the last seller putting forth the standard refrain that I will sell if others sell. This will mean that negotiations will not even start, leave alone being completed!

Thus, a pure market solution may not work, or be desirable, given these three problems—high transaction costs, disparate bargaining strength and the ability of the sellers to hold up all negotiations.

Interestingly enough, this is not a unique problem. Similar issues arise when a publicly traded company is being acquired. When an acquirer wants to take over a company, h/she needs to buy up at least 50 per cent of the outstanding shares. The problem again is two-fold—large numbers of small share holders and unless majority shares are obtained by the acquirer h/she cannot generate the value from the take-over. Again, we have high transaction costs (large number of small share holders), disparate bargaining strength (small share holders *versus* a large acquiring company) and a hold-up. The hold-up problem is slightly different here because not surrendering the shares is the best strategy for the small share holder; remember that in the land case "not selling" is not the best strategy but "selling last" is. Nevertheless, in both cases transactions do not take place. In the take-over of publicly traded companies, markets and institutions that govern them (the stock exchanges and corporate governance laws) have addressed and solved the problems through the mechanism of the "take-over code". The obvious question to ask is why we cannot develop similar procedures, sanctioned by law, to enable transactions in land.

# 12 A Programme to Accelerate Infrastructure Spend in India through PPPs

Hari Sankaran

## Overview

It is now accepted that India's continued economic performance is predicated on significant investments being made in the building of its infrastructure. While estimates abound, the magnitude of investment, across an array of infrastructure sectors, has been variously estimated at between US$500 billion to US$1.5 trillion. This paper seeks to develop a case for a more holistic and integrated approach to infrastructure development so as to link such spends to specific socioeconomic outcomes. In the absence of such an approach, there is a real danger that the significant positive externalities associated with economic growth would be dampened whilst exacerbating its negative externalities.

If actualised, this quantum of investment would radically address issues of inclusiveness and sustainability; transform the economy and provide a significant boost to India's deep and rich tradition of trade and entrepreneurship; and, force more effective governance by aligning public policy, institutional development, and on-the-ground delivery mechanisms. In the process, issues related to public indebtedness and systemic efficiency would also be favourably impacted.

I quote Dr. Vijay Kelkar: "For coming decades, water, environment and urban infrastructure are going to be the key binding constraints on India's growth ambition. To remove these binding constraints, we will require large investments to accelerate country's march towards high quality growth."

It is the central thesis of this paper that these quantum of infrastructure spends are eminently realisable within defined time frames, provided a more strategic, outcome-oriented, and pragmatic approach to PPP is adopted. In essence, the paper argues that India's rapid urbanisation provides the country a potential urban dividend that can form the bedrock of a PPP programme for infrastructure improvement. It goes without saying that, as a corollary, poor infrastructure services will exacerbate the current urban situation with increasingly glaring socio-economic distortions.

Over the past decade, significant progress on the legislative and policy fronts have been made to support PPP interventions across sectors. These changes provide a sufficiently robust platform to devise intervention strategies in urban areas. What is lacking presently is clarity on the principles on which implementation should be structured on a systemic basis, the platforms through which multiple parts and layers (as would inevitably be required) of government can come together to support such interventions, and the nature of financial support that the government should provide to actualise such a strategy. This paper provides a perspective to (try) bring clarity on some of these issues.

The strategy to exploit the potential of urbanisation is built on three axioms: first, that the cost of development must include both direct and indirect costs associated with such development. Second, that land for urbanisation must be treated as a scarce resource. And third, that the development must be socio-eco-environmentally sustainable. As this paper will demonstrate, the urban dividend refers to the significant improvements in productivity and quality of life that could be achieved if a focused strategy of "Housing for All" were implemented along with infrastructure on an integrated basis. In essence, PPP investments of US$800 billion could potentially be realised if such a programme were implementable over a 10-year period with a positive impact on the exchequer matrix.

## Leveraging Affordable Housing to Improve Urban Infrastructure Services

The rapid pace of urbanisation, largely on account of the increasing migration from rural to urban centres in search of livelihood, has resulted in a severe mismatch between demand and supply of urban housing in general, and affordable housing in particular. The pace of migration will continue apace as long as urban incomes grow six times faster than rural incomes in India.

At present, 99 per cent of the housing shortage of 24.7 million as at the end of the 10th Plan pertains to the economically weaker sections (EWS) and low income groups (LIG) sectors. Given the fact that 26.7 per cent of the total poor in the country live in urban areas, the issue of affordability assumes critical significance. In terms of numbers, 26.7 per cent of the total poor implies 80.7 million persons or about one-fourth of the country's total urban population. The shortage is expected to significantly increase during the Eleventh Five Year Plan.

The Jawaharlal Nehru National Urban Renewal Mission (JNNURM) supports 63 cities (7 mega cities, 28 metro cities and 28 capital cities and towns of historical/religious importance) across the country to help implement City Development Plans (CDPs) that cover infrastructure gaps in water, sanitation, sewerage, drainage and roads and deficiencies in housing and basic services. In addition to these 63 cities addressed through the JNNURM, urban infrastructure and slums are also being addressed in the remaining non-Mission cities through the Urban Infrastructure Development Scheme for Small and Medium Towns (UIDSSMT) and Integrated Housing and Slum Development Programme (IHSDP).

The Basic Services for the Urban Poor (BSUP) seeks to provide a garland of seven entitlements/services through IHSDP—security of tenure, affordable housing, water, sanitation, health, education and social security—in low income settlements in the 63 Mission cities and in towns/ cities other than Mission cities. Despite these missions and programmes, very limited progress has been seen on the ground in relation to affordable housing despite its relevance and dire need.

The Government of India approved the National Urban Housing and Habitat Policy (NUHHP) (2007) with a goal to achieve affordable housing for all. One of the principal strategies of NUHHP (2007) is to use urban planning towards creating an enabling framework for affordable housing. The NUHHP states the following mechanisms:

(a) Encourage state governments, urban local bodies, development authorities to periodically update their master plans and zoning plans which should, *inter alia* adequately provide for housing and basic services for the urban poor.

(b) Promote balanced urban-rural planning by following the regional planning approach, take the whole state/UT as a region, under the town and country planning acts in the states.

(c) Plan Mass Rapid Transit Systems (MRTS) at the city metropolitan planning area and sub-region levels.

## Node-centric Regional Development Plans

(a) The GoI has been actively encouraging states to submit proposals, on a priority basis, to establish new nodes in the proximity of existing urban centres that cater to its requirement of affordable housing needs. New nodes around existing urban centres with adequate infrastructure and connectivity have become the order of the day. It has been estimated that over 500 new urban nodes would be needed to cater to both the backlog and future demand in the country.

(b) In the node-centric regional development plans, new urban nodes will need to be master planned, designed and implemented on an integrated basis. Affordable housing will need to include all infrastructure including physical, social such as hospital and medical services, education and civic services. To provide economies of scale, each node optimally should provide housing and associated services for a minimum of 200,000 families on a minimum land parcel of 2500 acres.

(c) These new urban nodes would need to supplement efforts in existing urban centres and leverage on its proximity to such centres to achieve sustainability. By integrating public transportation and connectivity systems as an integral part of the new node, it will also augment and supplement the capacity of facilities in the existing node.

(d) In the medium to long term, these nodes will integrate and become a long urban continuum as envisioned by the NUHHP. In the absence of this scale and pace of development, it would be difficult to meaningfully address the urban challenges faced by the country, its associated housing shortage or achieve the economies of scale required to make it truly affordable.

(e) The NUHHP (2007) clearly states that it seeks to enhance the spotlight on 'habitat' with a 'regional planning approach' as well as further deepen the role of Government as a 'facilitator' and 'regulator'. While the NUHHP (2007) underscores the importance of PPP in this perspective, it does not spell out how to strategise PPP at the programmatic, project or process levels. There is a need to quickly develop, implement and support operational formats and mechanisms in this direction.

## Affordable Housing and Sustainability

(a) The environmental impacts of affordable housing provided on an accelerated basis to this scale are going to be substantive. It would lead to significant depletion of resources (in terms of extraction, transportation and use) as well as pose challenges in the treatment and disposal of wastes and residues. Unless mainstreamed, it would simply not be possible to mitigate these adverse environmental impacts.

(b) Mainstreaming will require specific incentives to bring in new technologies and materials, innovative methods of building construction and new systems of building management. This will, in turn, significantly influence lifestyles of people, stimulate new markets and result in technology transfers.

(c) In this context, strategic partnership with the private sector becomes critical as a means of augmenting capacity of government and in channelising available resources to meet a national priority. Whilst the government needs to ensure that there is flexibility of engagement, it must also ensure that the programme is process-driven involving all key stakeholders. In this context, the case of the Liverpool ULB and the Ministry of Defence in the UK, discussed later in this paper, shed light on issues of stakeholder participation and process management.

(d) In any case, the PPP contracts will need to be evolved surrounding "affordable housing" for implementing and managing renewable energy based solutions, supply of eco-sensitive construction materials and fixtures and operating intelligent building management systems. Figure 12.1 outlines the key ingredients to balanced development of the regional nodes with low ecological footprint resulting in affordable housing with sustainability.

**Figure 12.1**

*Multi-Sectoral Interventions needed to Reach the Goal of Affordable Housing with Sustainability*

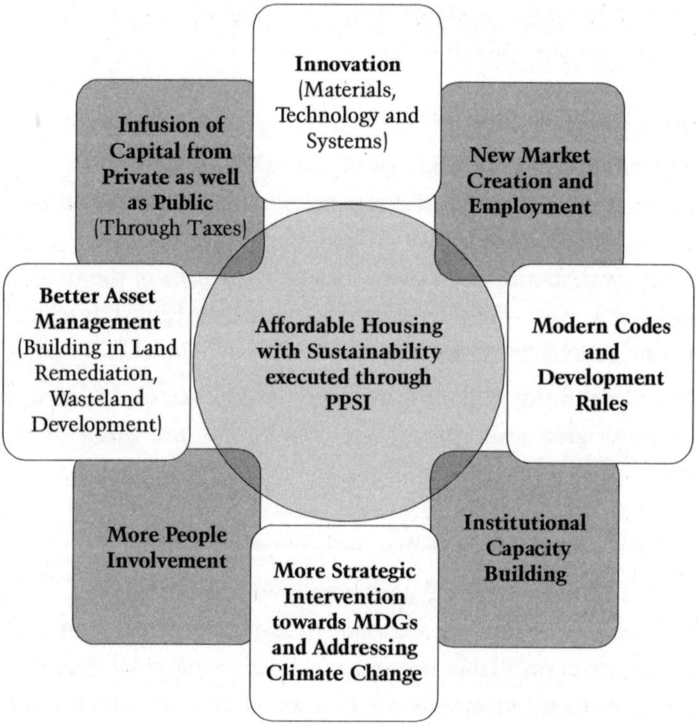


(e) There will also be a need to infuse sustainability considerations in the existing missions and programmes that are aimed to catalyse and promote affordable housing. These include the National Slum Development Programme (NSDP) and the Swarna Jayanti Shahari Rozgar Yojana (SJSRY) that was designed to provide gainful employment to the urban poor by encouraging the setting up of self-employment ventures and provision of wage employment opportunities for families below poverty line in urban areas. The Two Million Housing Programme (TMHP) and the Valmiki Ambedkar Awas Yojana (VAMBAY) aimed at providing subsidies for construction of housing and sanitation for urban slum dwellers may also be examined in this context. Urban Development Plan Formulation and Implementation Guidelines (UDPFI) may also be reviewed and strengthened in this direction.

(f) The benefits of such inclusive consideration could be far-reaching. These will include: (i) infusion of capital from international investors, (ii) catalyse innovations in materials, technology and management systems leading to new market creation and employment, (iii) capacity building of institutions and establishment of modern codes of development rules, (iv) more people involvement in the "process", and (v) creation of assets (e.g. by recovering degraded land) and their improved management. In addition, affordable housing with sustainability using PPP frameworks will greatly assist Government of India to meet the Millennium Development Goals (MDGs) and reduce carbon emissions. Figure 12.2 graphically depicts the strategic benefits of operating an affordable housing programme by mainstreaming sustainability.

**Figure 12.2**

*Strategic Benefits of Operating Affordable Housing Programme while Mainstreaming Sustainability*

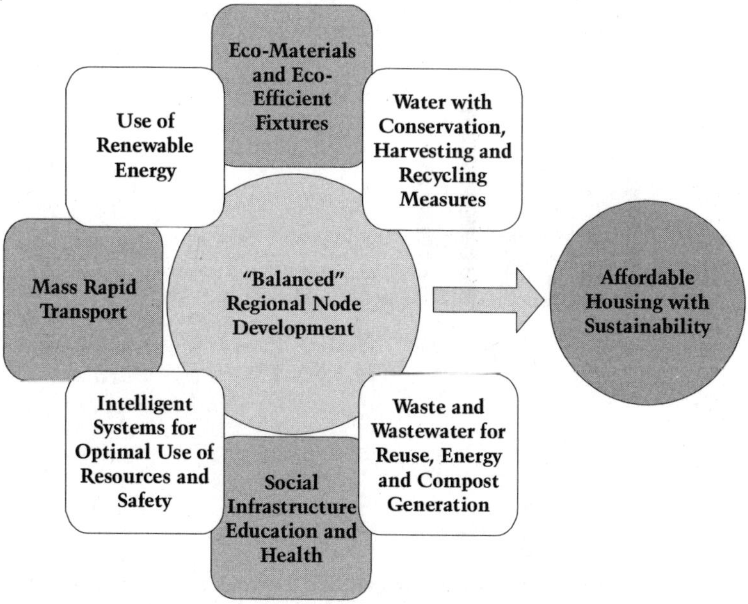

## Reaping the Urban Dividend

Essentially, the growth of any economy depends on the growth in factor inputs and such as labour and capital, the growth in productivity and entrepreneurship which exploits market opportunities. In all these areas, India is indeed very favourably placed today. As far as human capital is concerned, in the coming decades, India will have world's largest working population and given our emphasis on education, we will have increasingly better skilled human capital. People are calling this phenomenon as "demographic dividend". This factor is cited by many economists, including Dr. Vijay Kelkar.

(1) Notwithstanding the significant challenges faced by urban bodies, the extent of investment that has flown through PPPs in India's urban infrastructure is miniscule.

(2) Figure 12.3 clearly shows PPPs in the South Asian region at a much lower intensity compared to other regions. The trend of PPP in the South Asian region is however increasing with the dominant sectors being energy and telecom followed by transport.

**Figure 12.3**

*PPP Infrastructure Investments in Developing Countries by Region, 1990–2006*[1]

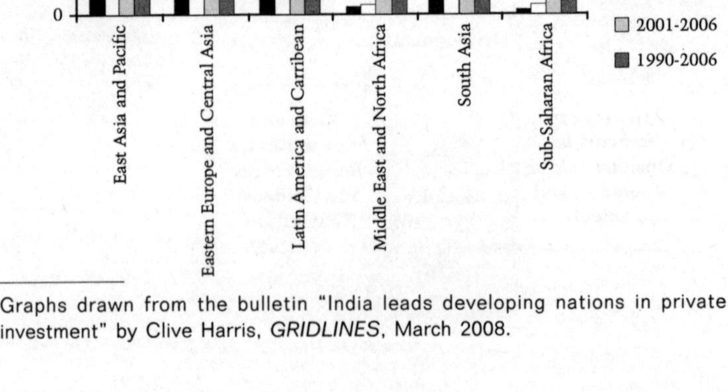


1. Graphs drawn from the bulletin "India leads developing nations in private sector investment" by Clive Harris, *GRIDLINES*, March 2008.

(3) The 2006 statistics on PPP as analysed by the World Bank (2006) in India shows that there were at least 86 PPP projects for which a contract was awarded and underway. The estimated project cost of these PPPs was Rs. 339.5 billion. Over 70 per cent of these PPPs (by number of projects) were in the roads sector. The other transport sectors have seen much fewer projects, with 8 ports (4 major and 4 minor ports), 2 airports and 2 rail projects underway. In the urban infrastructure sector, 11 PPP projects were awarded, with 8 solid waste management, 2 water and sanitation and 1 bus terminal projects.

(4) Figure 12.4 shows the sectoral distribution of PPP projects in India by number whilst Figure 12.5 shows the sectoral distribution by investment.

**Figure 12.4**

*No. of PPP Projects*

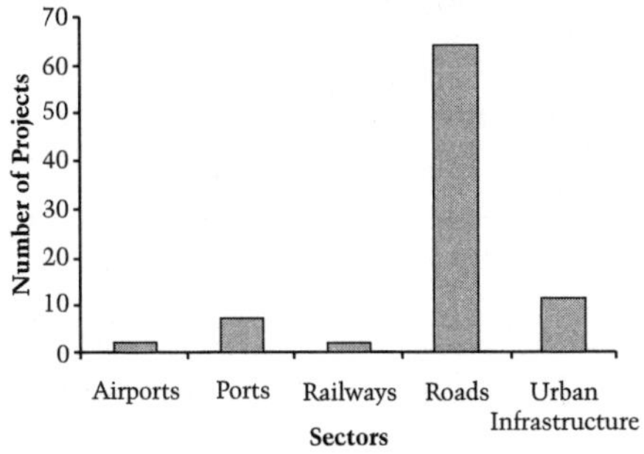


**Figure 12.5**

*PPPs by Investment*

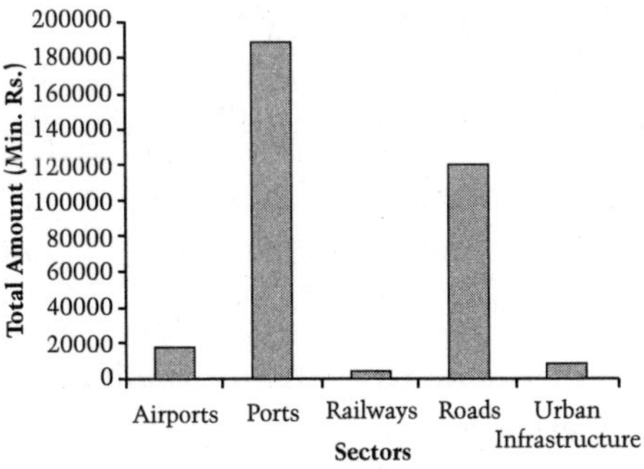

(5) Ports, with a much larger average size of investments, account for 56 per cent of the total investment. Urban infrastructure, where PPPs have perhaps one of the largest potential, is less than 1 per cent of the total. It is evident from the foregoing that a far greater impetus will require to be provided by government if PPPs are indeed to play a more credible and meaningful role in addressing India's urban housing and infrastructure shortage.

(6) To reap the urban dividend, government will need to consider the following measures to give a boost to the entry of the private sector in taking up the development and implementation of new nodes:

    (a) Declare a national mission for 100 million affordable homes across India over a 10-year period. States that wish to participate will contribute land in the proximity of existing urban centres. The mission will design, develop and implement the node through a PPP framework.

    (b) Contiguous blocks of land will need to be made available on terms and conditions that ensure the affordability of the housing to be provided in the new node. Speedy acquisition under relevant state government laws would be essential. In this connection, the Town Planning (TP) scheme of the Government of Gujarat must be reviewed as a possible framework to acquire land without compensation.

    (c) Declare the selected node as a priority sector project. Its approval as a priority sector project would be determined on the basis of the employment, income and housing it provides below median income families.

    (d) Allow the benefits under JNNURM and other schemes, such as the UDSSMT, available for such projects, including for utilities like water supply, sewerage, transport, etc.

    (e) Allow specialised machinery imported for construction purposes to be allowed as a "Project Import" with associated duty concession.

    (f) Set up an empowered group to facilitate requisite clearances from different state government agencies on a priority basis and to monitor progress with a view to ensuring speedy implementation.

(g) Declare each node as a special area under relevant state and Central legislations to enable the designated agencies/SPV/JV to plan and implement the approved node on a fast track basis and to operate and maintain the node on an ongoing basis.

(h) Establish mass transport solutions to the existing urban centres as an integral part of the master plan of the node.

(i) Consider special, but significant, fiscal incentives to encourage migration, investment and employment to and within nodes: income tax (individual and corporate), indirect taxes, etc.

(7) The infrastructure sector is a difficult sector for establishing project bankability with returns predicated over an extended time frame. Given the foregoing, existing fiscal benefits need to be extended to improve the financial attractiveness of projects to potential investors and lenders.

(8) Perhaps, uniquely, India has an opportunity of making its growth inclusive through a mission node approach to affordable housing and infrastructure, through a PPP framework. The successful implementation of new nodes around existing urban centres with the full complement of infrastructure services and connectivity would serve to accelerate growth on an inclusive basis. It would also serve as a powerful tool to reform existing urban local bodies: as an instance, the new nodes would provide GIS-based legally vetted title to land and property, etc.

## The Exchequer Matrix

The PPP approach to housing and infrastructure builds on the significant progress that has been made in legislation and policy frameworks in this regard. If there is a lacuna, it is because this carefully crafted enabling environment is not resulting in an adequate realisation of projects on the ground, thereby undermining the momentum of growth. At a more insidious level, the non-delivery of projects is eroding the case for inclusiveness, environmental and social sustainability, and the potential leveraging of budgetary resources.

From a programmatic point of view, the case for "Housing for All" provides an elegant solution to strategically structure a PPP model and leverage budgetary resources:

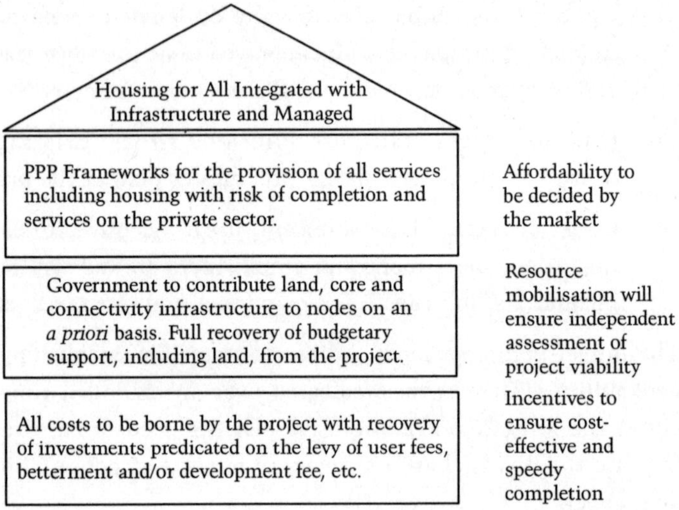


The broad ratio of project cost between land, core and total project cost, including connectivity and building infrastructure, works out to a rough ratio of 10:20:70. In other words, to kick-start the process, government will be required to contribute to at least 30 per cent of the total project cost by way of land, core and connectivity infrastructure. Thereafter, the programme should be self-sustaining with return cash flows adequate to recompense the government for the initial tranche of funding and with enough surplus to contribute to other projects.

There is a widely held belief that the test of a successful PPP is the extent to which it leverages budgetary resources. In itself, such a test would appear perfectly reasonable and valid. However, in computing leverage there is a need for a more considered approach: for instance, exempting infrastructure projects from the levy of duties may result in a reduction in current tax receipts. However, the fact that such projects come into existence on the back of such incentives would unleash a significant stream of externalities which, if discounted to present value would wholly justify such exemptions: maximising such streams is rarely an explicit criteria in the design of projects, especially on a life cycle cost basis. Neither is minimising timelines for project completion assigned importance.

The BOT (Build-Operate-Transfer)-Annuity approach of the NHAI (National Highways Authority of India) is an excellent example of how government can minimise its liabilities over the life of the concession by implementing projects on a PPP basis whilst retaining the rights to collect tolls subsequently as traffic grows:

(a) In a BOT project, the concessionaire assumes traffic risk and as a result, all the revenue upsides from the growth in tolled traffic. In an annuity project, the concessionaire finances the creation of the assets and its maintenance for the period of the concession but does not take traffic risk. The concessionaire assumes project completion risks and the government assumes revenue risk. From a government perspective, project cost is capped with liabilities commencing only after the asset comes into existence (revenue realisable) to the specified standard.

(b) By definition, where a BOT on a tolled basis is feasible, annuity model would be even more attractive, from a budgetary point of view, as it provides for the upside to be captured entirely by government. Where BOT on a tolled basis is not feasible, an annuity approach designed strategically provides the best chance for such projects to be implemented with a cap on costs. If the design of the project is well-conceived, government should recover its investment through the socio-economic gains of the project over the life of the concession.

(c) As any liability on government commences only after the project is commissioned, the risk of project completion is minimised. Appropriate safeguards in the concession will ensure a superior outcome in quality of asset created and/or service levels. Despite the foregoing, there is a continued reluctance in government to adopt an annuity-based approach.

(d) Post-commissioning, it is expected that government would auction a basket of annuity projects to secure back-to-back guarantees to back-stop annuity payments. In the process, the fiscal impact of the annuity structure should be minimised.

The annuity model (and variations thereof) provides a very attractive method of attracting the private sector to build infrastructure assets and to work with government in maximising the impact of the project from a socio-economic developmental point of view. In the "Housing for All" programme, it is recommended that the government consider an annuity approach to land, core and connectivity infrastructure.

In the provision of core and connectivity infrastructure in the "Housing for All" programme, for instance, the annuity approach provides interesting possibilities to strategically design the PPP programme:

(a) The concept of a betterment charge is well-established. A whole range of infrastructure service improvements could be conceptualised on an annuity basis where the recovery of such investments is predicated on a betterment and/or user pay charge levied and collected by and/or on behalf of government.

(b) The introduction of partnership forums, such as the Liverpool model, discussed more fully in a subsequent section of this paper, involving community representatives could be used to prioritise investments, establish service standards and link these with the levy of betterment charges.

(c) Technology permits government to introduce a targeted and progressive pricing strategy linked to the delivery of services. Equally, a more rational zoning and property tax system based on GIS platform would witness a significant increase in the revenues of ULB.

(d) It is thus feasible for government to conceive of infrastructure interventions in urban areas which significantly improve infrastructure service on a user pay or annuity basis whilst concurrently putting in place frameworks that improve revenue buoyancy.

An interesting case in point is the implementation of a high-speed metro. In itself, such a project is not commercially viable. The only exception, to date, is the Hong Kong Metro where even a cursory examination of its balance sheet reveals that its viability is entirely due to its real estate development activities rather than on its fare box or advertising revenues.

If a development charge were to be levied on all new construction within a defined "zone of influence" along the metro line, a predictable source of revenue could be generated for the ULB to backstop its annuity commitment to the concessionaire over the fare box and advertising revenues. Where sufficient new construction in the corridor is expected, such a strategy would suffice. Where such developments are not expected, it would be interesting to explore the possibility of increasing FSI/FAR (floor space index/floor area ratio) where the additional FSI/FAR is subject to the development charge. In any case, master planners have recommended an average FSI/FAR of 3 across urban agglomerations which should release significant resources for infrastructure spend whilst bringing huge housing stock into the market, thereby reducing overall costs.

The logic for the increased FSI/FAR rests on the case of improved transportation and infrastructure services which, in turn, would allow for higher densities in urban areas. Further sophistications could also be added to such an approach; for instance, annuities could be reduced upfront by granting development rights which are transferable, etc.

Transportation corridors also provide interesting possibilities to rationalise revenue administration of a ULB as also enable below grade channels along the right of way to provide other urban infrastructure services. Perhaps most interestingly, this approach provides a real tool for ULBs to address issues of pricing on existing services as it can be linked to additional development rights and to improved service standards.

By adopting an annuity-based approach, government would be able to discharge a large portion of its obligations under a "Housing for All" programme through the private sector: in other words, the government will use the private sector strategically at multiple levels to maximise budgetary leverage. In the process, it is estimated that the overall impact of the "Housing for All" programme will be positive on the exchequer matrix. Far more importantly, the foregoing approach internalises costs that are typically borne by the government whilst sharing the upsides which is almost entirely excluded from the purview of the public exchequer in the present context.

Income multipliers have been estimated by a large number of experts: for the housing sector, it ranges between 4 and 7 depending on definitions and the activities included:

(a) Thus, every Rs. 100 per annum spent on affordable housing (including infrastructure as defined above) will generate a minimum of Rs. 400 per annum in terms of incremental income. Similar estimates have been worked out for employment multipliers.

(b) Assuming a tax to GDP ratio of 8 to 10 per cent, this would translate into additional tax revenues of around Rs. 40 per annum.

(c) The implementation of an accelerated programme of affordable "Housing for All" through the concept of node-based development could double gross tax receipts. If the employment multiplier is taken into account, wherein a percentage of those who move into a new node are assumed to enter the formal workforce, the impact would be even more dramatic.

## Perspective on Financing

The significant unmet demand for affordable housing in India along with an associated need for improved quality of infrastructure provides a robust platform to support the financing of such a programme on a PPP basis. Indeed, India is unique in terms of the scale of its urban population that needs to accommodated over the next 25 years. No other country in the world will have the absolute densities of urban population over the next 25 years as India will.

With improving per capita income levels, the proportion of urban population willing to invest in affordable housing is increasing significantly every year. The creation of new urban nodes caters to this growing unmet demand: with high population densities, it is feasible to amortise the cost of land and core infrastructure across a large span of built-up area, thereby reducing the ultimate cost to the homeowner to a reasonable level. Equally, affordable housing with on-site urban amenities would be largely self-financed. The institutional markets, instruments and frameworks to support such a programme are largely in place.

To reduce costs further, measures to extend the tenor of financing for capital-intensive infrastructure assets (such as mass transportation, water, etc.) would be critical. India's urban densities provide an opportunity to amortise costs at a point in time; extending the tenor of financing for housing and infrastructure further would assist in improving the case for affordability. Together, these measures would hugely incentivise home ownership and infrastructure development.

In the current market, maximum tenor of financing is around 15 years. Multilaterals, with significantly limited appetite for greenfield project risks, may extend tenors up to 20 years. As against these tenors, infrastructure assets have design lives in excess of 50 years. There is thus an argument to develop appropriate mechanisms to extend the tenor of debt to finance such projects. New instruments such as take-out financing, mezzanine financing, and a host of other innovations have begun to enter the Indian market. Measures to further widen and deepen the financing framework in this direction will clearly impact the "Housing for All" programme favourably.

Given the current level of maturity of urban governance, especially with respect to project implementation, service standard and financial management, instruments that distribute or mitigate risks of ULBs run the danger of under-estimating the consequence of moral hazard. The recent global crisis bears testimony to such dangers.

There is nevertheless a strong case for the creation of a secondary market for debt instruments. The case for urban financing improves significantly where such markets exist. The financial discipline imposed by the markets may, in this context, provide ULBs with the incentive to reform so as to access larger quantum of financing at attractive rates.

Finally, the present concession structures are inefficient in enabling risk capital to "circulate" as they do not distinguish between contractors and sponsors. As a result, a significant quantum of equity (risk) capital remains committed to projects beyond the construction period when other more risk averse capital are willing to participate. In the road sector, for instance, over US$4 billion (of capital by value) is estimated to be locked in projects. Such values, if unlocked, will provide the necessary risk capital to support additional infrastructure programmes.

## Extending the Strategic Design of PPPs *ala* "Housing for All" across Sectors

From the above, it should be a self-evident proposition that all PPP projects must be designed to maximise the net benefit stream and seek fiscal support only to the extent of the shortfall between the net present value of the resultant benefit stream and the desired hurdle rate. In actual fact, PPP projects are rarely subject to such a test and are almost always designed, structured and implemented without such considerations. As a result, most PPP projects realise a fraction of the benefits that they could have generated, provide less to mitigate negative externalities, and overall catalyse lower levels of investments.

The case for a strategic design approach works at three levels: programmatic, project and process. Over the past decade, government has recognised the utility of PPP as a tool to help meet gaps in the provision of basic infrastructure and associated services. Over this period, the country has made real progress in attracting significant private investment in three sectors: telecom, roads and ports. In most other sectors, efforts have been piecemeal and mostly project-specific.

At the programmatic level, there are innumerable examples of how such designs assist in accelerating investments:

(a) Linkages in policy to leverage and exploit capacities created in telecom for e-governance, financial inclusion, tele-medicine, energy efficiency, etc., will hugely impact telecom penetration in rural markets. As a result, large gains (outcomes) relating to efficiency in public distribution, governance, availability of government services at the doorstep of citizens, health, value addition in agriculture, etc., can be secured in addition to the convenience and benefits of making available access to modern telephony. Such an integrated approach, led by line ministries, responsible for the outcomes, could result in additional investments of US$40 billion, within the next five years, with direct links to outcomes that are already an integral part of the national priority and agenda.

(b) The Electricity Act of 2003 provides an exemplary framework for the development of an energy market in India: generators would be free to choose where to site plants and compete in the supply of power, through a national grid, in securing off-take. However, select rules issued subsequently under the Act and the extant fiscal regime has ensured that very few power plants, especially merchant, have been commissioned over the past few years. It is no longer specious to argue that the non-availability of power is resulting in significant environmental degradation, loss of habitat and bio-diversity, in addition to negatively impacting the quality of life, productivity, competitiveness and costs. Over US$200 billion in additional investments could easily be secured if an integrated "Power to All" programme were implemented. Delays in improving the energy sector is singularly placing a huge opportunity cost on the economy.

(c) The absence of explicit policy and programmatic linkages between water, waste, health and environment has ensured that the case for investments in the water sector has been under-served. Representatives of community interest continue to maintain that water should remain under-priced despite the huge savings that would be gained if India's water sector were improved on an integrated basis. The environmental damage caused by mispricing this resource is severe. The issue, as once famously stated, appears to be more of an unwillingness to charge rather than an unwillingness to pay. Over US$100 billion of investments could easily be secured if an integrated approach to the management of water and waste resources, health and environment were adopted. Where an integrated approach has been adopted, issues of pricing and recovery have not been deterrents.

(d) India has over 4000 dams in various state of disrepair. The world over, dams support multiple socio-economic activities: fisheries, tourism, real estate, sports, hydroelectricity, command area development. Structured holistically, they provide an extraordinary opportunity to maximise socio-economic returns: income, employment, investment, environmental sustainability, social inclusion, agricultural productivity, optimisation of subsidies, etc. It is estimated that a little under US$3 billion is required to renovate and make safe existing dams. An integrated approach would provide additional investment opportunities of US$200 billion with dramatic economic rates of return and positive externalities.

(e) The tourism industry is a great employer: from people of low-skill sets to the most sophisticated, this industry provides a huge opportunity for uplifting vast sections of the population and diverse regions of our country. The absence of a strategic thrust, at a programmatic level, means that a cross-sectoral plan across infrastructure and service sectors, all oriented to leave the tourist with the best experience, would be simply impossible to implement in the country. As a result, India remains a laggard in the global tourism industry, whereas its tourism content continues to remain rated amongst the best in the world. The socio-economic impact of developing tourism is well-established and hardly needs to be emphasised; it is estimated that the integrated tourism multiplier for India is the highest across all sectors, at between 25 and 30.

(f) The past decade have seen huge strides in information, communication and technology (ICT). Its application to service delivery will result in huge gains in administrative efficiency, transparency, revenue to cost ratios, reduction in subsidies/leakages, etc. The introduction of ICT-based managed services in the urban sphere has obvious benefits: efficiency in revenue collection, energy use, cost control, etc. Efforts at introducing such platforms to secure the benefits of intelligent urbanisation are a low hanging fruit in the agenda of urban reform with profound implications for business and the quality of urban life. Across sectors, the migration to managed services based on ICT platforms will unleash massive investments, efficiencies and savings in budgetary resources. Strategically designed PPP provide the mechanism to implement such a programme.

(g) The Prime Minister's Gram Sadak Yojana (PMGSY) is an outstanding programme whose implementation has provided all-weather connectivity to a large number of otherwise unconnected villages/regions. There is now a need to integrate a number of other initiatives that could utilise the available road network to maintain the momentum of development: food processing, biomass-based power generation, integrated water management, etc. Structured under a PPP framework, the PMGSY and other myriad schemes of this genre that already exist in government, could be converted into a transformational programme for rural India. The institutional and financial resources required for this purpose already exist.

If approached strategically, over US$700 billion of investments could be secured linked to the achievement of specific socio-economic developmental outcomes in the infrastructure sectors outlined over and above the investments that could be mobilised from the implementation of the "Housing for All" programme. In essence, such an approach will use capacities and investments within the system in a more efficient and meaningful way. The induction of the private sector within a strategically designed programme as outlined above, through the PPP framework, provides huge systemic gains: the government knows why its undertaking a programme/project; the private sector knows the national priority and its targets; and, the wider community has a clearer idea of the intended outcomes of the programme.

The success of the Mission mode approach in telecom in the mid-1980s perhaps points the way forward: a similar approach, on a strategic basis, may perhaps have to be adopted with each Mission entrusted in linking infrastructure sector interventions to outcomes of national priority. Ownership for the implementation of the programme would continue to be driven by line agencies best suited to secure targeted outcomes.

A singular outcome of the reform programme has been the emergence of an increasingly strong private sector. Unlike in the 1980s, the private sector brings capabilities, both managerial and financial, that can be made to work, in a partnership mode with government, to support the implementation of such programmes. Such an approach will require government to progressively change its institutional frameworks, processes, language, intent and actions to treat the private sector as partners rather than as mere vendors/service providers. In the alternative, programme implementation will be tardy, ridden with conflicts of interest, ineffective and unable to secure the significant socio-economic outcomes that are potentially available.

Two very diverse and interesting initiatives in the UK amplify this point. In the UK, every local authority is required to establish Local Strategic Partnership (LSP) frameworks. LSPs are groups of organisations involving key stakeholders such as businesses, government, public sector agencies and representatives from community groups, to discuss important issues about an area. Working together in partnership, they look at how well their area is doing, where improvements could be made, and provide solutions on how to tackle problems. The partnership targets are set in light of a Local Area Agreement with targets based on a set of 198 indicators. Liverpool First makes an interesting study in this context.

(a) *Glendale Liverpool:* Glendale Liverpool, formed in 2006, is the company responsible for the maintenance of the parks, golf courses, cemeteries and crematoria within the city. The partnership helps create, develop and maintain a diverse network of green spaces and public facilities to safeguard natural and historic resources, provide recreational and educational opportunities and help promote sustainable communities and services. The partnership was recently awarded the Green Flag, a quality environmental management award for increasingly public interest, usage and enjoyment of these historic green spaces. A recent programme that is focused on developing Liverpool's horticultural capacity and sustainability for the future is the launch of a horticultural 'green' apprentice scheme.

(b) *2020 Liverpool:* 2020 Liverpool provides the city with a broad range of professional and technical services to assist the city in the development and maintenance of the council's buildings and highway infrastructure. The partnership assists the local authority in delivering a high-quality built environment responding to major regeneration activities across the city, such as the Big Dig, Liverpool 1, gateway improvement and the cruise liner terminal, etc.

(c) *Liverpool Direct Limited:* Liverpool Direct Limited (LDL) is a pioneering partnership, created with BT in July 2001, that has helped to change how the council's services are delivered by putting the customer at the heart of service delivery on a ICT platform and on a 24-hours-a-day, seven-days-a-week, 365-days-a-year basis. LDL was recently awarded the 'Customer First UK Standard' for its clear vision, set of objectives and for demonstrating how ULBs can dramatically improve customer service.

(d) *Liverpool Vision:* Liverpool Vision is a private sector-led board and is the city's lead economic delivery partner established during 2008 to promote and secure support for a wider vision for the Liverpool economy of the future; identify programmes and projects that reflect the vision; and facilitate the actions necessary for delivery. The work of Liverpool Vision supports the vision of Liverpool to develop as a city to compete successfully on a world stage—a high growth, high value-added economy, creating prosperity for all its citizens.

(e) *Liverpool Science Park:* Liverpool Science Park is the UK's newest and fastest growing science park. In 2006, the innovation centre attracted 22 companies within its first year. This highlighted its key role in the redevelopment of the city's wealth and knowledge-based economy. The park provides a base for developing science and knowledge-based companies offering a combined package of first-class accommodation, business support, and links to the region's specialist experts. By 2008, the park had greater than 80 per cent occupancy, ahead of projections.

(f) *Enterprise Liverpool:* Enterprise Liverpool is the company responsible for all street scene works within the city. Citizens want streets that are free from disruption, are safe and accessible and create a lively and attractive environment. The partnership continues to deliver these aspirations through a customer-focused approach. The partnership is developing into a major element of the council's capacity to deliver quantitative and qualitative improvements to the way highway and street works are executed. It generates, through the innovative use of technology, the necessary changes to meet government targets for e-government. It vastly improves customer contact through the interface with Liverpool Direct Ltd., the council's contact centre.

(g) *Liverpool First for Children and Young People:* The primary purpose of the partnership is to consult, plan, monitor and evaluate the delivery of services across Liverpool in undertaking their statutory duty to cooperate in improving the well-being of children and young people. It also promotes and shares good practice, and aims to secure the engagement and commitment of key stakeholders in delivering the five outcomes of 'Every Child Matters': being healthy; staying safe; enjoying and achieving; making a positive contribution; and achieving economic well-being.

(h) *Citysafe:* The Citysafe Crime and Disorder Reduction Partnership (CDRP) has performed well over the last three financial years. It has contributed to successful partnership working and outcomes for the people of Liverpool and has improved its relative position. Crime rates have been reducing year-on-year, with violent crime in Liverpool reduced by 36 per cent last year.

The introduction of similar partnership structures in ULBs in India will be a key ingredient in the "Housing for All" programme. Efforts by individual ULBs in this direction are neither sufficient nor system-driven to make such efforts meaningful.

As PPP arrangements, by definition, involve multiple stakeholders, any process that is adopted must foster trust, not give cause to erode it. That requires transparency. Similarly, programmes that do not drive investments through projects to secure specific outcomes efficiently will find it difficult to engage and sustain PPP frameworks. A recent initiative of the Ministry of Defence in the UK makes an interesting case study in this regard:

(a) Land is often used as a monetisable asset to help finance infrastructure. Most governments have used this asset to secure specific infrastructure investments and/or to render a project more attractive from a commercial point of view. The key point of sensitivity is always the process adopted in integrating land parcels into project designs as well as the fact that property values tend to change over time, increasing the risk that the public sector is not obtaining maximum public value from the asset, while also heightening the uncertainty for the private sector.

(b) The UK Ministry of Defence (MoD) adopted an innovative but strategic process to PPP to address these challenges. The model project essentially targets to relocate military and civilian personnel from different 14 MoD sites into a single location. To part finance the acquisition of land and design and construct the facilities at the new location, the MoD proposed that the land at the 14 sites be packaged and sold for re-development. It was also determined that a classic "procurement"-driven PPP approach would have been either unbankable or unacceptably expensive.

(c) The MoD appointed an integrator (termed Prime Plus Contractor) to take the principal risk of delivering initial phases of the project and to competitively procure specific works within the project subsequently. The integrator is provided incentives to maximise the net revenues from surplus land/properties and is responsible for schedules and quality standards being met.

(d) The cash from the sale of surplus sites is paid into project-specific accounts that the MoD controls and are used to pay debts, direct project costs, and the integrator's management fee to deliver on the project. Any amount in excess of a guaranteed minimum payment is shared with the MoD and the integrator on a pre-determined profit-sharing mechanism so as to align and incentivise the integrator to maximise revenues over time.

The integrator model is an interesting study in process management for several different reasons. First, the government itself undertakes a procurement (read more as a selection of a partner) process only once. Thereafter, the integrator is responsible for all procurement. Second, the onus is on the integrator to ensure that pre-specified outcomes of the PPP are achieved and not the government. Third, it caps government liability despite the future revenue stream being uncertain. Fourth, it enables dynamic changes in project design as at each stage of the project, a process of re-definition is permitted so as to maximise desired outcomes. Finally, such a process ensures that project outcomes are the focus of the partnership as it aligns economic incentives with continuation of such an arrangement. At each stage, the test of transparency, efficiency and integrity is established.

From a strategic point of view, the Indian landscape in PPP is relatively under-developed. A Deloitte report concludes that India remains at Stage 1 compared to other countries that have also adopted a PPP approach. Nevertheless, it is interesting that where similar innovations/approaches (as have been tried out in more mature markets) have been experimented in India, programmes and projects have been generally successful. Indore's efforts at providing water and sanitation is a case in point.

## Conclusion

Overall, the case for using PPP as a delivery mechanism in infrastructure is well-supported by both domestic and international experience. For India, the next phase of infrastructure development will require a more holistic, integrated and strategic approach to PPP, to scale up its initial efforts in this regard. With its legislative and policy framework largely in place, the focus now needs to shift to enabling genuine partnerships that build institutional capacity across sectors. The response of the private sector to projects offered till date would certainly appear to suggest their willingness to support such a drive.

As Dr. Vijay Kelkar has said, the interesting and important question that we should all be asking ourselves is: What should the portfolio composition of the government be? What assets should be held by the state? We need to think about this question, and once we have a consensus and clarity about what the portfolio composition ought to be, we should embark on a set of adjustments that take us to a different, and hopefully better, asset (Kelkar, 2010).

A Report commissioned by the UK Treasury found that among a sample of PPP projects, the average savings were close to 17 per cent of project cost at the time of commissioning, on a standalone basis, and up to 45 per cent on a life cycle cost basis. In the United States, the costs of completing construction for segments of the Denver E-470 toll road that used a PPP approach came in $189 million below the original cost estimate of $597 million. In Australia, eight Partnerships Victoria projects were on average 9 per cent less expensive than under the typical procurement process. In addition, PPPs provide a number of other advantages including superior customer experience and services, avoided costs of operation & maintenance, leverage of budgetary resources, accountability, transparency, etc.

The "Housing for All" programme provides an immediate opportunity to government to galvanise public and private sector resources to address the challenge of urbanisation in a positive way. In the process, it is the central thesis of this paper that the country could reap a significant urban dividend: affordable housing, improved urban infrastructure, especially commuting infrastructure, and a more rational approach to the provision of services (both pricing and service standards) resulting in a massive unleashing of urban productivity and a reduction in urban poverty.

An integrated approach to "Housing for All" embedded within its ambit concepts of sustainability would also provide the government with the necessary tools to impact socio-environmental considerations, including the Millennium Development Goals (MDGs). The programme would be demonstrably designed to be inclusive and cater to all sections of society.

Such a programme will introduce new consultative mechanisms, across diverse stakeholders, to ensure a more inclusive approach to project implementation. For instance, the sheer scale of land acquisition will require a far greater balance between stakeholders if it is to succeed. Improved consultative mechanisms would also ensure that the benefits of urbanisation spread to all sections of society.

A well-structured "Housing for All" programme will provide the economic bedrock for improvements in urban infrastructure and services. Over 500 new nodes would need to be established (in proximity to existing urban agglomerations) to accommodate an incremental urban population of 500 million people, on a full cost recovery basis. Each new node will require to be connected to existing urban agglomerations through mass transport systems, and develop "surround" infrastructure that is environmentally and socially sustainable. Given the scale of the new nodes, their level of infrastructure services at affordable prices, it is expected that existing urban agglomerations would also be motivated to improve systemic efficiency on a more rational basis.

The "Housing for All" programme is estimated to cost over US$800 billion. Whilst the majority of the investment requirements of such a programme will be mobilised through the private sector, government will require to assume responsibility for land acquisition, core and mass transport connectivity infrastructure. In turn, it is recommended that these elements of the programme be undertaken through an annuity model where full recovery of investment could be through a variety of innovative schemes administered by government. In the process, it is estimated that the impact of the programme on the exchequer matrix would be positive.

Finally, it is argued, that a strategic approach to infrastructure, through PPPs, would enable government to build on its considerable successes across sectors. Such an approach could support a further investment of US$700 billion over the next decade.

In the final analysis, it would be a fitting testimony to a journey that commenced 18 years ago, if the Government of India were to launch the world's largest "Housing for All" PPP programme dedicated to the alleviation of poverty, improved quality of life for all its citizens on an inclusive basis, and environmental and social sustainability. Structured and implemented in an integrated and intelligent manner, the programme would bring about significant systemic efficiencies whilst establishing new standards in governance, urban management and standards of service.

## References

World Bank (2006). *India: Building Capacities for Public Private Partnerships: Energy and Infrastructure Unit and Finance and Private Sector Unit*, South Asia Region, June.

Kelkar, Vijay (2010). "On strategies for disinvestment and privatisation", 26th Sir Purshotamdas Thakurdas Memorial Lecture. Chairman: Finance Commission, Mumbai, 29 January.

# List of Dr. Vijay L. Kelkar's Publications

## Monographs/Lectures

1. 2010, "On Strategies for Disinvestment and Privatisation", *26th Sir Purshotamdas Thakurdas Memorial Lecture*, Indian Institute of Banking and Finance, Mumbai, 29th January.

2. 2009, "Flawless" Goods and Services Tax for Promoting Growth and Employment, *Address at the FICCI National Executive Council Meeting*, Bangalore, 12th October.

3. 2009, "Towards a New Natural Gas Policy", *Inaugural Rajiv Gandhi Lecture* at the Rajiv Gandhi Institute of Petroleum Technology, Uttar Pradesh, 22nd August.

4. 2009, "GST For Accelerated Economic Growth and Competitiveness", *Special Lecture at the Annual Conference of Associated Chambers of Commerce*, New Delhi, 29th June.

5. 2008, "Financial Inclusion for 'Inclusive Growth'", *N.P. Sen Memorial Lecture*, Administrative Staff College of India, Hyderabad, 13th January.

6. 2005, "India's Economic Future: Moving Beyond State Capitalism", *Gadgil Memorial Lecture*, Mumbai, October 26.

7. 2005, The International Monetary Fund: Integration and Democratization in the 21st Century", *Working Paper submitted to G-24 Technical Group*, Philippines, Manila, 17-18 March.

8. 2004, "India: On the Growth Turnpike", *Australian National University 2004 Narayanan Oration*, Canberra, April 27.

9. 2002, "South Asia in 2020: Economic Outlook", in *South Asia in 2020: Future Strategic Balances and Alliances*, edited by Michael Chambers, Strategic Studies Institute, USA, November.

10. 2001, "India's Reforms Agenda: Micro, Meso and Macro Economic Reforms", *Annual Fellows Lecture*, Centre for the Advanced Study of India, University of Pennsylvania, USA.
11. 1997, "Transforming India's Oil Industry: The Agenda Beyond Pricing Reforms", *Second Vasant J. Sheth Memorial Lecture*.
12. 1996, "India: Development Policy Imperatives", Vijay Kelkar-Bhanoji Rao (eds.). Tata Mcgraw-Hill, New Delhi.
13. 1996, "Strategies of Privatisation: An Approach to the Oil Industry", in *Liberalising India—Progress and Problems*, edited by Dietmar Rothermund, New Delhi.
14. 1996, "India's Oil Policy in the Coming Century", *3rd Lovraj Kumar Memorial Lecture*, Indian Society for Chemical Engineers.
15. 1990, "Efficiency of Public Sector Enterprises", *The Eighth Dr. Deepak K. Merchant Memorial Lecture* at the Indian Institute of Technology, Mumbai, India, September.

**Selected Publications**

1. 2009, "Towards a New Natural Gas Policy", *Economic and Political Weekly* XLIV(36), September 5.
2. 2005, "Time for Change at the IMF", *Finance and Development*, March.
3. 2004, "The Evolution of 'Homegrown Conditionality' in India-IMF Relations", *The Journal of Development Studies* 40(6): 59-81, August.
4. 2004, "Reforming the Governance of the International Monetary Fund", *The World Economy* 27(5): 727-743(17), May.
5. 2003, "R&D in India", *Issues Paper No.9*, Administrative Staff College of India, Hyderabad, India, March.
6. 1999, "India's Emerging Economic Challenges", *Economic and Political Weekly*, August.
7. 1991, "Pricing Policy for Bulk Exchange of Power", *Asian and Pacific Journal of Energy:* 109-124, December [new series].

8. 1991, "India's Information Economy: Role, Size & Perspective", *Economic and Political Weekly*, September.

9. 1991, "India and the World Economy: A Perspective for the 1990s", *Second U.S. India Bilateral Forum*, The Institute of East Asian Studies, February 19-22, Berkeley, California.

10. 1990, *India's Industrial Sector: Performance Policy and Reforms*, Report for the Asian Development Bank, Manila.

11. 1989, *Towards a New Energy Policy*, Bureau of Industrial Costs and Prices, Government of India, New Delhi.

12. 1989, "World Trade in Manufactures", in *World Economy in Transition*, edited by K. Ahuja-Patel, Pergamon Press, U.K.

13. 1985, "Manufactures Exports in India's Development—Policy Options for the 80s", Development Research Institute, Tilburg, The Netherlands.

14. 1997, *Long Term Perspective for Management of India's Non-renewable Resources*, Planning Commission, Government of India, New Delhi.

15. 1982, "Growth Possibilities in OECD Economies: An Alternative View", *Trade and Development Review*, UNCTAD, Geneva, Spring.

16. 1980, "Gatt, Export Subsidies and Developing Countries", *Journal of World Trade Law*, Geneva, July-August.

17. 1980, "India and the World Economy: A Search for Self-reliance", *Economic and Political Weekly* (Annual Number), February.

18. 1977, "Growth Possibilities in the Indian Economy", *Economic and Political Weekly*, December 24.

19. 1997, "Evaluation of India's Trade Policies", *Economic and Political Weekly*, June.

20. 1976, "An Economic Analysis of the Impact of Private Foreign Investment in India", in *Some Problems of India's Economic Policy*, edited by Charan Wadhva, Tata Mcgraw-Hill, New Delhi.

21. 1973, "Problems of Employment and Income Levels in Nepal", Center for Economic Development and Administration, Kathmandu.

22. 1973, "Road User Charges and Route Licensing Policy in Nepal", Center for Economic Development and Administration, Kathmandu.

23. 1970, "Optimal Borrowing and Development Planning", Center for Research in Management Science, *Working Paper No.298*, University of California, Berkeley.

# Index

## F

## I



## J



## K



## L

## R



## S

ACADEMIC FOUNDATION
E-mail: booksaf@gmail.com
www.academicfoundation.org
Price: Rs. 995